'Handling'

Please return/renew this item by the last date shown
on this label, or on your self-service receipt.

To renew this item, visit **www.librarieswest.org.uk**
or contact your library

Your borrower number and PIN are required.

Libraries**West**

MARINE A
'MY TOUGHEST BATTLE'

MARINE A
'MY TOUGHEST BATTLE'

SGT ALEXANDER BLACKMAN

FOREWORD BY
FREDERICK FORSYTH

MIRROR BOOKS

Born in Brighton, Alexander Blackman served 16 years in the Royal Marines, completing six operational tours of duty in Northern Ireland, Iraq and Afghanistan.

He now works for a company helping veterans back into work.

He lives in rural Somerset with his wife Claire, their dog Dave and their cat Madam Fifi.

First published in hardback by Mirror Books in 2019

This paperback edition published in 2019

Mirror Books is part of Reach plc
10 Lower Thames Street
London EC3R 6EN
England

www.mirrorbooks.co.uk

ISBN 978-1-912624-50-8

Typeset by Danny Lyle
DanJLyle@gmail.com

Printed and bound in Great Britain by
CPI Group (UK) Ltd, Croydon, CR0 4YY

A CIP catalogue record for this book is available from the British Library.

It will come as no surprise that I am dedicating this book to my wife Claire for her unfaltering support and tireless campaigning for my release. I would not be without her.

Also, to our families and friends and the Royal Marines family who brought me here and got me through.

FOREWORD
by Frederick Forsyth

In what eventually became a nationally prominent case, under the title of The Marine A Affair, I was very much a Johnny-come-lately. I missed the original court martial that found Royal Marine Sgt Al Blackman guilty of murder and sentenced him to a life term. My attention was only drawn by the appeal trial, which confirmed the verdict and sentence of the original court martial a year earlier. Even now, I do not recall the exact reason why my old hackles began to rise.

Journalists are not the most beloved of our fellow citizens, but there is one branch of this flaky calling that merits our appreciation: investigative journalism, always my preference. A good journalist never dances to the tune of an Establishment which is probably corrupt, certainly self-serving and will sink to shameful levels of cynicism to cover up its many mistakes. The job of journalism is not to endorse the bastards but to expose the fiascos and name those responsible.

On nothing more than a hunch, I started to research the background of a veteran Marine Sergeant with decorations and a chain of foreign tours, mostly in combat zones, suddenly being converted to a murdering criminal serving life for shooting a prisoner. Almost at once I ran into official obstruction. The only effect this had was to confirm my internal red lights were not deceiving me. There was something rotten here.

I started by going back to the military trial, seeking out those who had witnessed it but from a detached viewpoint. One of those was a retired colonel who had attended several courts martial in his career. He was adamant: the whole circus had been fundamentally flawed.

The relentless prosecuting counsel, David Perry QC, had run rings round a blitheringly useless defence team under the benign gaze of the bench. There were two corporals in the dock, but they were acquitted.

I learned weird things about that trial. After the verdict, the seven jurors pulled on their headgear and saluted the man in the dock. For the record, British officers do not salute murderers. So what the hell were they saying? I suspect it was: "We have done what we were ordered to do."

More research revealed that Al Blackman's J Company had been abandoned in the hideously dangerous hellhole of Nad-e-Ali for far too long, surrounded by the cream of the Taliban, under fire day and night, ambushed on every patrol but visited just once by their commanding officer. In short, there had been a complete breakdown of chain-of-command norms in that sector. At six months, they had been there far too long.

I found a professor of psychiatry who was adamant that even tough men will crumble under such conditions, until no longer mentally stable – but he was never called to testify. The shot Taliban had been torn apart by a helicopter gunship and was dying in unspeakable agony. This was not seen as a mitigating circumstance. But then, nothing was. The whole trial screamed the word 'scapegoat'. So I began to write articles.

I was far from alone. In Parliament, Tory MP and ex-soldier Richard Drax led the charge. In response to the 100,000 public signatures on a Government petition, he demanded, and was granted, a commons debate. The affair went nationwide. Then the *Daily Mail* weighed in with an appeal for crowd funding to secure Sgt Blackman, in his prison cell, the defence he never got at trial. In an eye-watering response, the British public sent in £804,000 – for a man they had never met or even seen.

That kind of funding brought in probably the most effective defence QC at the bar. Jonathan Goldberg had defended in 80 courts martial and never lost one. He was engaged and brought with him his two brilliant juniors. Then the fight was really on, with a frantic Establishment in full retreat.

It took time, of course, but then we all know that the aphorism 'justice delayed is justice denied' is listed in any decent thesaurus as a pseudonym for codswallop. A few senior brass to their shame dug their heels in against the sergeant, but in street demonstrations the sea of green berets of RM veterans were an angry tide.

Finally, five law lords under the Lord Chief Justice sat in the Appeal Court in the Strand and listened. They heard all the technical evidence on the effects of grief, shock, horror and exhaustion on the human mind, and finally pronounced what the country had already decided. Sentence of murder quashed, replaced with manslaughter – meaning a variable sentence. They pronounced seven years. Divided by two for exemplary behaviour. Al Blackman had served three and a half. He walked.

The key was not an old codger with his articles, letters and phone calls, nor yet a decent MP. It was partly a brilliant barrister and his team. But mainly it was the British people and their £800,000. God bless 'em.

Frederick Forsyth

PROLOGUE

Helmand Province, Afghanistan, 2011

It had been four years since I took my first breaths of the hot, urgent Afghanistan air, and I thought I knew the country well.

But here is a lesson I learned in the heat of the deserts of Iraq and Afghanistan, a lesson that would follow me back to England and dog me into my life beyond:

Every time you think you know the way the world turns, you are wrong.

A person's life can turn on an instant, and for me – although I didn't know it – that instant was going to happen today.

It was approaching the most scorching hour of the day, mid-afternoon on 15 September 2011. The lads under my command in J Company, 42 Commando, had already been on patrol for eight hours. Eight hours: a lifetime in Helmand Province, southern Afghanistan. We were lucky that day: of the eight men who went out, all eight returned. That hadn't always been the case, so when I watched them tramp back into the compound I did so with a sense of unbridled relief.

At the end of the patrol they were weary, depleted, sun-kissed and ready to recuperate behind our compound walls. I knew how they felt. For eight hours I'd hurtled around the compound, or else been sequestered in our ops room – which amounted to little more than a sweltering shipping container dropped down in the desert, where the air grew thicker, more humid and close, with every breath. As the lads dekitted around me, or made for the twin tents that were what passed for home, I could feel the utter fatigue. There had been days when I'd come back from patrol, already having drunk the 10 litres of water I carried with me, and yet still been close to collapse. But after a day as brutal as this, it wasn't just our bodies that needed rest. Our minds were full to bursting as well.

The heat of the desert is exhausting. The hours spent in the 40-degree heat, your skin coated with sweat so thick and viscous it feels like oil, your body laden down with weaponry and ammunition, radios and armour – it drains men much stronger than I am. In Afghanistan, the body armour alone can weigh 9kg. The supply chain might find itself severed at any moment, so a soldier might carry between five and 10 litres of water on top of their other kit. All in all, it might mean he's carrying the equivalent of a 10-stone man over his shoulders: eight hours a day, through the searing heat. There is no more vivid way of saying it than: a British soldier in the Middle East is encumbered by the same burden as a medieval knight in full plate armour.

PROLOGUE

Yes, the physical demands of Helmand Province can feel incalculably large. But soldiers are trained for this. From basic training through to pre-tour exercises, the focus is on developing our bodies to handle the rigours of war. What so few of us mention are the mental demands. Afghanistan is a war in the desert, but even more than that, it is a war of the mind. We might not have engaged the enemy in open combat in the course of today's patrol, but that did not mean we were not fighting from the moment we left the compound gates. By 2011, the war in Afghanistan was already 10 years old and had long since stopped being a war of skirmishes and open confrontations. In 2011, our enemies were not only the insurgents who grouped together and stormed our compounds, nor those who set up ambushes at the sides of the road and launched RPGs (rocket-propelled grenades) at our convoys as we passed. No, in 2011, a British soldier was more likely to be killed by an IED, an improvised explosive device, than they were in armed engagement. And so we ran the gauntlet on every patrol: we would walk, metal detectors in hand, scouring the ground, knowing that every step might trigger an explosion.

Back in the days when the Taliban openly attacked our compounds, or ambushed us where we walked, at least we knew the rules, at least the nature of 'us' and 'them' was well defined. But the horror of Afghanistan in 2011 was that a local man smiling at you one moment might be your killer the next, when he activated the bomb expertly buried in the path of your patrol.

A man might rake you with gunfire one moment, then abandon his weapon and pick up a farm tool the next. The enemy was all around us, hidden in plain sight, and all we as soldiers could do was... endure.

No form of combat is free of its stresses, but at least when you are engaging an open enemy there is something to fight back against. But what do you do when your troop numbers are constantly being chipped away by deaths and life-changing injuries, courtesy of the booby-traps buried in the roads along which you have to walk? What do you do when the body parts of your friends and fellow soldiers, which you haven't been able to recover in the aftermath of a sudden violent explosion, are strung up in the trees around you to taunt you as you march by? In the past weeks, the tension of this tour seemed to have hardened even further. We were depleted, we were on edge – and for me, the belief that the local Taliban were specifically targeting my patrols because I was this location's commander added another frisson of threat.

Today had been a long, gruelling day, but at least it was near the end of a long, gruelling tour. Another month and we would be out of this hell-hole. Another month and these days of constant watchfulness, constant dread, the constant anticipation that any moment could be your last, would be over.

Then the radio began to crackle, and everything changed.

The patrol was barely over when the silence of the sun-washed afternoon was broken by machine gun fire. As the lads divested themselves of their kit, the air was suddenly alive with the sounds of attack – distant enough that we were not under immediate threat, but close enough that we could hear each individual burst. Somewhere north-west of us, one of our neighbouring compounds was coming under attack.

The lads were only just out of their body armour. The relief that comes with the end of a patrol, knowing that you don't have to don 65kg of kit and go back into the unearthly heat for another day, can be palpable. But with an attack in progress on a friendly location I stood the lads to and said, "Better get suited and booted." The looks they gave me were understandably aggrieved. I understood that. I'd have been aggrieved, too. But these were my lads, Command Post Omar was my responsibility, and it was on me to make sure they were safe, whatever the cost. I took that responsibility seriously. I always had. Most of the lads under my command were here on their first tours. They had mothers and fathers and girlfriends and wives waiting for them to come home. Not all the men we started out with would be going back. That is war. But I was determined to do whatever I could to keep these lads safe – and if that meant pissing them off here and there, I had no problem with that. Our neighbouring compound was scarcely two miles away; if they were taking fire, that meant we could, too. In war, though you don't always get the choice, it is better to be safe than sorry.

As the lads got kitted out again, I went back to the radio and listened to the voices crackling back and forth. Beyond our compound, the machine gun fire ebbed away, then built up again. The voices on the radio were not frantic – these were professional soldiers – but their uncertainty was plain. At first they thought the fire was coming from further north, then from further west. The truth was, nobody knew where the insurgents were. These are the most unnerving moments in a theatre of war. When you are being openly confronted, you can always attack back. But what do you do when your attackers are unseen? When you can't tell where they're coming from, how many of them there are, how orchestrated the attack?

We waited.

We waited some more.

Eventually, the radio crackled back into life. "One possible enemy moving east."

I gathered the lads. Outside our compound an irrigation canal led north, and scarcely 800 metres further along sat a row of houses, the kind of adobe mud structures they build in this part of the world. Command had been watching the besieged compound on the remote feed, its cameras mounted in balloons high above the battlefields, and they'd tracked a figure they believed to be one of the insurgents until he reached these same abodes, where he'd cached what appeared to be his automatic rifle behind its earthen walls.

"CP Omar, take your unit up and search the place. Secure the weapon."

PROLOGUE

It was not a task any of the lads seemed to relish. The truth was, I didn't relish it myself. The machine gun fire at the neighbouring compound had died away, but that did not mean the men who'd been firing had evaporated into thin air. Only one of them had been spotted making his getaway. There had certainly been more than that. But wasn't that just another day in Helmand? Knowing you were under threat, but not knowing who or where from?

One month, I told myself. One more month and this would be a part of my past.

"It's only 800 metres," I said, nominating seven of the lads and telling them to be prepared. "That's 800 metres there, and 800 metres back. If we find a weapon, we secure it. If we don't, well, we did what we needed to do. We can be there and back in an hour. But that's what we're doing."

You don't get used to the heat. Sometimes you think you will, but then you step back into it, your armour insulating your body even further, and you're reminded: it isn't like this back on Salisbury Plain. No amount of training can prepare you for conditions like this. You get thrown in, and you learn to survive it.

We hustled through the compound gates, back into the light.

Perhaps 800 metres doesn't sound far, but after eight hours already on patrol, with the sun beating down, it feels it. What a long-distance runner might cover in three minutes took us – laden down with packs and metal detectors, constantly scouring our whereabouts for would-be attackers and signs of

IEDs – much longer. When we got there, it was to discover that the building we'd been asked to search was a farmer's adobe house, short and squat. It took a matter of moments to force the door open and, startling the lone figure inside, fan out into his home and conduct a search.

We recognised him straight away as a local, but that did not necessarily mean he was not one of the insurgents. Six months stationed in a particular part of Helmand and you quickly get to know the local characters, and they get to know you, too. We were not here as an occupying force, we were here, ostensibly, to keep the peace, to maintain order, to give Afghanistan the time and space to recuperate after Taliban rule had ended. Keeping up good relationships with the locals was paramount to that – even if, on occasion, our orders were to force our way into their buildings and conduct thorough searches.

Once we had ascertained that the farmer was unarmed, I focused on keeping the location secure while one of my corporals led the search.

Some time later, he reappeared from the structure with nothing but a hunting rifle in his hands.

"Is that it?"

My corporal nodded.

With something approaching relief, I got on the radio. I will not say that there was no frustration. We were already exhausted and had been asked back into the field, and all to chase a red herring. Whoever had assailed our neighbouring compound, it wasn't this farmer with his hunting rifle. But relief was the dominant emotion, it always is, when you find that you don't need to engage.

"That's all he has," I reported back. "A single-shot weapon. He's allowed to have that. We're heading back."

"Roger that," came the reply.

I gathered the lads together. As we left, retracing our steps, the farmer watched us noncommittally from the threshold. It wasn't anger on his face. If anything, he looked bemused. Perhaps when eight British soldiers burdened by half a tonne of military equipment kick down your door, mutter darkly about your hunting rifle and then leave without seizing a thing, it's the only rational response.

Just 800 metres; 800 metres and, surely, we would be done for the day.

We almost made it.

Less than 200 metres from the compound gates, our radio burst back into life.

"Moving north…"

"Is he armed?"

"He's one of them. He's armed."

I stopped the lads. The chatter across the radio seemed more certain this time. Another insurgent, presumably one who really had attacked our neighbouring compound, had been sighted making his getaway, his automatic rifle half-hidden beneath a blanket in his arms.

We were close enough, now, to see the compound walls, but I knew what we had to do. The insurgent had been spotted back the way we'd come, heading past the drainage ditch and adobe houses and into the scrub country beyond. There was no point in going back to the compound, not if we'd be needed out here. If any of the lads were particularly disgruntled, they hid it well. But whoever had attacked our neighbouring compound was still out there, and now it seemed that command had a positive ID.

In summer, the landscape of Helmand Province changes dramatically. Trees and shrubs burst forth in full leaf. Some banksides grow dense and entangled, so much so that we have to blaze our way through with machetes and knives. At the edge of the track we were on the tree line was not as entangled as that, but it still afforded camouflage of a sort. I ordered the lads down into the trees to take up a defensive position. There would be little protection from gunfire, but at least we could await the next move here.

It sometimes feels like you spend your whole tour waiting. When the kinetic activity comes, it comes quickly. An RPG is loosed at the convoy you're travelling in. A grenade is hurled over your compound wall. One of the corporals in your patrol triggers an unseen explosive device, buried in the road; one moment he's a human being, with all the lives and loves and hopes that that entails, and the next he's just viscera: memories and blood. But between those times, a soldier's lot is to wait, and to wait, and to try and control the dread that builds in him as he is waiting there.

PROLOGUE

I cannot remember how long we were waiting. Time plays tricks on you. It elongates and stretches, or else it seems that everything happens at once. All I really remember is that some time later, as we maintained our defensive position and listened to the chatter across the radio, another sound arose, somewhere on our peripheries, the familiar thudding, the heavy chopping of rotor blades making a vortex out of the air. I turned my face upwards, and it was then that I saw the Apache helicopter for the first time. It arced over us and off to the north, searching for the insurgent that command had identified.

Something was happening out there, so we waited some more. Over the radio, the higher echelons at command were debating with the crew in the Apache and others on the ground. Dimly, we could still hear the helicopter, but now we knew it had stopped its circling. The insurgent must be in their sights.

The chatter continued. A voice from the Apache seemed to confirm that the insurgent was, indeed, armed. A voice from command asked for corroboration. Voices flitted back and forth, short staccato bursts across our radio. Only when they had established to their satisfaction that the insurgent was carrying what appeared to be an AK47 did the conversation change. It seemed clear, now, that we would have to take him out. But the question was: should he be taken out from the air, or from the ground?

At that moment, I got on the radio myself. He was just one bloke. I informed them of my position. "I'm available for taskings," I told them, and awaited my next command. There were eight of us from CP Omar already out here. I had little doubt that we could take charge of one insurgent, even if he was armed. I was beginning to envisage it. It didn't have to be messy. In all likelihood, nobody would get hurt. With eight of us, we could encircle him, take him by surprise, force him to disarm. If we played it properly, there didn't have to be any collateral damage at all.

But none of that mattered, because the Apache was already in play.

While we waited, the decision had already been taken. Moments later, we heard the burst of chain gun fire from the helicopter itself. The noise is unmistakable. This is not a weapon designed to kill lone enemies; it is designed to puncture and incapacitate tanks. From our hiding place, we listened as the gun pumped away: 50 rounds, 60 rounds; 80, 100, 120. All in all, before the thunder stopped, 140 rounds had been dispatched.

Into the silence that followed, the radio crackled on.

"Is he down?"

"Is the target deceased?"

"Is the target moving?"

The debate continued. In this way, 10 minutes passed. Then 15. Then 20. Finally, command established that, yes, the target was hit; that, yes, the target had been killed. "Three-two-A," the voice on the other end of the radio ventured. "The target is down, north-by-north-west of your current location." He read off a series of grid references, which we quickly co-ordinated with our own maps. "Can you get out there and retrieve the weapon?"

PROLOGUE

This was the presiding goal after any remote attack, to commandeer whatever weaponry the target had left behind. That way it did not fall back into the hands of enemy insurgents and, piece by piece, one weapon at a time, we might stop random attacks just like this.

The grid references located a stretch of land, a farmer's field, more than a mile from our current location. It would take us some time to get there, but it took an age to get anywhere in Afghanistan. The hours were ticking by, but the sun was still unforgiving.

"Roger that," I said.

So that was it. We had our orders. We'd left the compound on one search-and-retrieval, but found nothing. This time, it seemed, we would at least be coming back with *something* to show for the extra hours we'd put in out here. I turned to my lads. They were young and didn't like to show it, but all of them were exhausted. I was exhausted, too. But one last push. One last foray. It didn't have to take long. Longer than we'd like, perhaps, but since when had a war ever gone smoothly? Somewhere to our north-west lay the insurgent, cut to ribbons by ordnance meant to take out tanks. We would get out there, retrieve his weapon, and then – finally – we could be recuperating in our compound. This day had already lasted too long.

In some ways, it will last every day of my life.

Sgt Alexander Blackman

CHAPTER ONE

My name is Alexander Blackman, but that isn't how you'll know me. The chances are you'll have read some portions of my story already – but in those stories, I am not "Alexander" or "Al" as my friends and family call me. In those stories, I am "Marine A", the moniker I was given during a well-publicised court martial of 2013, when I was convicted of the battlefield murder of a Taliban insurgent and sentenced to life in prison. It's a name that has stuck with me ever since.

To some I have been a pariah. To some I have been a symbol of the ongoing war in Afghanistan. But to the many hundreds of thousands of people who contributed to my defence, who marched together to Westminster on my behalf and who rallied around my wife as she battled for me through the press and law courts, I was a soldier who needed a nation's support. Yet throughout it all, very little has been told about me, the person I am, and the experiences that shaped me. All anyone has really known of me is that I am "Marine A". All anyone has really seen is the empty silhouette of a man's face and the vague sketches courtroom reporters are allowed to make. But ever since I was released from prison, my conviction for murder and life sentence overturned, I have been searching for a way to tell this story. Not just the story of what happened in Helmand Province in 2011 and the actions for which I was convicted, but the broader story of a life spent in the service of my country, the story of the effects war can have on a person, and the story of the one thing that kept me anchored, kept me sane, through the darkest years of my life: my wife Claire, who kept the flames of hope alive, even while they were fading to embers inside me.

I have thought long and hard about how to begin this story. Does it begin in the courtroom where I was sentenced to life in prison? Does it begin in the deserts of Iraq and Afghanistan? Does it begin in Northern Ireland, where I was posted in the final months of the Troubles, when the peace process between Catholics and Protestants was at last taking effect? Or does it go back even further, to my basic training, or the days before I knew being a Royal Marine was going to be part of my life at all?

The truth is, none of us really know where to start telling our own stories. So I will do what feels most simple – and, above all, most honest. I will start at the beginning.

Here, then, is the story of my life, honest and unvarnished; for better, for worse.

I was born, Alexander Blackman, at the start of the sweltering summer of 1974. Ours was a busy, ramshackle kind of family – but however chaotic it might have been, it was filled with the most enormous amount of love. I was the third of four children. By the time I was born, my mother Frances and father Brian already had my elder brother John and sister Lorraine – and, a while after I came along, we would all be joined by my younger sister Melody. Looking back, I can see how much of a miracle-worker my mother had to be: running a household of four children, often while my father, a long-distance lorry driver, was away, is not a challenge that I would like to accept myself, not even after all the years I spent marshalling my lads in Iraq, Afghanistan and in the Royal Marine training camps here in the UK.

Home was a constant whirlwind. Four children, all at different stages of their lives, created a household where things never seemed to stop. There was always something going on. The door was always open to members of the wider family, friends from school and neighbours – and my mother anchored all that chaos beautifully. She was, and remains, an extraordinary woman. While Dad was away on work, Mum was the law – and if at times we disagreed, well, when she made a decree, all four of us leapt to it with military precision.

I was not an academic boy and, since I am being completely honest here, I can say that I did not particularly enjoy school. My childhood was as happy as it could have been, but being stuck in a classroom, learning for learning's sake, was not something that the young Alexander Blackman really relished. I would rather have been out there, experiencing life outside the school gates. But I understood, too, that schooling was important – and, with my parents' encouragement, stuck at school until I was 18, resitting the GCSEs I hadn't done well at first time around.

After that, it might have seemed that the world was my oyster. But the truth was I didn't have a burning ambition in life. I hadn't grown up dreaming of a particular profession, nor yearning to get away from Brighton and make something of myself. I was one of those countless millions who leave school without a firm idea of what to do, and stumble into the first thing that comes along. And that was how, at the age of 18, I began working on a local dairy farm, not far from where I'd grown up. It might not seem much, but these quickly became the best years of my young life.

This work was, in a way, what I had needed, although I didn't know it. I liked the outdoors. I liked the structure. I liked knowing I was contributing to something bigger than myself. In this way, one season passed into the next, and I got to know the ebb and flow of life on a dairy farm. It might have gone on that way forever, but five years later, for the first time, I was beginning to wonder what I might do with my life.

The fact was, I was unusual in the family. My elder brother John had trained as an electrician. My elder sister Lorraine was the first in the family to go to university, studying business studies in Southampton and going on to find work as a specialist in IT. Even my younger sister Melody would, one day, go on to achieve a PhD in physics and find work designing and building new lasers for engineering firms. Would I really, I had started to wonder, work on the farm all my life? There was no doubt how much I loved it, and no doubt how well I got on with all the people there. They had become some of my firmest friends. But I knew, also, that people sometimes stay in jobs that they ought to move on from simply because they love turning up every day and being among people they know and care about, and perhaps that was not the thing for me. For the first time, I got the itch.

A military life had never actually occurred to me. So often, being part of the military runs in the blood, but we Blackmans were not an armed forces family. My father had been in the army, choosing to join the Royal Horse Artillery as a regular rather than be conscripted for his national service, and for a time he'd enjoyed it. It had taken him to Cyprus, then to the Middle East – but that had only lasted four years, and afterwards he had gone happily back to civilian life and provided for his family. Further back, my grandfather and his family hadn't been allowed to go and serve in the second world war because they had reserved occupations on the railways here in Britain. Tasked with keeping the national infrastructure in safe working order, they were expressly barred from going off to war, and this was something that my grandfather in particular found difficult to bear. So that was as far as the military tradition went for the Blackmans.

I don't know why it occurred to my sister, Melody, that a military career might be for her – but by the time I was 23, she was approaching the age where she had to make a decision about what to do after college, and something in the idea appealed to her. She'd been planning on visiting the Brighton recruiting office to discuss her options with the careers advisor there, but she was nervous as well – nervous, perhaps, that the guys down there might intimidate or joke around with her. It was here that I, the protective big brother (of not insignificant size) stepped in.

Accompanying Melody to the recruiting office was not meant to start the next great phase of my life. I lurked around while Melody chatted with the careers advisor, picked up some pamphlets and leafed through them as they spoke, and that was that. Yet in the days that followed, as I drove back and forth to the dairy farm and went about my duties there, an idea started to niggle at me. Something sent my mind spinning back to the things Dad had told me about his own period in the army – how much he'd enjoyed the experience, and all the tools it had given him to use in the rest of his life. It was there that he'd got his specialist driving licence that later allowed him to drive heavy goods vehicles for a living. But there was more than that to it: it had given him skills in structuring his life, managing his relationships and knowing how to react when faced with unexpected conflict. The idea grew on me over the following days and soon enough, I had returned to the recruiting office to find out more.

Melody never did sign up for a military life, as it happens, but somebody in the Blackman family ended up devoting their life to the British armed forces.

CHAPTER ONE

In October 1997, I got off the train at the request stop at Lympstone, near Exeter in Devon, and walked to the rear gate of the Royal Marine training centre with all the other potential new recruits, my pack slung over my shoulder like a boarder going off to school. As we walked up the hill, I could see the assault course, the trainee barracks, the weapons ranges all arrayed before me. An hour later, I had been sized up for combats and boots, and a matter of hours after that all the other new lads and I were being put through our paces.

For three days we trained and ran, trained and ran, worked long hours in the gym, were put at the mercy of an intense Royal Marine PTI (physical training instructor) – and on top of that we were questioned and interviewed throughout. Royal Marine basic training, we were repeatedly told, is one of the most arduous programmes in the world and, over those few days, we saw why it had that reputation. Some of the lads couldn't make it; they were sent away, told to spend six months getting fitter and to come back and try again. Yet by the end of the three days, I had proven myself. I was far from the fittest person there, but work on the dairy farm had given me enough upper body strength to get me through the various assault courses and other physical challenges. Perhaps I could have done better, but they'd seen enough in me for my Royal Marine career to begin.

The idea that I might one day go to war was not, I have to admit, particularly prevalent in my thoughts when the new year came around and, having finally told my boss at the dairy farm that I was leaving, I decamped to begin my full training. 1998 is not so very long ago, but from a warfare perspective, the world was a very different place. The peace process in Northern Ireland was already in full flow. The Berlin Wall had come down some years before, removing the spectre of old enemies that had lasted so much of the 20th century. The old membership of the Warsaw Pact was breaking apart, many former members even petitioning to join NATO. It had been nearly 20 years since the Falklands, the last major war in which the British armed services were deployed. And we were still three years away from the events of 11 September 2001, when the attack on New York's twin towers would precipitate the "war on terror" and an entirely new chapter in the history of the world at war. There was always work to do for the British soldier and I was not ignorant of the fact that situations can develop rapidly, but in 1998 I had little idea that soon, I would not only have completed a tour of Northern Ireland, but would have been promoted to corporal, taken part in the invasion of Iraq, returned to the country for a second tour of duty after Saddam Hussein was toppled from power, completed my qualification as an anti-tanks specialist and been promoted, again, to the rank of sergeant. In 1998, all this was in the future – and yet it all happened in the fastest, most frenetic seven years of my life.

Then, one night in August 2005, after I had long since settled into my life as a bachelor soldier, everything changed.

CHAPTER ONE

I've heard it said that any successful relationship must start with a truly memorable meeting, something that stands out against the ordinariness of life. Well, that wasn't my experience. There were no great dramas on the night I met my future wife, Claire. But, no matter how my career was going and what wars it would take me to, this was the start of the greatest adventure of my life.

In 2005, I was 32 years old. A few months away from being promoted to sergeant, I had only recently returned from my second tour of Iraq, having joined the invasion force in 2003. Like all Royal Marines coming back from a tour of duty, I was looking forward to some rest and relaxation – and if that also meant a few drinks with the lads in a local nightspot, well, I was game for that. At 32 you can be a veteran in the armed services, but you're still at an age where you want to have fun. A few old friends of mine had planned a night out in Taunton, Somerset, where they were stationed and, for want of anything better to do, I decided to join them. It's lucky that I did, because it was the night my life truly began.

The nightlife in Taunton might not be the most electric, but it has its charms. Besides, anywhere that a few Royal Marine friends and I could get together was all right by me. The night started early and by the time midnight loomed, we found ourselves in one of the local nightclubs. I am not the sort of man who spends his nights on the dancefloor, but I was happy enough, propped by the bar with the lads, soaking up the atmosphere. After six months in the deserts of Iraq, even a Taunton nightclub can feel like the grand ballroom at the Savoy.

Perhaps I wasn't fully aware of it at first, but at some point one of the ladies on the dancefloor caught my eye. It was not only that she was tall and blonde (I am not that shallow!), there was something undefinable about her, something that drew my eye in a way that nobody else had – in the club or, in fact, anywhere else in the world. Although I'd had girlfriends before, none of them had lasted very long, and I had never been particularly bothered about that. I'd enjoyed what fleeting relationships I'd had but I'd enjoyed my own company just as much – and, truth be told, in my 20s I was probably too selfish for anything to last long term. I suppose that was why the Marines suited me fine – I liked the structure and opportunities it had given me, I liked the sense of advancing myself piece by piece, and in my spare time I enjoyed being able to do what I wanted to do when I wanted to do it. And perhaps I was not so different from many other lads in their 20s for that.

In the nightclub, I tried not to stare, but it seems I was not successful. The dancer was distracting me from my chats with the lads so much that I hardly noticed when another lady separated herself from the throng, marched right up to me and said, "That arse has a name, you know!"

The words hit me fast, but I quickly realised she wasn't being serious. In fact, it was one of those fortuitous moments that would, quite unwittingly, direct the course of the rest of my life. The stranger quickly introduced herself as Carly and, as one song ended and another began, she returned to the dancefloor and dragged the girl I'd been watching up to the bar.

CHAPTER ONE

"Al," Carly ventured, "this is Claire. Claire, meet Al. He's the one who's been watching you all night."

Nightclubs are not the best place for getting to know someone you've only just met, but we did our best. Claire was a little older than me, only recently out of a long-term relationship, and she'd come out for the night to let her hair down, just to live a little. She probably didn't expect to be chatted up by a Royal Marine just back from Iraq, but then again, I have never been the best sort of person at chatting anyone up. Even so, in spite of the flashing lights and thumping music, the conversation flowed. It was flowing so well that, a few drinks later, Carly decided that she'd had enough, said her goodbyes and left Claire and me to it.

I told Claire a little about my own background, and she shared a little of hers. Claire was a local girl now, but she'd been born down in Kent, she was the eldest of three siblings and the boss of her two younger brothers, Anthony and Phillip. Her father, a telephone engineer for the Post Office and later British Telecom, had suddenly announced, when she was 11, that he'd successfully applied for a new job, and that the family would be relocating to Somerset, on the other side of the country. But what was traumatic for the 11-year-old Claire soon became one of the best decisions for her family life. Moving to Somerset opened up the joys of country living to Claire and her brothers. They roamed the hills and rode their bikes down winding country lanes, and camped out overnight – all the Enid Blyton things they hadn't been able to do in suburban Walderslade, Kent.

Even from that first conversation, making our voices heard above the cacophony in the nightclub, I knew that Claire had brains. She'd thrived at school and studied environmental sciences at King's College in London, after which she'd worked for the BBC on various television programmes – Crimewatch, Horizon, Watchdog Healthcheck – as well as for Radio 4's You and Yours. Yes, she was talented and ambitious, that was clear. After London she'd moved back to the south-west to work in PR for a conservation charity and, by a roundabout way, that was how she'd wound up working in communications for the hospital in Taunton. A life story in miniature, but I knew straight away that this was somebody about whom I wanted to know much more.

Right now, however, it was time for another drink. I reached for Claire's glass, meaning to go back to the bar, but she stopped me. It was, she insisted, her turn. Claire is like that. She is independent and forthright, and certainly didn't need some soldier she'd only just met to play the chivalrous gentleman and insist on paying for everything.

"What will it be?" she asked me.

"Jack Daniels," I said, "and Coke."

She looked at me as if I had said something unforgivable. "Why on earth," she uttered, "would you ruin your whiskey with… *Coke*?" She rolled the last word around as if it was some sort of curse.

What can I say? It was the way I liked my whiskey.

She's ribbing me about it still.

CHAPTER ONE

Later, Claire would tell me that on the night we first met, she thought I was a gentleman. That I was funny, generous and kind. That she saw something in me that I didn't really see in myself, at least not outside a military context, a quiet confidence in my own skin. But in the days afterwards, I really wasn't sure what she'd made of me. Like I said, Claire had only recently come out of a long-term relationship, while I was well on the way to becoming an eternal bachelor. She was, I learned much later, looking forward to some time on her own. Perhaps it's fortunate that I didn't know that at the time – because, knowing myself as I do, I might have backed away. All I knew was that I didn't want to back away. Claire had sparked something in me and, as things developed, I knew that I wanted her in my life – no matter how hard she tried to get rid of me!

But the truth is that I didn't really expect to hear from her again. At the end of the night I'd given her my phone number, hoping she'd be in touch but not truly believing she'd call. The problem was, I wasn't stationed in Taunton. I was only there visiting friends for a few days before I had to return to my own posting. In 2005, freshly back from Iraq, I had been posted to Faslane Naval Base in Scotland. Since the 1960s, Faslane – on the shores of Loch Gare, barely 30 miles from Glasgow city centre – has been the home of the United Kingdom's nuclear deterrent. For military personnel posted there, it can be one of the least eventful tours of duty, and for that reason many see it as less attractive. But I'm not the sort of person to kick up a fuss about things. In the military, it doesn't help. You have obligations. There are strictures that need observing. Causing trouble doesn't get you anywhere, and in Falsane there was a job to do. So I'd gone up there to do it.

The morning after the night before, though, Claire called, and we met for breakfast. Over bacon and eggs, I discovered that I liked her even more than I had in the nightclub setting. At least here we could talk and learn a little more about each other. I'm not one to automatically think people are romantically interested in me, but after breakfast we agreed to meet for drinks later that same day, before I had to make the long trip back up to Faslane. Something in me started to believe that this might be the start of something I had not yet experienced in my life.

Over the next weeks and months, Claire and I took the first tentative steps in our relationship. Maybe it helped that I was so many hundreds of miles away from her! Claire is a confident, independent woman. She had bought her home in Taunton and didn't need a man lumbering about, getting under her feet all the time. One of the benefits of being slightly older when we met was that we were both more mature and rational, especially about things we had little control over. My posting to Scotland didn't have to derail things. It might even have been the making of us. Claire enjoyed her own space and time – and, by now, after seven years as a Royal Marine, I was used to being shuttled back and forth and keeping the company of the lads in my unit.

CHAPTER ONE

In those days before smartphones and being connected to everyone all the time, communication wasn't easy. We spoke on the phone every week and caught up. Claire even sent me parcels. Sometimes, as I unwrapped one, I would get the sense that she was playing a kind of game – that she'd spent time finding unusual gifts, things that might raise my spirits until I found the time to venture back south and see her again. Perhaps it sounds silly, because of course we hadn't known each other long, nor spent long in each other's company, but a letter or package from Claire could change my outlook entirely. Especially when it contained a small bottle of my favourite port…

Soon, I was in the habit of travelling down from Faslane to Taunton on weekends, arriving late on Friday nights and returning at the crack of dawn on Monday, and all so that I could see Claire. Perhaps the time apart made those weekends feel so much more important, but one particular weekend has always stuck in my mind as signifying when I first understood what Claire was beginning to mean to me. A crisis at work had meant that I wouldn't be able to get down for the weekend – and, though we were both disappointed, one missed weekend was not a disaster for us. Claire seemed to understand and we agreed we'd see each other again soon.

As it turned out, it was sooner than I'd thought. On that Friday night, Claire arrived in Glasgow. If I couldn't come to her, she had said, then perhaps she would have to come to me. After all, even though I couldn't travel, I still had time off that weekend, and we spent it together, exploring Glasgow's highlights. That Sunday, as I took Claire back to the airport and watched her leave for the terminal gate, it dawned on me that here was somebody who – rather than miss me for one weekend – was willing to cross the country to see me. I was waking up to the fact that perhaps I wasn't the kind of man I'd been in my 20s, content with only my work and friends. Claire had changed something in me. I wanted more.

I knew, some months before I proposed, that Claire was the woman I wanted to marry. The fact was, I'd built myself up to asking for her hand in marriage a couple of times in the year before I finally did it, but each time I'd chickened out. The irony was not lost on me that by that time, I'd been on multiple tours of the Middle East, come close to losing my life on more than one occasion, seen friends and colleagues maimed and killed, and been able to soldier through it all – and yet the idea of asking Claire one simple question had filled me with such nerves that on two separate occasions, the words had withered on my tongue and I'd beaten a retreat.

It was 3 July 2008 – my 34th birthday. For some time, now, Claire and I had been living together in the house she'd bought in Taunton. After Faslane, I'd been attached to 40 Commando, fortuitously based outside Taunton, and although I'd sorted out my own accommodation on camp – never wanting to presume anything of my relationship – Claire had suggested that we try living together. What began as an experiment, both of us certain of our love for one another but anxious not to spoil a beautiful thing by living together too soon or for the wrong reasons, had slowly transformed into real life. Taunton had become the first permanent home I'd had since leaving Brighton and the dairy farm 10 years before, and I wouldn't have had it any other way.

We went out to celebrate my birthday at one of our favourite restaurants, just outside Taunton itself. I'd been building myself up for the moment throughout the meal, but somehow the words hadn't yet come; and by the end of the meal, I was wondering if they ever would.

By this point in our relationship, Claire knew all my idiosyncrasies, just as I knew hers, and when I got up to use the bathroom, she knew only too well what it meant. I had a habit of paying the bill on my way back, and this was something that Claire, as passionately independent as she was, couldn't stand. Ever since that first time we met in the Taunton nightclub, when she'd bought me that Jack Daniels and Coke and reprimanded me for the sacrilege, she had wanted to split things evenly. Sometimes I got away with it, but tonight, of all nights, she steadfastly refused to let it happen.

"It's your birthday," she opined. "You're not paying a single penny on your birthday…"

At that moment, my intended marriage proposal bubbled up in my mind. It wasn't a case of now or never – if I bottled it now, as I'd bottled it before, I would stoke myself up for it all over again – but in that moment, something told me that the time was right.

"I promise I'll let you pay," I said, "as long as you promise to marry me."

As wedding proposals go, it was not perhaps the most beautifully worded, nor the most romantic. I am sure that history is littered with men who have made more florid proposals – men who have dropped down on one knee, or hired string quartets to play while friends and family watch on. But that is not me, and that is not Claire.

She was just staring at me, shocked, but I'd already said it once and it gave me the courage to say it again.

"I promise I'll let you pay," I repeated, "as long as *you* promise to marry me…"

Claire was silent a moment longer. Then, "As long as *you* promise you're not joking," she said.

But from the way she looked at me, I could tell that she already knew.

Once we knew we were going to be married, we could make plans for the life we meant to live together. Claire would often roll her eyes when I talked about retiring in my mid-40s – as many Royal Marines do – and joked that, rather than continue as a man of action, I would be happy as a househusband, a man of leisure, perhaps holding down a part-time job in B&Q. Claire, it seemed, had other ideas about me sitting around making the place untidy.

CHAPTER ONE

"We'll move to the country," she would sometimes say. "Find an old house and make it ours. Learn how to be self-sufficient out there. Get a couple of dogs and a cat…"

It was the rural idyll, I suppose, but very quickly Claire's dream became one we shared.

Being with someone had changed the way I thought about life. I was starting to think about 10, 20, 30 years into the future. I've already said that before I met Claire, I had a tendency to be selfish – not, I hope, in a malicious way; but I had enjoyed having nobody to look out for in civilian life but myself. Yet, as my relationship with Claire changed and deepened, that selfishness seemed to evaporate. Suddenly, I cared about someone else's opinion. Suddenly, it mattered to me what somebody felt. Suddenly, I wanted to spend every spare moment I had with someone else, not out there in the world chasing my own adventures and entertainment.

Four years after that night in the Taunton club, Claire became my wife. On 19 December 2009, we gathered in the parish church close to Claire's family home and, surrounded by our friends and families, made our marriage vows.

As we came out of the church, husband and wife, it was a perfect winter day. This deep into December there was certainly a chill in the air, but the skies above were crisp and blue, and when fat flakes of white flurried down upon us, it was not a fresh fall of snow but the confetti our loved ones were throwing up into the air. Somewhere, unstoppable, a group of my Royal

Marine friends were belting out Christmas carols at the tops of their voices. Later, as we repaired to a fantastic manor house in nearby North Newton for the reception, I got to thinking that life couldn't be more perfect than I felt it was just then. Claire and I were the first to arrive but, as we stepped through the doors, our guests fanned out around us. Fires were roaring in the manor's many splendid hearths. Magnificent decorations in red and green were strung up. Silver stars sparkled and the scent of the roast pheasants we had ordered for the wedding dinner was already strong in the air.

I took a moment to breathe it all in. Christmas was coming, Claire had become my wife – and over there, there was a free bar. In that moment, I wanted for nothing in the world. With so much to look forward to, what else could a man ever want?

CHAPTER TWO

2003: al-Faw Peninsula and Abu al-Kasib, Iraq

One moment we were riding in convoy through the dusty streets
of Abu al-Kasib, outside Basra in southern Iraq. Moments later,
I was lying in a ditch, the air above me alive with the splutter and
report of automatic rifle fire. The Pinzgauer all-terrain vehicle –
or "Pinz" – I'd been travelling in was an obliterated wreck in the
middle of the road, the quad bike my troop sergeant had been
riding, a blackened shell.

Things happen in an instant. An hour ago, all was calm. We'd
achieved our objective, which was to start setting up checkpoints
and a defensive perimeter at a junction south of where we now lay.
Then orders had been issued over the radio: we were needed to
the north. Somewhere up the road, closer to Basra itself, another
of our units was in difficulty. So my troop sergeant and I rallied the
lads, formed a convoy with our Pinz vehicles, and set off.

The suburbs were a sprawl of low buildings of mud and
stone, with cornfields in between. In convoy we came, my five
lads and I in the lead vehicle, more in the Pinz behind, and our

troop sergeant riding the quad bike alongside. From somewhere out there, we could hear the rapid percussion of automatic rifle fire, not close enough to shock or startle, but enough to tell us in no uncertain terms that this war was *live*.

Then we rounded a corner in the road.

It took me an instant to recognise that the Iraqi standing in the middle of the road was holding a rocket launcher in his hands. In that same instant, a rocket burst forth. I could see its head blazing directly toward me.

I will not say that my life flashed before my eyes. This was not a war movie, and sometimes the cliches simply aren't true. If I felt anything, it was only the momentary shock that the rocket existed at all. *What is that?* I remember thinking, in the fraction of a second it took me to understand what was about to happen. After that, there was only the preternatural calm that takes over in a crisis. It's at moments like this that you have your training to thank for keeping you grounded, for helping you overcome the very human instinct to panic and freeze.

The last thing I remember thinking before the rocket struck was how *unexpected* the whole thing was.

Then the chaos began.

We hadn't known for certain until three days before the invasion that we were going to enter Iraq. Naval Deployment 03 had been planned for years in advance, and when my current unit, 40 Commando, had embarked from the United

Kingdom aboard HMS Ark Royal, all we had in mind was a tour of the Mediterranean, stopping off to train with NATO allies along the way.

But this was 2003, an era of uncertainty at home and abroad. I'd enlisted as a Royal Marine in 1998, when the presiding conflicts of the 20th century seemed to be over. Nobody was foolish enough, or so unversed in history, to believe that we were entering a time of unending peace, but it is also true that nobody really knew what the world's next flashpoint would be – or when it might come.

All of that changed in 2001.

I can vividly remember where I was on 11 September, when al-Qaeda terrorists hijacked and flew planes into the twin towers in New York City. In 2001, I was a lance corporal with D Company, 40 Commando, and in the September of that year I found myself in Cyprus on a training exercise. When the first hijacked plane struck the World Trade Centre, my lads and I were just off-shore, aboard the RFA Sir Tristram. As news of the atrocity spread, my fellow marines and I gathered around the small television screen in the ship's mess hall. There was silence as we watched the devastation. Occasionally, an errant voice would pipe up, wondering if what we were watching was real. But in our guts, we knew that it was transformative: not only to the world, but to every one of us there in that room. Soon, somebody said, we would be going to war. In a few brief moments, the future direction of our careers had changed. It was just a matter of finding out where we would be going and who we would be fighting against.

The world had its defining war once again. George Bush, then president of the United States, dubbed it the "war on terror", and in October 2001, a little less than a month after the al-Qaeda attack, the United States invaded Afghanistan, whose Taliban regime harboured al-Qaeda itself. Joined initially by forces from Canada, Australia and the United Kingdom, the invasion would soon be bolstered by forces from every single member of NATO.

By the time we had embarked on Naval Deployment 03, the war in Afghanistan was 18 months old, and the clamour at home – in the press, in parliament and on the streets of London, where protestors turned out in their hundreds of thousands – was about whether Britain's wars in the Middle East should be extended into Iraq. The UK had already joined the US in one war in the Persian Gulf, helping to lead the coalition that drove Iraq out of Kuwait after it invaded and tried to seize its oilfields in 1990. Now the question was whether we would join them a second time. It already seemed clear that the US would invade, and in London, parliament debated fiercely the necessity for the UK to do the same.

I have never played a political game. I have always been very clear with myself: as a Royal Marine, I was employed by Her Majesty's government, and whatever decisions were made further up the command chain, it was my duty to carry them out.

Duty matters to me. It always has. And, at least at the start of my military career, I was good at compartmentalising the different parts of my life. When I was at home, I was at home. When I was with 40 Commando D Company, I was with 40 Commando D Company. Accordingly, when I was aboard HMS Ark Royal on Naval Deployment 03, my head was not back in England, where the newspapers raged with the arguments for or against war, or in parliament, where the "dirty dossier" was being turned inside out. I was a Royal Marine, doing my job, and until I was told otherwise, that job was to train with our allies in NATO and put all thoughts of future war out of my head.

Of course, that was easier said than done. None of the lads on board were oblivious to the resupplies of ammo, body armour and other pieces of kit that turned up on ship. Even as we turned south to cross the Mediterranean and enter the Suez Canal, the chatter on board was still that if Saddam Hussein opened Iraq up to UN weapons inspectors, we'd be sailing back north. But one day turned into the next, yet more days flickered by and then, three days before the land invasion began, on the same day that US artillery began to bombard the country from the air, seeking to disable its military, we got the word – we were going in.

Five years a marine, and I was about to embark on my first war.

The lads and I gathered on the vehicle deck aboard HMS Ark Royal, waiting for the signal. Some of the Chinook helicopters had already embarked. I watched them dwindle into the skies above Iraq's al-Faw peninsula, their rotary blades making a familiar thunder as they tore holes in the air. Soon, our turn would come.

I had never been the sort of person who looks too far into the future. In 2003 I was not yet 30 years old and I had spent my 20s taking life as it came, one day at a time. It was not something I particularly worked on, it was in my nature not to catastrophise. But now, waiting as the Chinooks arced back in to ferry the next set of lads out onto the peninsula, the anticipation felt different. All of this was a genuine unknown. But so is everything until you do it, so I fell back on my old defences, one step at a time, never thinking too far ahead.

Then word came, spreading across the vehicle deck with the ferociousness of any rumour. One of the helicopters taking in elements of 42 Commando had gone down.

It was enough to sober me and all the lads around me.

"Downed?" somebody asked.

The answer was: nobody knew. Whether the Chinook had gone down under enemy fire or from simple mechanical failure wasn't yet clear. All anybody knew was that it was gone, and of the multiple lives aboard it there was no sign.

Intellectually, you know that there will be casualties in war. You know that you are going out there to do a job, and that that job might mean that you kill, or perhaps get killed. In my career I have lost colleagues whom I considered friends. But in 2003, I had not yet killed and I had not feared for my life – and though I knew the chances were real in my head, it was only in moments like these that they sunk into my heart. The thought of the lost Chinook brought possibilities so much closer. Lives lost, perhaps, before the land invasion had truly begun. In that moment, whether it was due to enemy fire or simple bad luck didn't matter to me. The end was the end, however it happened.

The air filled, again, with the relentless *whomp-whomp-whomp* of rotary blades. Across the vehicle deck, our troop sergeant was directing us. It was time.

"Best of luck," he said as we assumed positions in the belly of the Chinook.

The rotary blades turned faster, faster, faster, and we lifted, haltingly, into the air above HMS Ark Royal.

As we climbed higher, Iraq's al-Faw peninsula opened up beneath us. To the west sat Kuwait, to the east, the border with Iran. In formation, the Chinooks taking 40 Commando onto the peninsula fanned out, filling the skies above the Persian Gulf with noise. Then we were dropping down, the coast falling away behind us, and touching the earth of Iraq for the first time. This, I realised as I stepped out of the Chinook, with its blades still beating a rhythm above me, was invasion.

40 Commando was part of the second wave into Iraq. The artillery bombardment had lasted three days, and US Navy Seals had already made landfall here on the peninsula. The port city of Umm Qasr was one of the coalition's primary targets, vital for establishing a supply of humanitarian aid into the nation, but we

were here with an altogether different objective. This portion of the peninsula was home to the Manifold Metering Station, part of the vast infrastructure of Iraq's oil industry.

Our mission: to secure the metering station and ensure it remained viable and intact. We had not come to wage war and destroy this country. Operation Iraqi Freedom's primary goal might have been the toppling of Saddam Hussein and a change of regime, but in the longer term the coalition was meant to stabilise the nation, give it room and security to rebuild, and allow a new democratic government to flourish. If any of that was going to be possible, the country needed its economy functioning at its best, and in Iraq, that meant oil. The metering station had to be preserved. As the Chinook had come over the coast and descended onto the peninsula itself, I had seen the station's shape, its tall funnels and pylons, standing shrouded on the horizon, then the station and its surrounding installations came into stark relief as the Chinook began its descent.

I have already said this was not a war movie. As we stepped out, there was no instant enemy fire, we had not burst directly into a gunfight. But there was something otherworldly about the landscape – something lunar, something eerily quiet and still, in spite of the remaining Navy Seals who bombed around in their off-road vehicles and the elements of 40 Commando who had landed before us, waiting in their mustering areas while their vehicles came in.

CHAPTER TWO

We gathered at our own mustering point, the Chinook that had brought us in now nothing but a speck in the sky.

It was the silence that was oppressive. In other areas of Iraq, the invasion was in full force as the coalition battled back the forces of the Iraqi Republican Guard. The northern front of the invasion was bitterly fought over as US troops strove to secure Kirkuk, Mosul and the northern oil fields – and to stop divisions of the Iraqi army falling back to reinforce Baghdad. But our own welcome to Iraq was ghostly and still.

The Iraqis around here had bugged out some time before. All the men who worked here and the armed forces set to guard them had evaporated into thin air, most of them ditching their arms on the way. It wasn't difficult to understand why. Many of the men down here would have seen service in the Gulf war of 1990–1991. They knew what they were up against, that the military might of the US-led coalition could not realistically be resisted. And so, in the days that followed, we moved from installation to installation, locking them down, making sure no resistance remained, and piece by piece collecting all the weaponry they'd left behind.

Sometimes news would come in from further north. Other elements were having live engagements, bursts of intense kinetic activity that flurried up in the vast emptinesses of warfare, but here at the Manifold Metering Station and in its immediate surrounds, the silence remained.

Three days later, a new tasking came in.

Now we travelled north.

The landing site on the peninsula had been dominated by oil infrastructure but, as we pushed on, that faded behind us and we caught our first glimpses of civilisation. This was the road to Basra, which hunched somewhere on the horizon, surrounded by the sprawl of its various suburbs.

As our convoy moved on, the land changed around us. On one side of the road, desert stretched into the distance; on the other, where the land was cultivated and irrigated, palm trees stood tall and signs of agriculture began to abound. Fields were dotted with mud-walled compounds, then with buildings built from solid stone. Soon those buildings grew denser and our primary objective came into view.

We had been tasked with clearing an old university complex on the edges of Abu al-Kasib, on Basra's southernmost border. As we drove into its grounds, the building loomed above us. The lads in my unit fanned out, swiftly securing the ground floor, while other elements of D Company began clearing the surrounding buildings, going door to door in search of anyone who remained.

The sun was just coming up. It could have been like any other day.

As the search continued, my troop sergeant and I rounded the back of the complex to make certain nobody was there. For a time it seemed that this complex, too, would be as barren as the metering station we had first flown into. Perhaps 40 Commando, I thought, would have a quiet war.

Then there was movement, up ahead.

About 200 metres from where we crouched, an Iraqi soldier in green fatigues had appeared. My troop sergeant and I held position. For the moment, fortune was with us – he hadn't seen us yet. But there was no doubt about it, this was our first sighting of the enemy. The automatic rifle in his hands was everything we needed to know.

I took the shot.

Though it was my first live engagement of the war, and in fact the first live engagement of my military career, I had had no second thoughts. One of the greatest strengths my training had given me was the ability to make a decision quickly. In my later career, it would make the difference between life and death. Yet no sooner had the enemy combatant dropped to the ground than others appeared. I heard the splutter and burst of incoming fire for the first time in my career.

The sky erupted. Bullets arced past, exploding into the walls of the university buildings around us. My troop sergeant Craig and I wheeled around, locating the new combatants. First one, then another, then a third – men were lifting themselves up from a trench line we hadn't previously seen, their automatic rifles sputtering fire.

It had all happened so quickly, but the fire had brought the rest of our lads into the action. The vehicles we had come in on were mounted with medium and heavy machine guns, and only moments after we'd come under fire, the machine gunners returned it, felling the combatants who'd emerged. Clean, functional, methodical, this was the way we had been trained.

From beginning to end, the engagement lasted seconds.

After it was done, we held position, waiting for the rifle troops to come down from the university building they'd been scouring and sweep through the area from which the combatants had erupted.

The men we'd encountered were not the only ones in the grounds of the university, but they were the only ones we had to engage. Others saw us fanning out across the grounds and immediately gave up their weapons, handing themselves over as prisoners of war. Chatting to one of them through our interpreter, it quickly became clear that most of them were reluctant soldiers at best. Conscripted that morning, or in the days leading up to the invasion, they had been pressed into uniforms, handed weapons and told that if they did not stand and defend these locations, they would be shot by their superior officers. Faced with a decision like that, they'd held to their positions while many of their commanding officers bugged out, and it was with quite some relief that many of them surrendered and handed themselves over.

It was the same story everywhere as we pushed on. Clearing the grounds of the university was only the first part of our overall objective: to push into the low suburbs and set up defensive positions in anticipation of the battle for Basra itself. As we went, although we had the occasional sudden engagement with an enemy prepared to put up a fight, we took yet more prisoners, disarming them and bagging their personal belongings before passing them back through the company chain to our military police and, later, internment. In this way, we moved north through the suburb, eventually reaching our intended grid reference and establishing a defensive position at the junction there. Here we bedded down, awaiting our next tasking.

Somewhere up that road, trouble was waiting.

The rocket blazed towards me.

I have said that some cliches simply aren't true. Well, some of them *are*. As the rocket cut its path toward me, the world and everything in it seemed to fade away, move in slow motion. I could see the rocket's every detail as it turned closer, and closer, and closer...

But, though the world moves more slowly at moments like these, it does not follow that *you* can. By the time the rocket bore down on us, we had only just recognised its existence.

It struck the front of the Pinz I was commanding.

There was no time to contemplate the death that was powering our way. Nor was there any time to get out. The rocket hit the Pinz...

...and, by some strange mercy, bounced off the rucksack that was mounted there, then headed skyward and obliterated something beyond my field of vision.

I looked up, staggered that we were still alive. But the relief was short-lived. No sooner had I registered the fact that I was still here than I saw that another of the Iraqi soldiers – so many of them suddenly flocking to the road – was bringing a second rocket launcher to bear.

This time, there was time enough to react. We could count our mercies later.

"Get out!" I cried, grabbing my rifle.

The lads needed no encouragement. Rolling out of our vehicles, we threw ourselves into the drainage ditches at the side of the road. Seconds later, my face buried in the dirt, I heard the reverberation as the second rocket hit its mark.

It was some time before I could look out. The Iraqi soldiers had opened up with automatic rifle fire. The short, sharp bursts exploded through the air above my head. Though there was scant shelter where we had landed, the ditch offered some vague protection. Using it, I craned sideways and saw the vehicles we had been in only moments before engulfed in flames in the centre of the road.

I saw something else, too. Most of the lads in the unit had banked right out of the vehicles. Now they were squatting low in the cornfields on that side of the devastation, returning fire at the Iraqis at the top of the road. But on this side of the road, *my* side of the road, there were only three of us. Craig, my troop sergeant, our troop signaller Simon and I had our bodies pressed into the basin of the drainage ditch, more exposed than the lads on the other side.

CHAPTER TWO

We were out here on our own.

"How many are there?" I asked.

It was difficult to know. When the first rocket was launched I had seen only one man, but by the time the second had ravaged our vehicles, the road ahead was alive. I tried to gauge a number, but the rifle fire was keeping me down.

On the other side of the road, beyond what was left of my Pinz, the rest of the lads were gathered. They might have had more cover than us, but an undulating wave of grain does little to impede a steady flow of automatic rifle fire. If the three of us on this side were pinned down, unable to extract, perhaps there was still a way the other lads could beat a retreat of their own.

My eyes were drawn south, back down the way we'd come. Only moments before we'd been met with the RPG-wielding Iraqi soldier, we'd passed a farm building, a simple stone structure crouched on the side of the road. And there it was, scarcely 200 metres from where the lads had found cover.

I reached for my personal role radio, or PRR. "The farm building, 200 yards back down the track. You see it?"

The reply was drowned out by the screech and explosion of an incoming rocket, but by the way they looked back, I knew the lads had registered it.

"Best as you can, try and make your way there. We'll lay down fire. Pull back, boys. I'll try and see you there…"

They got the message. All we had to do was buy them a little time.

In short, sharp bursts we fired on the Iraqis further up the road. I saw one man go down, saw another stagger back where the rifle fire hit him, but there were already too many of them to count. Risking a glance across the road, I could see that the rest of the lads were drawing back, joining the fray as they went. Yet, in the chaos, it was near impossible to see what was happening. Bullets tore through the sky above our head. Yet more rockets carved their arcs over the decimated vehicles, erupting in violent blooms in the cornfield through which my lads were retreating.

Through gaps in the fire, I caught sight of some of the lads. Whether any of them had gone down, I still could not say. Still, they were doing what they needed to do. In the chaos they were falling backwards, out of my field of vision. Sometimes you have to accept that there's little you can do to help. From here on in, they were on their own.

Now was the moment to think about ourselves.

I turned to my troop sergeant, meaning to make some plan, when suddenly the air was ripped apart by another shriek. Instinctively we dropped back into the ditch for cover, just in time to see another rocket hoving in towards us. In the corner of my eye I saw it glance off the lamp-post that still stood above the burning wreck of my Pinz – but the impact was not enough to make it explode. Instead, it dropped to the floor and started spinning wildly on the spot.

My eyes locked with my troop sergeant's. Both of us knew what the other was thinking without having to say it: any moment now, the rocket was going to explode. Every second that passed as it danced its frenzied dance was a second closer to the detonation – and here we were, stranded in its blast radius.

Without a word, Craig picked himself up, extended his right leg and kicked the rocket hard with his boot.

The rocket arced away from us, up and across the road. Seconds later, it detonated, pieces of earth and road and obliterated Pinz raining down over us.

Craig scrabbled back into the ditch at my side. "Al," he grinned – and never before had I seen as sudden and unexpected a grin as this – "I think we're fucked here."

I couldn't help it. The automatic rifle fire was sounding again above our heads, but I started laughing, wild and uncontrolled. Soon, Craig and Simon were both laughing as well.

"Yeah, we are," I said. "So let's get on with it, shall we?"

I levered myself up a few inches from the ground and returned fire up the road. I had no hope of knowing if I had hit anybody, but perhaps it was enough that the enemy soldiers momentarily stayed their attack, and together we were able to scrabble a little further backwards along the ditch. When the attack started again, we hunkered down, returned fire, and once again managed to withdraw. By increments we retreated until, finally, we reached the sanctuary of a low stone wall. Scrambling behind it, at last we had the cover we needed.

We could wait here, but we couldn't wait indefinitely. What ammo we had was already dwindling. As soon as it died, all we would be doing was sitting here, waiting to be picked off.

Simon finally managed to get clear comms with the rest of D Company. Soon, he was relaying a message up the line. Reeling off our grid coordinates and our urgent need for support with an understandable nervousness in his voice, he passed back that three of our vehicles had been destroyed and we were attempting to fall back to one of the larger buildings to our rear.

A voice crackled back, acknowledging the request.

"What's the word?" I said, when he had put the radio down.

"They're coming," Simon replied.

Craig looked back over the wall, releasing a spray of automatic rifle fire along the ditch. "Best hurry," he uttered.

He was right. When next I looked, I could see the Iraqi soldiers gathering down the road, making ready to advance on where we were hunkered down.

"You know what we're going to have to do."

I did. From this position I couldn't make out the farm building the others had beaten a retreat towards, but I knew it was out there.

We were going to have to reach it ourselves.

We made it back.

Later, I would recall little of those moments as we drew back along the road, Craig, Simon and I frustrating the enemy where we could, throwing ourselves into what little cover rose up when we couldn't. Later, all of that would be a blur of pumping legs and burning chest, the rattle of automatic rifle fire and shriek of rockets over my shoulder. But it was the lesser of two dangers. We could stay and be killed for certain, or we could make a break for it and take the chance we might survive. So we took the chance.

On our bellies, we scrabbled backwards three or four metres. Stopped. Fired back on the enemy, if only to buy ourselves a few more seconds to scrabble back another few metres. In those seconds, the hail of automatic rifle fire started again. Bullets impacted on the walls above us, exploding into the road on our right. Rocket-powered grenades thundered up the road, slamming into the two gutted vehicles, or spinning wildly as they collided with the streetlights. In a frenzied situation like this, you have no time to think about the danger you are in. All my mental processes were devoted to correlating how far we had to go with how much ammunition I still had. There had been so much ammo on the vehicles – but by now those vehicles were black shells, licked by tall, hungry flames, and whatever ammunition remained on board was lost to us forever. We could not have reached it even if we'd tried. Instead, all I had on me were six magazines, 30 rounds loaded, and perhaps another 240 rounds on bandoliers that I could use once the magazines were emptied.

We were outgunned and too far from cover.

I still cannot recall how long we were on our bellies, pressed hard into the earth as the bullets arced above us, listening to the shriek of rockets exploding somewhere behind. But at some point when we looked up, the road banked to the left and, scrabbling around it, we had our first real cover. Craig, Simon and I grouped up. By now we were almost parallel with the local structure that the rest of the lads from the convoy were piling into. I still could not see if they were all safe. Perhaps one or more of them had gone down on the way. We just couldn't know.

Somehow, we were going to have to get to them.

But what that meant was crossing the open road.

Voices flew back and forth across the radio. The rest of the company were nearing now, but our convoy had walked into an ambush and there was no way they were going to do the same. We'd already lost three vehicles to the rockets, the company could not risk losing anything further. They had grouped up some distance back down the road. Elements of them would soon be here. Perhaps, with them, we'd be able to push up and drive the Iraqi soldiers back.

From our cover, we watched as the rest of the lads reached the cover of the farm building. At least where they were was defensible. At least, now, they'd be able to return fire. We waited as they fixed themselves in position in the windows and doorway. Listened as another rocket shrieked, devastating the surface of the road.

Then the return fire began.

The lull it bought us would be everything. The way across the road was not so very far, but even so, timing was everything.

As the lads in the structure returned fire, forcing the Iraqi insurgents to take cover, Craig, Simon and I made our break. Bullets arced down the road, exploding against the gutted vehicles and masonry of the buildings further along. By the time we reached the other side, taking advantage of a moment's respite in the fire to crash through the farm building's doors, only seconds had passed – but moments like that can feel like hours.

The sense of relief I felt at seeing all the lads here, every last one of them accounted for, was immeasurable. One of them had lost his rifle in the haste of the retreat through the cornfield, and at some point we'd have to get out there and retrieve it rather than let it fall into enemy hands, but everyone was here, and everyone was alive. That was what mattered.

But it wasn't over yet.

The lads had already set about securing our position. The big stone walls of the structure would allow us to minimise the risk of returning fire, but they also meant that the enemy could begin to push down the road towards us – and with all of us in one location, we were a prime target. One after another, rockets thundered, coursing over the relics of our burnt-out vehicles, exploding against the farmhouse walls and the surrounding structures. A constant hail of automatic rifle fire came with them, pinning us inside the building.

We had ammo to return fire, but we'd already expended so much getting here, and the lads had expended yet more covering us in our crazed dash across the road. Time mattered now, more than ever.

In the corner of the farmhouse, our signaller was busy notifying the company of our location. One after another the rockets came, but the gaps between them became longer and longer – until, finally, we understood that the soldiers up the road were exhausting their supply. At least this gave us a modicum of hope; the automatic rifle fire may not have abated, but there was this, at least.

We hunkered down. There was nothing more to do. The automatic rifle fire was intensifying, and this could mean only one thing: that the insurgents were converging on the structure where we were hidden.

One minute passed.

Two minutes.

Three. Four. Five.

Returning fire with what ferocity we could, revolving in and out of the vantage points from which we could loose fire, we counted down the minutes. Six minutes passed. Then seven and eight.

Then, in a thunder of ordnance, the rest of D Company arrived.

They arrived en masse, assuming strategic positions around the farmhouse and returning fire at the advancing Iraqi soldiers. Without any rockets left, the Iraqis were quickly outgunned. As the company moved down the road, we emerged from the farm building to join them, pushing back the way we had come. Moments later, understanding at last the level of resistance they were facing, the Iraqis broke, beating a retreat into the buildings further up the road.

CHAPTER TWO

Finally safe from immediate attack, the company gathered. The Iraqi soldiers were broken, but not defeated. We still had little idea how many of them there might have been, and the day was already growing old. The idea of pursuing them deeper into the suburb, where the buildings grew taller and more populous, was quickly discounted. Yet we could not remain in situ all night. The structure we had been using might have been defensible by daylight, but by night it would become a trap. There were too many avenues of attack, too many potential lanes by which we might be taken unawares. Perhaps that was what the Iraqis were hoping for right now.

Nor could we bug out. Our orders were to hold this position, so that by morning – resupplied with fresh vehicles and ammunition – we could continue to clear the path through Abu al-Kasib and to the edges of Basra itself. What we needed was somewhere to get through the night.

"It'll have to be the desert," our company commander finally announced.

Perhaps it seems counterintuitive that somewhere as open and unprotected as the desert was the best place for our company to be, and there is no doubt that it feels very exposed. Yet out there, we would be able to see in every direction. Through all 360 degrees, we could sense anyone coming within range of a viable attack. What's more, our night vision capability vastly outstripped that of the insurgents we were facing. In a built-up area, even one as modestly built up as the junction around which we had just fought, the Iraqis might be able to spring an attack on us. In the open, exposure worked to our advantage. We could see them before they saw us; the emptiness between us would be our defence.

The decision was made. I gathered the lads together and, alongside the rest of the company, we ventured across the cornfield through which they'd first beaten their retreat, and out into the desert. Stopping about half a mile from the last line of buildings, we established a perimeter.

Here we waited as darkness descended.

The night was long and vast. The emptiness stretched in every direction. Sometimes we could see shapes moving on the edges of our vision. Our night vision apparatus revealed the movements of insurgents beyond the range of our weapons – while we remained beyond the range of theirs. Hours passed in this way: walking the peripheries of our makeshift encampment, listening to the hiss and crackle of radio chatter telling us where other Iraqis had been spotted, where engagements were still alive. That night, what sleep I had was in the form of a few scarce, snatched moments with the black vaults and stars above, while others in the company protected our periphery. Then, as dawn approached and the skies paled, we reassembled, moving back across the open terrain to the site of the prior day's devastation.

The junction where, yesterday, I had come closer to losing my life than at any other moment, was barren and empty. The signs of the day's engagement were clear, the ghosts of two Pinzes and a quad bike still sitting forlornly in the middle of the road, the cavities in buildings and road where bullets had been sprayed or rockets exploded, the streetlights wrenched into crooked angles and, more than anything else, the way the road at our feet was marked with pools of dried viscera and blood, the only real evidence that we had inflicted mortal damage on the Iraqis who ambushed us. They had collected their dead and retreated with their wounded, and now there was only a ghostly silence.

Today we would continue the journey north, sweeping into the first properly built-up district and forcing its Iraqis out. The suburb of Abu al-Kasib had yet to be fully secured, and if Basra was ever to be controlled by coalition forces, this was the road we would have to travel. At least we now understood the kind of perils that might await us, how quickly a simple drive could turn into a full-blown battle. But for now we would regroup, take advantage of this momentary respite and begin anew.

We had made it through our first major engagement unscathed.

* * *

Some time later, I waited by an airstrip in the Kuwaiti desert. We had come to Iraq via a sea voyage that had taken weeks. Our return voyage would be much shorter. I searched the skies for incoming planes.

The invasion had been short, sharp and bloody. By the time I was pulled out of Iraq and waited here in Kuwait for repatriation to the UK, Saddam Hussein had been overthrown and dug out from the hole in the ground where he was hiding. In Baghdad the famous statue of him had been toppled, what was left of the Iraqi army had surrendered, and the country's oil infrastructure – on which so much of its future relied – had been secured. All this, and I had been in Iraq for scarcely 12 weeks. And yet, as we boarded the plane, there was a distinct feeling at the back of my mind that I was not finished with Iraq, and neither was Iraq finished with me. My tour in Northern Ireland towards the end of the Troubles, when the peace process was finally taking effect, had opened my eyes to the role the British army plays not just in achieving the peace, but in maintaining it as well. And so, as the plane took off and the desert sands of Kuwait and Iraq fell away from me, I knew I would return. The British armed services would be in Iraq for some years to come – but, in that instant, all I was thinking was that I had survived my first tour. I was going back home.

CHAPTER THREE

Helmand Province, Afghanistan

I wasn't to return to Iraq until 2004 and then again in 2006, a year after I first met Claire. Although the invasion's original goal – of toppling Saddam Hussein and forcing a change of regime from his Ba'ath ruling party – had been accomplished in a short, sharp timeframe, in many ways the war went on. By the spring of 2004, the insurgency was developing in new, brutal ways, targeting in particular the Iraqi security forces still being developed and trained alongside the coalition. In March, insurgents launched an assault against private US security contractors in Falluja, and although the devastation was limited, by November Falluja was the epicentre of the fiercest urban fighting of the war. For 46 days, coalition soldiers battled thousands of Iraqi insurgents, devastating the city – and, although it was defended from falling into insurgent control, 95 coalition lives were lost in the process.

The year 2005 was supposed to be when the coalition withdrew from Iraq, leaving it to the autonomous control of its own people and new government, which had been elected democratically that same year. Yet, across the year, the insurgency only strengthened. By 2006, sectarian violence was becoming widespread, as Iraq's Sunni and Shia populations renewed ancient rivalries. Groups with contrasting interests launched assaults against each other. Baghdad, with its melting-pot population, became the centre of various attempts at ethnic cleansing. Entire neighbourhoods of Sunnis were driven out of Basra. In Baghdad and its surrounding towns, Shias were massacred. And with Iraqi forces unable, yet, to function at a level strong enough to combat all these threats, the 'peacekeeping' role of the coalition forces became so much more paramount.

It was in this capacity that I had returned to Iraq in 2004 and 2006, first as part of a detail providing security for other members of the coalition while they were training the Iraqi security services, and then to assist in training the Iraqi naval infantry themselves. In neither tour did I see active combat, but the experience of watching a fractured country try desperately to knit itself back together, the sudden eruptions of violence and the permeating atmosphere of nervousness and dread, would stand me in good stead for my next tour of duty: Helmand Province, Afghanistan, in October 2007.

Taunton had been home since I left Faslane and rejoined 40 Commando. My original plan had been to take accommodation with the rest of the unit at Norton Manor Camp, north-west of the town. The site has a long and rich history, having begun as a hill fort in prehistoric times, slowly becoming one of the earliest settlements in the Taunton area, a Roman military base and, much later, a logistics depot and prisoner-of-war camp during the second world war. It became 40 Commando's permanent garrison in 1983 and has been ever since. If I was based here, I would be only a few miles from where Claire lived in Taunton itself.

I wasn't expecting it, but it wasn't long after I'd arranged my accommodation at Norton Manor Camp that Claire suggested we might try living together. Having moved down from Scotland, I'd been content with the idea that we'd be closer on a semi-permanent basis. The thought of moving in to Claire's Taunton home had not been at the forefront of my thoughts. Both of us were uncertain. Claire was a homeowner and would be inviting me into her world. I'd spent most of my adult life shuttling between various military garrisons and bases, living primarily with groups of other men. Did Claire really need a big Royal Marine stomping all over the place? Would the patterns of our lives, which had been so different until now, slide so easily together? Was it too soon for us?

I have always felt that the advantage of us having met a little later in life than many couples was that Claire and I were able to look at things on a more pragmatic basis. Living together would be a test, but I quickly realised it was a test I wanted to take – and one that I wanted to pass. If it didn't work out, well, that would be a sadness, but Claire and I are the sort of people who would rather regret the roads taken in life than those avoided. We hadn't known each other long, but – nothing ventured, nothing gained.

We agreed to try it and see how we got on. And so, keeping my accommodation at the camp open just in case, I turned up at Claire's door with my pack on my back, and called it home for the very first time.

We haven't looked back since.

By the time autumn 2007 came around, we'd been living together for almost 18 months. In that time, I'd been sent to Iraq on a security posting that lasted four months, as well as having gone away on various training exercises, at home and abroad, with 40 Commando. But living with Claire felt as natural as I had hoped it would.

For some months now, I'd known that with the next cycle coming up, 40 Commando were going to be deployed into Afghanistan. The rhythm of Royal Marine life means that there isn't time to dwell on or worry about what's coming, this is the job we signed up for and, with the war in Afghanistan ongoing, it had always been only a matter of time before I was deployed out there. It was only as our pre-deployment exercises began increasing in frequency and intensity, across the summer of 2007, that the reality of being away from Claire for a full six-month tour dawned on me. Yet the truth was that since we met and became a couple in 2005, Claire and I had spent more time apart than we had together.

Neither of us minded. That is the lot of so many military families. But in recent weeks and months, we had begun to talk about the future. It was, perhaps, the first prolonged period in my life where I thought about what life might look like in five, 10,

15 years' time. Perhaps it was only that I was getting older and, necessarily, more mature, but there has never been any doubt in my mind that the greater part of it was because of Claire. Claire had rooted me – not just in Taunton, which I now thought of as home – but emotionally and psychologically as well. We were strong enough together that I didn't worry that six months in Afghanistan would test us as a couple, but for the first time when going away, I felt the inordinate pull of *home*.

Claire had always been independent. It was one of the things I loved about her. We were two independent souls who had found each other. Her favourite line was that I could get on with my work in Scotland or Sierra Leone, wherever it took me, and not have to worry that she had nobody around to take the bins out. But this is not to say that I enjoyed saying goodbye and, though the moment I went to join up with the rest of 40 Commando for deployment to Afghanistan was not particularly dramatic, somehow it felt more significant than the other times we'd parted.

Over the previous two years, every time I went away I was certain that I was coming back. This time, although I had every confidence in the British military, the guarantees weren't the same. I'd already seen, in Iraq, the way war changes in a moment, the periods of long nothings punctuated by sudden, violent flurries of action. It was conceivable, if you let your mind wander that way, to think that this was the last time I'd see Claire. But at times like these, pragmatism takes over. Emotions get put away in a box, to be dealt with another day. When we said our final goodbyes, I knew I'd speak to her again soon, and I knew I was keen to come back to Taunton and pick up where we left off when my tour was over. And that was enough to spur me on my way as 40 Commando set off.

By 2007, the war in Afghanistan was already six years old. The story was not an unfamiliar one. Although the Taliban had been defeated in swift order, by 2003 its surviving elements had regrouped and reorganised. From the relative stability of 2003, things had quickly unravelled. The surviving Taliban might have been outgunned and outnumbered by the coalition forces remaining in the country, and especially by the International Security Assistance Force – the NATO-led mission designed to support the Afghan forces in defending the country themselves – but they did not need to win in an open fight to make significant gains in their quest to destabilise the nation in the middle of its rebuilding.

Along with various other insurgent groups, they waged guerrilla warfare. They ambushed security details. They ran suicide attacks against strategic outposts. And they killed indiscriminately, especially Afghan civilians: anybody who allied themselves with the "occupying" forces was considered fair game. Little by little, the Taliban had been reasserting their influence in the rural, tribal regions of the country. And with that escalating influence came escalating, random violence.

By the time of our deployment, I had been with 40 Commando for a year. In my first position as troop sergeant, I had taken my lads through a year's worth of training exercises, not only along the coasts and into the mountains of England, but as far afield as Sierra Leone, where we had conducted jungle training and assisted in training some of Sierra Leone's military. But Helmand would be my first active deployment in Afghanistan – and, with 20 lads beneath me, I felt the responsibility keenly. That is to say, I was proud of it. I knew what my own troop sergeant had meant to me on my first Iraq tour, and the opportunity to be that figure to a younger generation was, I felt, of great importance – not only in my career, but in my life as well.

By now I was 33 and, though not yet old enough to feel a father to this group of 20-year-olds, I was old enough to think of myself as a wiser older brother. I had been in combat situations before. Few of the lads in my troop had. I was ready for the responsibility of seeing them through it. I'd never been into Afghanistan, but at least I had the experiences of Iraq to draw on.

I was going to need them.

* * *

Helmand in 2007 was to be my first active deployment as a troop sergeant. Although I'd already spent a year with the lads I was taking into Afghanistan, there is a new responsibility that comes with this role in an active warzone, and it was one I took very seriously indeed. Most of the lads were eager to get out there and start doing our bit. It was what they had trained for, what they had signed up for, and I remembered the feelings well from our insertion into southern Iraq some four years before. Once the bullets started flying, things would get real incredibly quickly, but that was a bridge we would have to cross when we came to it.

Our small group of 20 men would be providing fire support by means of anti-tank missiles, heavy machine guns and grenade machine guns. In a few weeks' time, we would board a military flight for Camp Bastion – the British military base founded outside Lashkargah, the capital of Helmand Province in south-west Afghanistan – and from there we would range far and wide, sometimes for days or weeks at a time, engaging the enemy wherever command had identified they might be hiding. Life as part of a mobile operations unit would alternate between lengths of time at Camp Bastion, training and recuperating, and periods out in the field where things could get kinetic very quickly. I knew from my first tour in Iraq how suddenly violence can flurry up out of seemingly nothing at all. The lads I was taking out there had trained for it, but there is always a gulf between training and reality – and only being actively deployed can bridge the divide. It was going to be a test, but as Royal Marines there is no greater test of your skills than being out there, where it matters.

We were up to the task.

Then, only weeks away from deployment, we were given news of a change of plan. Rather than be stationed at Camp Bastion and go out as a mobile operations group, Alpha Company had received new orders. We would be going further into the field, to man Forward Operating Base Inkerman – a place nicknamed

CHAPTER THREE

"Incoming" because of the ferocity and relentlessness of the attacks it experienced. Here we would spend six months in a fortified compound with only one objective: to provoke the ire and draw the fire of all the insurgents in the district, providing them with a clear and present enemy with whom to engage. Perhaps it sounds like madness that we should be sent out there specifically to draw the eye of insurgents, but there was method to it. The base stood barely six miles from one of the most important theatres in the whole of the war for Afghanistan, a place that had already been decimated in waves of conflict and which, if it were to fall back into Taliban hands, could have changed the whole complexion of the war. Its name was Sangin, and we were being tasked with its defence.

Sangin doesn't look like much. It is a small place, home to barely 12,000 people, with scarcely 50,000 spread across the neighbouring districts. Compared to its closest major neighbour, Lashkargah, which has almost a quarter of a million inhabitants, it is tiny. Yet its strategic importance cannot be overstated. Sitting in the basin of the Helmand river, Sangin's sun-baked adobe houses and ragged buildings barely separate it from the manifold other small towns and clusters of settlements in Afghanistan, and the cornfields and pomegranate farms beyond it do not immediately suggest how important it is. But the simple fact is this, this small river valley, where the farms only survive the intense heat of summer by virtue of irrigation from the river itself, is the heartland of Afghanistan's opium trade. It is here that vast fields of poppies proliferate to fuel the nation's opium production. From here Afghanistan's opiates make their way into the furthest corners of the world, often smuggled into Europe as heroin and, because of the power and money invested in the trade, it is here that the Taliban – financed, in part, by the riches generated by the poppies grown in these fields – traditionally had a seat of power.

The allied invasion of Afghanistan had sought to replace the Taliban, but in the years since then, the Sangin valley had been fiercely contested. Cutting off the Taliban's financial apparatus was seen as critical to preventing their resurgence, and to ensuring Afghanistan's democratic stability into the future, but the opium trade was worth many millions of dollars to the Taliban and they had proven, time and again, that they did not mean to give it up easily. In many ways, it was exactly what prevented their total annihilation. Sangin had become one of the central battlefields in their fight to survive.

Consequently, loosening the Taliban's hold on Sangin and its valley had become a central part of British foreign policy in the region. The fighting here had already been fierce, with the town itself having been under perpetual siege for almost a year, and relieved only six months before our arrival. In June 2006, after the Taliban executed a number of locals for "collaborating" with the new Afghan government helped into power by the allied forces, a force of more than a hundred British troops were newly stationed in a compound in the very heart of Sangin, a fortified base from which they could patrol the town and ensure its safety. The citizens of Sangin have traditionally distrusted outsiders almost as much as they fear the Taliban, but for a time there was little reaction to the presence of these troops.

Then everything changed.

In late June and July, the base was attacked by small arms fire. Soon after this, the Taliban began to focus their energies on it several times a day, launching attacks with automatic rifles and RPG-7 anti-tank rocket launchers. What became known as the Siege of Sangin was about to begin. With the British soldiers cut off and trapped inside their compound, depending on Camp Bastion helicopters for supplies, the situation grew desperate. Royal Engineers were able to enter the town and, under covering fire, surround the compound with new fortifications, including double-rampart Hesco barriers, but it didn't stop the attacks. Two of our signallers – one of whom was the first British Muslim soldier to be killed in the conflict – and a local interpreter were killed by a Chinese rocket fired at the compound and, although the British forces were able to repel the increasing waves of attack, they could not break the siege. A rapid response by British paratroopers was able to relieve it, but not permanently.

Over the next weeks and months, the situation intensified. A British paratrooper, Corporal Bryan Budd, part of a section clearing a compound in town, was taken captive in a Taliban ambush, and although a rescue mission succeeded in bringing him back, it was too late to save his life. He died of his injuries soon afterwards. As late as March 2007, the Royal Regiment of Fusiliers' C Company were attacked by Taliban forces 79 times in their first three weeks of service in Sangin.

It was only in April 2007, when an international force of more than 1,000 servicemen was sent to relieve the town, that the Taliban were finally driven out and the siege officially broken. US troops and Royal Marines from 42 Commando, along with forces from Denmark and Estonia supported by Dutch aircraft and Canadian artillery, converged on Sangin. By then, thanks in part to the advance warning NATO had given of the attack, the town had been largely vacated by both the Taliban and most of its inhabitants, and the coalition was, for the first time, able to occupy it. The danger of the Taliban still existed in the surrounding district – and they were forever seeking to regain a foothold in the town – but the Afghan authorities were able to return and appoint a new local governor who could, at last, look to the future. Slowly, citizens dared to return to their old lives and think about rebuilding.

It was into this new environment that Alpha Company were being inserted. In October 2007 the Siege of Sangin had been broken for six months. Over that time, the town had slowly repopulated itself, but it remained in disarray. The Taliban might have been driven from their seat of power in Sangin itself, but they were still at large in the rural areas beyond. The danger that the town might fall once more into their hands, and that the opium industry might once again flourish, financing the Taliban to yet more successes, was ever present. But by manning Forward Operating Base Inkerman with a heavy enough force, it was hoped that the Taliban still in the area would be too preoccupied engaging us to focus their energies on destabilising and recapturing Sangin. For six months, we would be the cannon fodder that drew Taliban fire – while, down in the valley, the schools and markets were rebuilt and reopened, and the peaceful civilian population came back to the homes that were once theirs.

My lads and I were about to find out what it was like to spend six months directly in the line of fire.

* * *

And so it began. Life settled into a pattern: guarding the base, running patrols. On this particular day, a patrol had barely been out two hours when the radio at Forward Operating Base Inkerman came alive with the sputter and crackle of a live engagement. This, in itself, was nothing extraordinary. Engaging the enemy was what we were here for, and hardly a day had gone by since our arrival when we hadn't confronted them, whether at the gates of our fortress or out there. That was what the patrols were for – if the enemy were harrying or being harried by us, they were leaving Sangin alone.

But it took only instants for the guys in the ops room to identify this as a particularly ferocious attack.

"We're incoming," the patrol's signaller crackled over the comms. *"Ten minutes out."* There was a beat, and then he continued, *"We're bringing trouble with us."*

Ordinarily, the first sign that an attack on FOB Inkerman was incoming was the sudden burst of small guns fire, or the shriek of a mortar as it was launched over the walls. The gunners permanently stationed on the base walls would return fire immediately, either downing or scattering the insurgents who had come to harry us. Ten minutes was more than enough to ready a defence, but precision was going to be vital if we were to get our boys back through the gates and into cover.

The word went out. An attack was coming.

Forward Operating Base Inkerman had begun its existence as the country residence of a relatively wealthy Afghan family who had, like many others, seen an opportunity in the invading coalition armies and leased it to the allied military as an outpost. Since then, engineers had come in to expand its environs with fortified Hesco bastions: thick, utilitarian boxes resistant to explosions and small-arms fire. When we first arrived to take over from the Royal Anglians, it was still a work in progress. Designed as a base for more than 100 servicemen, it looked at first an austere place, the central compound surrounded by a mish-mash of tents that we would now call home, without any hard cover to protect us from mortar attacks.

At least the base's peripheries were well armed. Behind Inkerman there was nothing but open desert – so with nowhere for the Taliban to hide out there, we could expect few attacks from that direction. In front of us, however, was the "green zone", where the land, feeding from the Sangin river itself, was more lush and fertile, and the vegetation grew tall and dense. It was from here that enemy combatants launched their regular assaults. Mostly it was small bands of insurgents, 10 or 12 strong, bursting out of cover to attack with small arms fire. Sometimes Chinese rockets would unleash their thunder against our fortifications. Mortars might sail up and over the walls to strike the centre of our compound, or Russian grenades might arc up and over the perimeter, exploding somewhere within. But our defences were robust and usually held. Ramps led up to the perimeter walls, where six-gun emplacements were permanently manned, with space for general-purpose machine guns and grenade launchers of our own. Behind that was the mortar line, and behind that the battery of artillery that we could unleash on our most fervent attackers. Many of the staff at Inkerman were engineers, here in support of the heavy guns and artillery. It was the job of my troop to defend the walls.

Ordinarily, the attacks were easily repulsed but, since we'd landed here, they'd come with such frequency that they sometimes seemed relentless. I hadn't been able to understand it at first, but it seemed as if the Taliban insurgents were infinite. Rather than vary their methods and approaches of attack, they would pop up in precisely the same places, take up exactly the same vantage points and loose their fire at us from there. There was a strange predictability to it, as though the insurgents were on an endless conveyor belt: even their commanders must have thought them disposable.

Today was different. I scrambled up into one of the gun emplacements and looked out on the green zone. From somewhere beyond the tree line I could hear the exchange of fire, followed by silence as our patrol beat the next stage of its retreat. Then the fire began again. By degrees, they were getting closer. I could hear it in the volume and severity of the attacks.

Up on the parapet, the radio crackled with life: the patrol was five minutes out, now they were three minutes out, now, two.

At last, we could see them coming through the line of scrub and trees, out into the open ring between FOB Inkerman and the green zone. Somewhere beneath me, the gates to our compound yawned open to accept the patrol back through.

But they had to get here first.

The insurgents had not streamed out of the cover of the green zone like our lads did. They took up vantage points instead, just beyond the line of the scrub, and from there unleashed bursts of small arms and automatic rifle fire at our lads as they charged, legs windmilling underneath them, for the safety of the barricades.

It was a long way to go with no cover. But thankfully that's what we were here for.

The order to return fire had gone up the moment our lads broke cover. Now, as they pumped hard to cover the ground to our Hesco fortifications, we opened fire. In the scrub, the silhouette of one of the insurgents dropped out of sight. Somewhere to the left, another reeled backwards, struck in the chest. Others disappeared from their vantage point in instants, retreating to the safer darknesses beyond the open ground.

How many of them were out there I didn't know. Nor did I care. All that we needed was seconds, and seconds was what we had got. I could hear the cry going up as the gates of FOB Inkerman were heaved back into place, all our lads safely back through.

The return fire went on for some time. The remaining insurgents continued their small arms fire, confident that we were not going to sally out and confront them. Then, when their interest in the escapade was expended, they evaporated into the unseen depths of the green zone.

They'd be back. They always were.

But none of us minded. Getting shot at out here, well, that was our job.

* * *

Another day, another attack. The rocket hit the wall before any of us knew what was going on. One moment there was just white noise, the staccato bursts of automatic rifle fire. The next, the fortified wall exploded inwards, absorbing much of the blow but bucking backwards under the blast. Four of my lads stationed up on the gun emplacements also staggered backwards under the force of the blast.

As others rushed in to drag the injured lads out of the fray, I joined the defence on the walls. The rocket blast had come from somewhere out there in the green zone, and now we could see the Taliban insurgents appearing to loose small arms fire at the gun emplacements up on the wall. In moments, we were returning fire. The Taliban were repelled easily enough that day, but that was not the point. The way they popped up in those same familiar positions let us push them back, time and again – but today the element of surprise had been on their side. The lads were injured badly enough that they could not be patched up here. Before the insurgents were beaten into retreat, a casevac helicopter had to be scrambled to get them back to Camp Bastion and the field hospital there.

But this was life at FOB Inkerman. We were the flickering candle flame that drew in the buzzing insects of insurgent attack. We were the oasis in the desert to which all bloody-minded insurgents were meant to be drawn. And every time a Chinese rocket exploded against our fortified walls, every time one of our patrols was ambushed and had to beat a retreat, under heavy fire, to our bastion at the head of the Sangin valley, every time an insurgent took a pot shot at one of us or hurled a Russian grenade up and over our walls, meaning to maim or kill as many of us as they could, we counted it a victory. We were doing our job.

* * *

CHAPTER THREE

Christmas Day dawned.

There had never been any talk of me going back home for Christmas. My R&R would come later, and I'd never questioned or even thought twice about it. If it had been offered me, I would have given it up in favour of one of my lads anyway. So many people at Inkerman had families at home, wives and children who wanted their daddies home for the special day. When I look back on my own childhood Christmases, I have so many memories to cherish – and there was my father, in the middle of every one. No, I was quite content to spend my Christmas in the desert while others who needed it more went back home. Claire hadn't thought twice either, she had always understood.

I woke to the sound of music.

"IT'S... CHRISTMAAAAAAAAS!"

I picked myself blearily out of bed, pulled my clothes on and reeled out of the tent where moments before I'd been sound asleep. Striding across the camp was the compound's psychological operations (psy ops for short) guy. On any other day, he might have been out in the field, driving around in an armoured rover blasting out messages on a souped-up sound system, berating the enemy, cajoling them to focus their attentions on Inkerman, drawing them away from Sangin and its surrounds, instructing them to give up because *we* were the more powerful force.

But not today. Today he marched across the compound, wearing only a pair of tight Y-fronts, combat boots and a

Christmas hat. The sound commander – a kind of ghetto blaster – strapped to his back was pumping out not incendiary warnings or taunts at enemy combatants, but Slade's hit song, 'Merry Christmas Everybody!' at a deafening volume.

As I stood there watching, a glut of other sleeping riflemen, soldiers and marines emerged from their slumbers, too. Slade had been replaced by Wizzard, who were soon replaced by Wham! It was Christmas, but not as I knew it.

I sloped off to the mess tent and filled myself with breakfast. At some point today I would grab one of the satellite phones and get hold of Claire. She already knew why I was here instead of there. It was not that I wanted to be away from her. It was that Christmas was for children, and we had none. I knew she would be with family of her own today, but it would be good to hear her voice.

Up on the walls, the gun emplacements were still being manned – but because of the wintry conditions, the undergrowth in the green zone had died back, leaving fewer places out there to hide and spring an attack. Consequently, the last weeks had been quieter than when we were first inserted. None of us were foolish enough to believe we were going to have a peaceful Christmas, but even so, we had been glad of the temporary respite.

Soon there came the sound of more singing, but when I emerged from the mess tent, not a single half-naked marine was in sight. Outside, the company Christmas carol service was under way. Some of the lads had erected a monument of stones and topped it with a Christian cross made out of wood. They were gathered around it now, their breath pluming in the chill of the morning air. Their voices, ragged around the edges, were raised in unison:

"Silent night
Holy night
All is calm…
All is bright."

I cannot say that all the lads had great voices, but nevertheless there was something stirring about it as they came together to fill the desert air with the refrain.

"Round yon Virgin, mother and child,
Holy infant so tender and mild…"

As the voices lifted and soared, reminding me of more traditional Christmases back home, a sudden shriek tore through the air. Instants later, something exploded against one of the fortified outer walls.

The song stuttered to a halt. In seconds, the company was lurching to the cover of the buildings inside Inkerman's fortified walls. I turned on my heel, hurtling inside with them. Moments later, another mortar exploded somewhere to my left. Something arced up over the wall and disappeared over the other side of the compound.

The call went out: the insurgents were camped out beyond the range of the direct weapons we had stationed up on the walls. This would be a job for our own mortars. Even high on the Christmas spirit as they were, our lads were a model of professionalism. It wasn't long before the mortars were unleashed, with devastating effect, upon the location where the insurgents had been sighted.

The sounds of devastation beyond the walls of FOB Inkerman had silenced the choir – but only momentarily. As our return attack came to an end, some of the lads picked up the carols again. *Oh Christmas Tree* rang out as the sound of the final mortars faded.

"*So this is Christmas,*" I thought, echoing John Lennon. "*And what have you done…*"

* * *

We left the compound in convoys.

Most of my duties at Forward Operating Base Inkerman involved its defence. But there was another side to my role, too. The base was not always resupplied by ground; air-drops made out in the desert played a large part in this, too. Having completed the Drop Zone Command course before deploying, it was my responsibility to make sure that those air-drops were made and received safely. Consequently, there I was, sitting in the front of the Land Rover as the gates of Inkerman closed behind me, at the head of a convoy going out into the desert.

We had barely moved on when we heard the gunfire. It was too distant to be directed at us and yet not distant enough to think we were out of danger, so we halted the convoy and listened to the chatter across the radio. The insurgents must have been monitoring the gates of the compound because no sooner had we left than the assault had begun.

"Stand to," we were told, and we readied ourselves for the order to turn around. If the base needed defending, the resupply could wait. It wasn't ideal to leave our supplies out at the drop zone, but things changed quickly in the Sangin district, and we had to stay close.

The gunfire came in concentrated bursts. In its midst, I could detect the return fire from the general-purpose machine guns up on our barricades, puncturing the fire from the insurgents.

Then, suddenly, all was silent again, the insurgents killed or scattered.

Word came over the radio: "Crack on for the resupply. We're finished here."

The convoy started to roll forward once again and, with Inkerman just over a mile behind us, we set off for the desert. Despite the base being so close, we were going to have to be careful. In around 100 metres, the gully would open out onto a flatter plain – and out there, across the desert expanse, was the drop zone marked on my map.

I turned to the driver. "We'll have to stop up there. Get out the metal detectors, clear the route ahead until we are out into open des—"

I didn't have time to finish the last word.

The world exploded around me.

Smoke...

The smell of burning...

An incessant ringing in the ears...

I opened my eyes to find the world was spinning off its axis. No matter how I concentrated, it would not come back into resolution around me.

As everything span, the Land Rover came back into view. Well, what was left of it. The front half had been obliterated. Its remnants were strewn like mangled litter across the gully. I was dangling over one bit of it, the scrub in front of me swimming in and out of focus.

Somebody was shouting out. I heard the voice cutting through the persistent drumming in my ears. Behind us, the convoy had ground to a halt. My lads poured out, bringing their automatic rifles to bear – but nobody had sighted the enemy, not yet...

Behind me, Jimmy, my driver, was clawing out, heaving me bodily back inside the part of the vehicle that had survived. With my head still ringing, the world still out of focus around me, I crashed back into the seat from which I'd been thrown.

I looked down.

I saw I had no legs.

The terror that hit me is difficult to describe. The world was still turning. My senses were only just coming back into being. I calculated I had been out for seconds, not even a minute, but in those instants everything had changed.

I had no legs.

CHAPTER THREE

I knew, now, what had happened. We'd hit an anti-tank mine, buried in the earth of the gully. Sometimes the insurgents did this: ours was not the only war to have been fought in Afghanistan, and the country was still brimming with the incendiaries and mines left behind by the Russians in the Soviet-Afghan war that had stretched from 1979 right up until the end of the 1980s. The Taliban had this stuff stockpiled – legacy stuff, to be deployed as and when they needed it. If we'd stopped 50 metres further back and got out the metal detectors, we'd have been able to dig it out and disable it, but as it was, the Land Rover I'd been in sat glowering at me from the other side of the gully. The mine had destroyed its front half, casting me and the driver straight up into the air.

Something clicked in me as the world came back into focus. I shifted, realised I was sitting awkwardly – and, with increasing fascination, watched my legs unfold again from beneath me. By some strange mercy, they hadn't been blown off at all. I'd been thrust up into the air and had landed to hang over the edge of the devastated vehicle. When Jimmy had hoisted me back in, as if to save me from any incoming fire, my legs had folded underneath me – and, in the chaos of those moments, my mind hadn't registered it at all. The absurdity of it almost made me crack a smile.

Ordinarily, an explosion like that would have spelled the end of our tours – and very possibly our lives. What had saved us, a vehicle mechanic later postulated, was one of those random twists of fate that no one can truly account for: the bottom of the vehicle had become packed with desert sand, providing another

71

layer of protection to insulate us from the blast. Without it, the explosion would surely have penetrated the floor of the cab, into the seating area, and made a ruin of us all.

Later, I would discover that I had a hernia in my navel, a result of being thrust up into the air by the exploding Land Rover. Matt, our gunner, had sliced his hand open where the grenade machine gun mounted up top had collapsed in the blast – but, if that was the extent of the human damage a buried Soviet anti-tank mine did to us that day, we could count ourselves lucky.

But the fact was that not all members of Alpha Company would be going home from this tour.

As 2008 turned into 2009 and we entered the final movement of our tour, it was my turn to take the R&R break that many of the lads in the troop had taken over the Christmas period. Transitioning back through Camp Bastion to board a flight home, I ran into one of my colleagues just returning from his own two weeks' leave. I'd known Damian since joining Alpha Company. A well-respected corporal in 2 Troop, he was a bear of a man. Even at my size – all six foot four and 16 stone of me – Damian, or "De" as his friends called him, was an imposing figure. He carried it well, a professional to the core; he took the care and development of those in his charge with the seriousness it truly demands.

After a short while in which we laughed and joked about the last few months in Sangin, as servicemen often do, I wished him goodbye.

CHAPTER THREE

It was to be the last time I saw him.

By the time I returned from two weeks' R&R with Claire, De had become the first fatality of Alpha Company. The Viking – one of our all-terrain armoured vehicles – he had been travelling in had run over a buried explosive device, and in the blast he hadn't stood a chance. This was no old Russian or Chinese mine salvaged from the war of the 1980s, but an improvised device put together by the Taliban – the kind that would, in the coming years, become their most prevalent form of weapon, but which in early 2008 was a new and nascent threat. De's death hung over FOB Inkerman as a stark reminder that, though we lived behind fortified walls, and though our firepower was superior to anything they threw at us, we were all still vulnerable in this place. But war is never neat. It is never tidy and organised. It can be chaotic and brutal and unfair, and the end of De's life, arriving in an unexpected instant, was a perfect example of that.

By the time April 2008 came around, and with it the time for my company to be withdrawn from Forward Operating Base Inkerman, I was ready for home. If there was a sombre mood as we checked out of base and made our way, by Chinook, back to Camp Bastion for repatriation to the UK, it was because we'd lost one of our number out here – and, though a few of us had been injured in the continuous waves of fire that swept at Inkerman, losing a friend and colleague at war is a wound that never quite heals.

Yet back in the comparatively cosmopolitan environs of Camp Bastion, I realised a truth I had not really considered since my days in Iraq, almost five years before – that in spite of the dangers and losses you endure at war, there is pride to take in your accomplishments. We had been sent to FOB Inkerman with one goal in mind. For six months we'd harried and engaged and drawn the attention of the insurgents who operated in the area. We'd run patrols, faced down countless Taliban assaults, and all so that the town of Sangin could repopulate and re-establish itself under new governance, grow secure enough that it would not fall back under Taliban control and become the hub of the area's opium industry once again.

And that pride I talked about, the sensation of having put yourself at risk, that some of you had even made the greatest sacrifice in pursuit of a shared goal? Well, here's the thing I realised as we left Afghanistan: it had worked.

Six months before, Sangin had been a ruin, a depopulated, bomb crater of a warzone where no life could endure. Across those six months, we'd pushed the Taliban up and out of the Sangin valley. At the start of the tour, they had been all around FOB Inkerman. By the time we picked ourselves up to get out of there, we were having to travel a fair distance from base to find any fight at all. Meanwhile, in Sangin itself, the bazaar was thriving again. Schools had reopened. People who had once lived in the town's streets had returned. Sangin had once been described as the deadliest area in Afghanistan, but now we were watching a wasteland returning to life, one week at a time.

CHAPTER THREE

The story of Sangin was far from finished. In spite of all we'd done on that tour, the Taliban still saw the town as central to their ambition to reclaim Afghanistan and ramp up opium production again. Soon, fighting would return to its streets – and so the dance of war would go on. But at the moment we departed for Britain again, we could see what we'd done. The good we had contributed to the area was tangible, there for all to see. And just seeing it made the cost of war more palatable. I could look at my lads and say: we'll never forget the friends we've lost, nor the ones who went home injured, it will stay with us, forever, that one of our guys is dead. But this was the job we were given. We came into it with our eyes open. And, though we should never forget the bad, lads, let's turn our eyes to the good as well. *That*, down there, is what we were trying to achieve. *That's* what we were here for. Take a pat on the back – because, whatever else happens out here, there's goodness too.

The sense of a mission accomplished can be more meaningful than any other to a soldier. It makes every sacrifice worthwhile. And, for me, that was my first experience of Afghanistan. A man can survive almost anything if he knows some goodness and light can come out of it.

I would need to cling onto that the next time I was here, when goodness and light seemed in very short supply.

CHAPTER FOUR

Return to Helmand Province, Afghanistan, 2011

By the time I returned from Helmand in 2008, Claire and I had been together for a little over two years. Together, and yet apart. Our separations had never been a problem for either of us. Two independent spirits need time and space, we had found each other, and for a time that had been enough. But by now I was in my mid-30s. Life was happening quickly. And my thoughts had, inevitably, turned towards what shape my future might take. The truth was, I wasn't sure how it would look – I had never been the sort of person to look too far ahead. But the one thing I was absolutely certain about was that I wanted Claire to be a part of it. Since we'd met, I'd been in Scotland, back to Iraq and now to Afghanistan. If we were going to be certain we were right for each other – not just for the here and now, but for the ever-after – we both felt that we needed some consistency, the opportunity to experience life together day to day, week to week, month to month.

And so, with this in mind, I asked my line manager about what might happen next: what the Royal Marines might want of me, and what I might want of them. On this front, the Royal Marines have always been an incomparable organisation. It is part of their very ethos that family comes first. This was precisely why I had forsaken a Christmas at home in 2007: men with families and children always came before men like me, who didn't yet have those things. The Royal Marines know that what matters most to a man is what is closest to his heart, and that without those things to hold onto, service is difficult. You need something to fight for. And that was why they took little convincing. After the time I'd been away, the months I'd given to my country in campaigns in Iraq and Afghanistan, I was "top of the tree" for some stand-down time.

That was how, soon after my return from Helmand in early 2008, I found myself back at the Royal Marine Commando Training Centre at Lympstone, near Exeter – the very same centre at which I'd arrived 11 years before as a fledgling recruit, uncertain about whether my future lay with the Royal Marines or back on the farm.

This time, I was here with a very different agenda. I would be part of the Central Training Team. Lympstone is responsible for training all new recruits, for training corporals and sergeants as well as officers. My role would be to train the trainers. As part of a three-man team, I would help ensure that Lympstone was turning out the best Royal Marines possible. It was my chance to put everything I had learned in active service and all the qualifications I'd gained to good use, and give back to the service that had given everything to me. As part of my work, I would also help run the first two weeks of the Junior Command Course, helping the young marines looking to advance to become corporals to refresh themselves, get rid of bad habits and get their "training centre" heads on, before they embarked upon the course properly.

It was a job I liked. After seeing first hand the value of good training in Iraq and Afghanistan, it made me proud to know that I was helping to lay the groundwork for further generations of Royal Marines, many of whom would leave Lympstone and move directly to commando units where they would prepare for deployment in Afghanistan itself. For me, it was a maturing moment. Helping others climb up the ladder that you have just scaled is one of the most fulfilling aspects of a Royal Marine, or indeed any military, career. It is the rhythm of give and take, of offering yourself and gaining something in return, that builds and rewards.

What it also did was allow me to start envisaging *life*. Not just the military life that I had grown used to across 11 years of service. Not just the phases of my career, the expectation of deployments and the long months spent in distant locations. These things had been the measures of my life since I was last at Lympstone. Many Royal Marines, and others in the armed services, will live their entire lives by these rhythms – and perhaps I would have been one of them if not for my chance meeting with Claire that night in the Taunton nightclub. Yet now that we were in our third year together, things had changed. And working at Lympstone not only allowed me to remain in the UK for the full duration of this draft cycle, it allowed me to live at home in Taunton, with Claire, and be a regular couple for the first time since we had met.

The home time mattered. Work could be busy, or less busy, depending on the season – but this time, I always knew that I could put it down at the end of the day, get in the car, and drive home to Claire. It was as close as I had come to a regular nine-to-five existence. And it did everything we wanted it to. Across the duration of my posting, Claire and I settled into a life that worked for us both. We discovered that we really could live together, day in and day out, for the rest of our lives. I asked Claire to marry me and, a year later, we became husband and wife on what was the happiest day of our lives. And though we knew that this nine-to-five, Monday-to-Friday existence might not last forever, for now the pattern suited us. As couples embarking on lives together do, we even began to fantasise, only idly at first, about what life might be like once my time with the Royal Marines was finished. At the time, I didn't think I would be ready to move on for perhaps another 10 years. But there was a whole life to be lived after that.

My time at Lympstone was always limited – that is just the nature of draft cycles with the Royal Marines – and by the time it was finished, it is fair to say that I was ready for the change. Life continued to move apace. I had always known that when I left the training centre, I would be sent back to a commando unit. The only question was which one it might be. So, when I discovered that I was to join up with 42 Commando in late 2010, it came as no great surprise.

As far back as 2008, when I'd returned from Helmand, I knew that Afghanistan wasn't finished with me. I'd seen so many lads come through the training centre, back from their second deployment, or about to embark on their third, that returning was a near inevitability. By 2010, the British presence in Afghanistan was close to 10 years old. But hostilities were ongoing and a withdrawal was not yet in sight. There was still work to be done, and because 42 Commando were about to go back to Helmand, so was I.

The build-up to deployment involves a succession of training exercises and drills designed to make you ready, not only for combat, but for the long months you will spend in unfamiliar and often uncomfortable conditions. By the time I got word that I would be joining 42 Commando, they were already in the full throes of that training. But I was in the middle of completing an "A Range" qualification, which would later allow me to run live firing ranges with all the standard-issue British infantry weapons, so I did not join them directly. It was not until Christmas approached that I found myself part of 42 Commando out on Salisbury Plain, looking ahead at a new year that would take me back to the Middle East.

Claire and I were looking forward to celebrating Christmas together at home, the kind of quiet Christmas we both cherished.

CHAPTER FOUR

But this year it would be marked by another occasion, one I will never be able to forget.

Some days before Christmas, my mother called me with news that, although not entirely unexpected, was still enough to rock the foundations of my world. For some time, my father had been in ill health. Over the years, an industrial accident he'd had many years earlier had continued to wreak havoc on his body – and, by increasing degrees, my mother had become his full-time carer. It was another expression of the love they'd found so many decades ago and which had continued to burn strongly across their lives. But, when mum called me that December, there was a tone in her voice that I had, in my more reflective moments, been dreading.

"They've taken him in, Alexander. He's in the hospital now." She paused. "You'd better come down."

I had not needed asking. I would have driven all night.

As fortune had it, 42 Commando were being given leave over the Christmas period in anticipation of our deployment, and I was able to reach the hospital in Brighton without having to ask too many favours of my commanding officers. By the time I got to the ward where my family was gathered, my father had stabilised again. Yet, as stable as the charts and signs claimed him to be, there was no denying the impact of seeing him in a hospital gown, propped up on a hospital bed, hooked up to all those machines. Perhaps it is a cliche, but I had grown up looking up to my father. I still looked up to him now, and seeing him brought low like this was its own kind of revelation. My father was mortal.

The doctors had already been in attendance that morning. They'd taken my mother through everything they could, and she explained it to us as we sat at our father's side.

"Hospital isn't the place for him. They've given him the all-clear. He's going to come home, but…" The "but" lingered in the air for some time. "They're looking into what they can do for us back there. What kind of support they can give."

Mum was a force of nature in our family. Ever since I was small, she'd been the glue that bound us together. When Dad was away driving his long-distance lorries, she was the stalwart, keeping the home fires burning, making sure all four of her children were washed, fed and cared for. The idea that she now needed support to look after my father seemed so unfair. But there was no doubting how seriously the hospital took her needs, nor those of my father. I'd heard of so many miracles being performed by army medics to save the lives of colleagues out in Iraq and Afghanistan, but I don't think I have ever been as grateful or as proud of our NHS as I was in those moments.

Knowing that Dad was going to be able to go home, and that Mum would have the support she needed to look after him, took an enormous weight off my shoulders – and, after spending a couple of days in Brighton, in and out of the hospital and back at my old family home, Claire and I retreated back to Taunton, where we spent a quiet Christmas together as planned. One day turned into the next – and, though Dad remained in hospital, every whisper that we heard was a positive one. As soon as his home support was established, he would be back where he belonged, in the family home where he had spent most of his adult life.

New Year came; 2010 was over, and 2011 had a sense of new beginning about it. My father would soon be out of hospital, and soon I would be leaving for my second tour of Afghanistan, this time as a troop sergeant responsible for a group of marines who had never seen active deployment before. If I was nervous for the future, I was optimistic as well. A new phase was beginning.

Yet I had only been back at work for a couple of days, going through more training with the lads of 42 Commando, when the telephone call came. I woke that morning on camp to the mobile phone trilling at the side of the bed. My sister Melody's name illuminated on the screen told me, instantly, that something was wrong. I have always been close to my siblings, but a call this early could only mean one thing. I answered it with a sinking feeling.

"Al," Melody said, and I could already tell from her tone exactly what she was going to say. "It's Dad..."

Scarcely 10 days had passed since we'd had the prognosis: things were looking better, they'd said; he'd be able to go home, supported, he'd be picking up soon. But Melody's words became imprinted on me in those moments. My father, who had been my rock and guiding light for all 36 of my years, had at most another week to live.

When I put down the phone, I was numb. The death of a father is so different to death witnessed in combat. Both blindside you, but this was a feeling unlike any I'd known before. Perhaps it was because the prognosis had, only days ago, been so positive. Perhaps I had acclimatised myself to the idea he was going home and that life, though different in some ways, would continue much the same as it had before.

But everything changes.

I gathered myself together and went straight to see my sergeant major. After I'd explained the situation to him, he didn't think twice.

"Go," he told me. "See him. Family comes first."

So that was what I did.

Very quickly, I formulated a plan. First, I would drive back to Taunton and pick up Claire, then together we would make the long drive to Brighton and everything that awaited us. Before any of that, I hurried back to my accommodation. I had only gone to collect a few things, to pack a small bag for the journey, but no sooner had the door closed behind me than something broke inside me. A sea wall crumbled and the waters came roaring through. For five, 10, 15 minutes I cried. I stopped myself. I cried again. I am not ashamed to say that in those moments I was a wreck, blubbering as wildly as I'd done when I was a small boy with only my mother and father there to console me. In those 15 minutes I railed against it, I pleaded, I made bargains, I opened myself up and poured out everything there was in me. None of it made a difference. My father was disappearing from my life. I felt untethered, uncertain, I think, of where to look, what to do, how to behave – except to know that I had to get there fast.

After grabbing a few things, I somehow found the strength to pull myself together. Courage under fire had never been as difficult as stopping myself fraying at the seams as I crossed the camp, jumped in the car and headed home, the roads and fields and hedgerows that I passed all blurring in my vision.

I'd already called Claire and she was waiting for me. Together, we made the long drive down from Taunton to the hospital in Brighton, where the rest of my family were already waiting.

And there was Dad. Lying in his hospital bed, readying himself to say goodbye.

Claire and I stayed in Brighton for three or four days, back at the house I'd called home for so many years. The feeling of family rallying around in anticipation of Dad passing away was incomparable. We were grown now, we had gone our separate ways, and yet here we were, brought back together by our love for our father. Across those days, the NHS proved itself, to me, to be an unparalleled organisation. Nurses and doctors went above and beyond the call of duty in caring not only for my father, but for his family as day after day we sat at his bedside. Normal visiting hours were forgotten. Nurses found a way for my mother to stay at her husband's side, even into the small hours of the night. While we camped out in our childhood home, coming to terms with what was about to happen, my mother and father spent their last nights together, under a hospital roof. From sun-up to sunset, somebody was with Dad at all times. Life, which for so long had been so vast and took in so much of the world, had devolved down to us few Blackmans, the route between our childhood home and the hospital in which our father was going to pass away. It seemed so big, and yet so small.

At nights, I looked back on all the years we had spent together. I had always been close to my father, even as a small boy, but we'd grown closer still in recent years. It is, I think, something that happens between fathers and sons. As I had grown older, the relationship between us evolved. I don't know how it happened, or when, but somewhere along the way, I'd stopped thinking about Dad as "just" my father, and him about me as "just" his son. The old dynamic of parent and unruly child had given way to something richer and more meaningful, a real friendship.

I have sometimes wondered if me entering the military changed things in some way. Dad hadn't been a soldier as long as I had, but there was something in the shared experience, I think, that drew us closer together. We'd both spent time in Egypt and, upon sharing stories and photographs of our respective time out there, Dad had commented on how little the camp I'd stayed in had changed from the one he stayed in 40 years previously – and the perennial joke between us was that while he had trained as a tank driver, I myself had become an anti-tank specialist, trained to take tanks down. But it was more than this that bound us together. Life with the Royal Marines is so different from life at home – so different that it must be difficult to envisage for someone who has never lived that kind of life. That Dad and I had seen both sides made us *know* each other so much more keenly.

On the fourth day in Brighton, as Claire and I drove to the hospital, we got the call: some moments before, my father had died peacefully in his sleep. None of the days of expecting it, none of the nights I'd spent anticipating the end, none of the goodbyes I'd said, fearing it would be our last, could prepare me for the reality. I walked into the hospital, numb in a way I had never thought possible, and looked down at my father at rest.

We'd spoken only the day before. My father and I had never been emotional men. To say out loud what each of us felt about the other would have felt... untoward, somehow. And yet, as I looked at him now, there was not a single iota of doubt in my heart – he knew how I had felt about him, and I knew how he had felt about me.

Even so, seeing him lying there blew me open wide. I might not have had any regrets, but the sadness was overwhelming.

I sat down by his bedside and cried.

Claire and I remained in Brighton for several days. There was so much to do before I returned to Afghanistan, but the Royal Marines had been clear – *family comes first* – and the accommodations they made for me could not have been better. Even so, the thought of what was coming up was beginning to weigh heavily on me. In a matter of weeks, I would be back in Helmand Province. This time, I would not be in the relatively developed and populous area of the Sangin valley where I'd been stationed across 2007 and 2008, but in a more remote area, the facilities stripped back, the support structure less robust. In 2007, there had been as many as 100 fellow soldiers around. In the months to come, there would be as few as 12 or 15 of us, small units, small patrols, with long distances in between. The thought of it did not yet unnerve me, but it did make me acutely conscious that things were not going to be the same as they once were. Three years had elapsed since I last set foot on Afghan soil. The war had moved on. The situation had changed. And I was going out there as a different man, a troop sergeant now, responsible for 15 lads who I didn't yet know. In the rare moments when I could push aside the sadness of Dad passing away, the responsibility of it all hit me hard.

I didn't want to leave. The greater part of me wanted to stay here, among family, to spend the next days with them as we prepared for Dad's funeral. But the responsibility I owed the lads in 42 Commando was not something I could take lightly, and Mum was already being looked after by my sisters. So, after a couple of days, Claire and I returned home. The emptiness I was feeling still seemed vast and unconquerable, but perhaps throwing myself back into the preparations for our tour would be useful. Shooting down to Plymouth, where the guys were about to go out onto Salisbury Plain for their final pre-deployment exercise, I then headed back to Folkestone to complete a course and catch up on a lot of information I'd missed. I have always been good at compartmentalising, able to shut one mental door as I open another, but keeping my two dominant preoccupations apart was increasingly difficult across that week. Trying not to think of Dad and everything he had meant to me was near impossible, and yet, every time my thoughts veered away from the lads in 42 Commando, I was wrenched back in that direction too. I needed to find some way to balance the two things in my mind, and honour them both.

Some days later, Claire and I made the long drive back to Brighton. I'd left the rest of 42 Commando at camp, just back from Salisbury Plain and our final pre-deployment exercise – but, although Helmand now lay on the immediate horizon, there was another duty I had to fulfil first.

We were going to my father's funeral.

My father was not an ostentatious man. In his latter years he had become very conscious of the ruin we have been making of our planet: consequently, his funeral was to be held at the local crematorium, where he now lay in the sustainably made coffin he had stipulated in his will. When Claire and I arrived, the crematorium was already filling up with all our family and all my father's local friends. We took our seats among our nearest and dearest, my brother, sisters and I all flanking our mother as we listened to the service. I can hardly recall the specific thoughts that cartwheeled through my mind as I sat there, contemplating everything that had happened in the past few weeks. I was aware,

I know, of my father being there with us. I was aware, too, of how the sadness at his death and the good feeling he had engendered in so many across his life infused the air around us. Dad had been incredibly proud of his short service in the army, and his association had arranged for a bugler to play the Last Post for him now. As I listened to it start up, it brought to mind images of my father from across the many stages of his life, both those I had known and those I had not. It was a nice touch and I remember thinking how very proud my father would have been, and how much little things like this mattered. People who have served their country once often feel as if they have served it forever.

Somewhere in it all, in between worrying about the lads preparing for Afghanistan and worrying about my mother and how she was going to navigate this next, uncharted phase of her life, I'd pushed aside the pain I was feeling myself. Perhaps, in retrospect, that is something a Royal Marine lifestyle teaches you, to be committed to others, even above yourself and your own well-being. But as I watched the curtains open up and my father's coffin roll through towards the furnaces beyond, I heard one of his favourite songs blast out over the crematorium speakers. The dulcet tones of Johnny Cash flurried up over a familiar guitar line I had heard so many times before. "*I stepped into a burning ring of fire*," Johnny sang, just as my father's coffin disappeared from view. It was everything my father would have wanted, and it was then that all the emotion poured out of me.

I was smiling, not crying.

My father's passing had hung heavily over me during the final pre-deployment exercise on Salisbury Plain, with all its immersive scenarios and simulated combat. It hung heavily over me some days later when Bickleigh Barracks in Plymouth was decked out for a "Family Day", when 42 Commando's families and loved ones would gather on camp to hear a lecture about what life was going to be like over there, see the base at which their sons, brothers and husbands had been spending so much of their working lives, and meet the other marines who would be shepherding them out there.

After the funeral service at the crematorium, everyone had moved on to a local golf club where, over food and drink, the sad farewell we had bidden my father became a celebration of his life instead. It was there that I had finally begun to put things in perspective. I was grateful for the life he had lived. Grateful that he had seen all his children grow up and embark on their own journeys. Grateful that he was loved so much that so many of his old colleagues and friends had come to toast him on his way. I was thankful for all the wonderful people in the NHS who had done what they could for him across his final days. None of that took away the emptiness I was feeling, but it was a salve of sorts to know he had been cherished. But now, faced with the formality of 42 Commando's Family Day, I had to switch off the part of me that was still grieving, and which would continue to grieve across the long months to come. The Alexander Blackman who had just lost his father and was still reeling from it had to be locked away, while the Alexander Blackman who was troop sergeant to 20 lads, who would be leading them out into one of Helmand Province's most remote and dangerous regions, had to step up.

There had been no Family Day like this in 2007, before I first went to Afghanistan. But things had changed. Hearts and minds mattered now, more than ever. And exercises like this were crucial in showing how the Royal Marines supported our lads. How much they, and their families, mattered.

I stood and watched as a parade of families and friends appeared on camp and converged on the welcoming hall. The memories of my father's funeral were still vivid in my mind, and the knot created by his absence felt as if it would be a permanent scar, but at least this day was something of a diversion. After the chaos of the last few weeks, the rush to join 42 Commando and having to hurtle back and forth between camp and my family home in Brighton, I still wasn't as familiar as I would have liked to have been with the lads for whom I was going to be troop sergeant, but in welcoming their families I took each of them into my mind. There was already so much information to absorb. I set myself to the task.

Much of the day was taken up with a tour the families and loved ones were given of the camp. Insights like this into the day-to-day lives their sons and partners had been living would hopefully settle some of the anxieties they must have been feeling, by showing what a thoughtful and attentive organisation the

Royal Marines is. After the tour, the families gathered in a lecture hall to listen to one of our commanders explaining exactly what life was going to be like where we were all going. Though the dangers, the austerity, the relentlessness of it could not be understated, perhaps just *knowing* could be a salve to a worried mind. There is nothing like anticipation to make a person afraid.

The truth is, of course, that none of the lads I was taking out with me could yet understand what lay ahead. Just as I myself could not understand what it was going to be like before the invasion of Iraq, or before my first tour of Afghanistan, so too were they unprepared for the realities we were about to face. I'd already detected some of the bravado of youth as we performed our final pre-deployment exercises – that vigour, perhaps even eagerness, to be out there putting all your training into action, to be getting on with the job at hand. I'd seen it all that time ago on HMS Ark Royal as we sailed for the Persian Gulf, not yet knowing if we would be inserted into Iraq or not. Before you see the reality of it, and no matter what the lessons of history are, it is all too easy for young soldiers to get swept up in the excitement of a first tour. Somewhere along the way, it was going to be my job to temper that excitement with some difficult truths.

After the lecture, the families and marines were shepherded through to the camp's dining hall, where dinner was being laid on. We were coming to the end of a useful, if exhausting, day, and the truth is I was eager for rest. I don't think I understood, even in that moment, how much my father's death had drained me, and would continue to drain me for the days and weeks to come. But in a few days' time, I would be flying for Camp Bastion, and from there to our location in Helmand, in advance of the rest of 42 Commando. I was confident that, once it started, the mental switch would be flicked in my head. I'd cross through that veil, embrace the job at hand, and be subsumed into life in Helmand.

As everyone filed in for dinner, I stood with the other commanders, greeting the lads and their families as they came. "Mum, this is Sgt Blackman," one of the lads began. "Sgt Blackman, this is my father," began another. By the time they had all taken their places, it felt as if I'd met the wives, mothers, partners or children of all of 42 Commando. And, although of course you always take a keen interest in the backgrounds and lives of the men under your command – because to know *who* they are and what makes them tick contributes to good leadership – the reality of meeting and greeting their family and friends is so much more visceral. People become more rounded, perhaps even more *real*, when you see their faces reflected in their mother's own; or when you see them standing closely with the partner that they love. By the time dinner was beginning, I felt as if all these people were fixed permanently in my mind.

Some time later, the formalities ended. As the dinner service was cleared away and waiters drifted around with drinks to bring the evening to a close, the lads from 42 Commando joined their families and mingled. I was glad to see it. Friendship and unity are important in many walks of life, but they were going to be

critical where we were going. And if I didn't yet feel that I knew
the lads as thoroughly as I wanted to, it was important to see that
they were bonded with each other.

I was mingling too, doing my piece to present the Royal
Marines in the light which I have always thought they deserved,
when one of the ladies I had been introduced to earlier
approached with her son, 23 years old and about to be deployed
on his first active service.

She fixed me with a look. It took me a moment to compute
what that look was. She was looking at me with expectation, but
with something that amounted to *trust* as well.

"You will make sure he comes back, won't you?"

The question hits you like its own kind of bullet. It's the natural
reaction of a mother, a wife, any loved one contemplating their son
or partner going off to war for the first time. It's a question that
mothers and wives have been asking in private for generations, a
kind of petition, or a prayer, an entreaty to somebody, to *anybody*,
to help, to give a guarantee. As she asked it, I felt the weight
of it immensely. I'd never been asked it before. There are never
any guarantees. That's the pact we make with ourselves when
we enlist. It's implicit in what we do with our lives. There is no
commander in the world who could offer a guarantee of the kind
she needed to hear.

And yet: "I'll do everything," I said.

Well, what else is there to say? What else, except to offer the
reassurance that somebody needs, in that particular moment, to

feel good, to feel right, to feel that – no matter where their son, partner, loved one is going, no matter what terrible things might happen out there – none of it is going to happen to them.

This lady might have been the first to ask me, but she was far from the last. As I met each of the families of the lads I was taking into Helmand that night, the same question lingered on their lips. Some of them dared not ask it. Others couldn't dare not to. So, over and again, I promised them it would be OK, that we would be doing everything we possibly could to bring their boys back safely – even though, in both my heart and theirs, we knew there could be no guarantees.

I repeated the same thing all night.

CHAPTER FIVE

Some days later, Camp Bastion stretched out beneath me as the plane began its descent towards the landing strip. In 2006, the then prime minister Tony Blair had called Camp Bastion the place "where the fate of world security is going to be decided", and looking at it from above, it was not difficult to see why: 20 square kilometres, constructed in the heart of the Afghan desert, Camp Bastion was more like a city in miniature than a simple military base. In 2011, it had already become the biggest British military base constructed since the second world war.

I'd seen Camp Bastion before, of course. The camp began its existence as a tactical landing zone set up by the Royal Air Force in 2005, and became of significant strategic value when operations in Helmand Province were first being undertaken. Back then, it had been a landing zone and a collection of tents, but as early as 2006 it was being fortified and constructed further, until eventually it became the central hub for British activity in Afghanistan. Now, it housed as many as 32,000 people – primarily British, but with others from Denmark, the

US and across the coalition forces – and facilities I would only be able to dream of out at our posting. Speak to most of the soldiers stationed at Camp Bastion and they would tell you they would rather have been further forward in the fight, in positions where they were more directly challenged, but there is no doubt that being stationed there was the closest facsimile of living at home that anybody on service in Afghanistan could get. There were air-conditioned tents, banks of computers with instant internet access, connecting you to friends and family at home at the touch of a button. There were coffee shops and games rooms, where off-duty soldiers could get some much-needed relaxation at the innumerable consoles. There were even some of the world's most remote franchises of Pizza Hut and Krispy Kreme Donuts.

There was something else as well. Something with much more significance than all those little touches that made the camp feel more a slice of home than a fortress in the desert, Camp Bastion was the site of one of the most advanced field hospitals in the history of warfare.

At the start of every tour, all officers are sent ahead of the rest of their units to familiarise themselves with their new locations and learn as much as they can from the unit they are about to replace. This is to make the transition between one unit and another as effective as possible. Soon, I would board a Chinook and fly to the outpost I would call home for the next six months – but before that, I was to be given a tour of the medical facilities.

CHAPTER FIVE

"You'll see what they can do," I'd been told. "The way they save lives. The way they can put bodies back together." If I passed it on to the lads I was about to lead, perhaps it would give them fresh courage. Perhaps it would reassure them that, even though lives could be lost out here and bodies could be ruined in so many different ways, there was always hope.

I hadn't seen this medical facility before, but I had known for some time of its overwhelmingly positive reputation. Even as far back as 2007, before the camp was as vast as it was now, the men on the ground in Helmand had known that if the worst happened to you, there was every chance you would survive if you could get back to Camp Bastion in time. Here were stationed some of the world's very best doctors and surgeons. New, cutting-edge surgeries were being developed and performed here at a rate far ahead of what might happen in the rest of the world. The kinds of devastating injuries soldiers receive in warfare demand swift, exacting responses. Here, the doctors and surgeons were devoted to emergency medicine. And no expense was being spared to provide them with the state-of-the-art equipment they needed to perform at their very best.

Along with a group of other team leaders, including our own company commander, I entered the hospital facility. When I had last passed through Camp Bastion on my way back home, the medical facility here had been a tented area, inside which various trauma and surgical areas were demarcated. By early 2008, however – and with the expectation that the war would be ongoing for some years to come – the construction of a semi-permanent facility had begun, and the hospital had grown exponentially since then. The benefits of having a permanent hospital here were clear. Patients could now be treated in a controlled environment, free from the ravages of the elements, and protected from the dust, heat and cold of the Afghan desert. And, because of the new "container" walls built around the facility, the state-of-the-art scanners brought into the hospital could now function without being interrupted by the air surveillance radar also on base. Previously, the electromagnetic output of the radar had played havoc with the CT scanners, but in the upgraded hospital, everything could work as smoothly as in any hospital back home.

The upgrades had never stopped. The years 2008, 2009 and 2010 had, we were told, been heavy for casualties, and Camp Bastion's hospital had had to grow even further to keep up with the demand. What had begun as a field hospital with an emergency department with eight resuscitation bays, an operating theatre department – known as "the Bastion right turn" – large enough to support two operating tables at the same time, and a radiology department, had continued to grow rapidly. At the start of 2011, when we were shown around, there were four operating theatres, an intensive therapy unit (ITU) with 12 beds, a general ward with capacity for 50 injured soldiers and a blood bank so big that, across 2009 alone, it provided more than 3,000 units of blood for transfusions to injured military personnel. The hospital had become yet more advanced with the enlisting of new expert radiologists, as well as primary health, dental and mental care facilities.

This was a working hospital in full flow. Only weeks had passed since I decamped to the hospital in Brighton to be at my father's side – and though the hospital environments could not have been more different, both were busy, thriving places with expert, dedicated staff.

For a brief period, the hospital at Camp Bastion had been – and in many ways still remained – the busiest trauma unit in the world. The years since I'd last been in Afghanistan had seen a dramatic upsurge in the number of serious casualties. Across 2009–10, there had been 200 British fatalities in Afghanistan. Compared to the previous years, this might seem a lot, but the fact is that without this hospital facility, the death toll would have been so much higher. In recent years, the war had intensified. People were being maimed and killed in ever-changing ways. And, although some of them did not survive, most were being saved right here, in this facility where we walked.

"There's one more thing I'd like you to see." The hospital director led us into the final corner of the field hospital, where two pristine white rooms housed some of the largest pieces of apparatus we'd yet seen. "These," he told us, "are our new scanners."

The huge machines stood as testament to how valued this hospital was, and how seriously the British military took its funding. The two CT scanners we were looking at had replaced the single, temperamental one housed here six months before.

Now, if one machine went offline, the doctors would never have to keep an injured patient waiting.

"They're more powerful, too," the medic explained. "The images we get from these are 10 times more detailed than the ones we had before – and they do it all in a fraction of the time. We can scan an entire body, head to toe, in as little as 18 seconds. And it's seconds that matter with traumas like these."

Later in the year, the hospital would also be augmented by an MRI scanner funded, this time, by the US military. With this piece of kit, the hospital at Camp Bastion would become one of the world's leading centres for research into mild traumatic brain injuries.

There was no doubt about it, behind these four walls, our doctors and surgeons worked miracles. Men who might have died only years before were now alive and back home with their loved ones because of the work these professionals did, and the research they were performing was advancing the science of trauma care further each day.

After showing us the scanners, the medic proceeded to show us a succession of photographs. Shots taken of injuries suffered out in the field, and of those same soldiers after the surgeons had attended to them. If the nature of the images – of men with their legs cleaved off by improvised explosive devices (IEDs), men after their life-saving surgeries, both legs now just stumps, as they learned to walk again – showed the kinds of wonders the medics at Camp Bastion could perform, they also showed the terrors that were being experienced daily out there in the field. One after another, the images coursed across my vision, a succession of different lives, all of them changed forever by being in the wrong place at the wrong time. In using IEDs with such prevalence, the Taliban insurgents were acknowledging that they could never hope to win in a stand-up fight against the might of the allied military. Instead, they had had to find other ways – and the way they had found was maiming more military personnel than ever before.

The images seemed to be endless, the medics here inordinately proud – and rightfully so – of everything they were able to achieve. But there was more to some of these injuries than first met the eye. So many of these injuries had necessitated the removal of both a soldier's legs. But as if this wasn't devastating enough, often the blasts had reached further. In too many cases, it wasn't just the survivor's legs that had been destroyed. It was everything that lay between those legs as well.

I'd seen injuries before, but not like this. Perhaps he could sense our unease, because the medic stopped and explained. The exponential rise in the way insurgents used IEDs and buried roadside bombs to resist the allied and new Afghan forces was dramatically changing not only the number of devastating injuries being flown back into Camp Bastion, but the nature of them as well. At the start of my 2007-08 tour, I had been surprised – perhaps even bewildered – by how Taliban insurgents seemed to throw themselves recklessly into our line of fire. The predictability of assaults – even though they could still be devastating – had begun to give way, towards the end of that tour, to a more nuanced and less predictable form of warfare. Buried explosive devices were so much more insidious, and in my time away from Afghanistan they'd transformed the types of injuries our boys were facing. "When you're hit by bullets, the injuries are localised. It doesn't mean they don't kill. You've all seen that. But buried explosives…"

Traditional body armour is built to protect the body's vital organs, the abdomen and chest, because that has always been seen as the most effective way of saving a life. IEDs changed all that. Buried or hidden explosives almost universally hit from below. A report in 2010 had suggested that up to 90% of injuries from powerful IEDs had led to double amputations of the legs. In fact, towards the end of my 2007–08 tour, one member of our unit had suffered a triple amputation and, in many of these cases, the scrotum area was badly affected. The images we were seeing today were a testament to that. One wrong step could not only make a ruin of a man's body, but limit the hopes and dreams he had of family and relationships for the rest of his life.

There was no doubt that the medical facilities on Camp Bastion were second to none. There was no doubt how much the people here cared. There was no doubt that they were pioneers in one of emergency medicine's most challenging environments. And yet, as I followed the rest of the officers out of the facility, it was not reassurance that I felt, it was the brutal reality of what was happening, with increasing frequency, in the locations to which we were all being sent – and the knowledge that these sort of injuries lasted a lifetime.

Outside, we stood in silence. I didn't need to speak to know what the others around me were thinking. The object of the exercise had been to fill us with confidence that, even if the worst did happen out there, there was every chance we would still survive. That was the message I was supposed to take back to 42 Commando. Right now, the message seemed obsolete. To reveal to them the miracles the doctors were performing here was also to acknowledge the kinds of life-changing injuries they might one day carry back home.

I remembered, starkly, my final moments in early 2008, when my vehicle had triggered the anti-Soviet tank mine that sent me skyward. I had been lucky then, as I'd been lucky under rocket fire in Iraq, but luck only lasted so long. If my body had been torn apart then, a facility like this could have saved my life. And yet there was something about *seeing* it, *seeing* the images of injury and recovery, that brought the realities home in a way no lectures or second-hand message had ever done before. I knew all the stories. But I don't think I had ever felt them as viscerally until now.

I thought I knew why that was. I could just about get my head around the idea of losing my limbs. I could survive without an arm. Having my legs amputated – as happened to so many lads caught unawares by a buried IED – would have a massive impact on life, but I thought I could understand how it might feel. What I couldn't understand was how you would go on living if you were like the man in that picture we'd seen, having lost not just his legs, but everything in between. And as I looked into the faces of the others, I fancied they were thinking the same thing. Ask any man what he would rather lose and I am certain his answer would be the same.

I was right. When the company commander next spoke, he confirmed everything I'd been thinking. "It's sobering stuff," he began. "What would you say if I said I was going to make wearing blast underwear compulsory for our company?"

Blast underwear is uncomfortable, especially in environments like Afghanistan, where the heat is already severe. US Marines wear protection flaps hanging from the waist of their regular body armour, but the British armed forces had always been reluctant to introduce them because of how much they restrict a wearer's movement. Yet new approaches were always being taken. Technology always improved. A military accessories contractor in Cardiff had developed a pair of "blast boxers" in knitted Kevlar, and it was said that the Ministry of Defence was looking at a version using tightly-woven silk – incredibly strong, and yet more flexible than Kevlar – in the future. For now, though, all of us outside the hospital facility seemed in agreement, blast underwear might be restrictive, it might be uncomfortable – "And I'm certain I'll get some push-back from the NCOs," our company commander said – but every last one of us would accept those things if it meant we could avoid injuries like the ones we'd just seen.

CHAPTER FIVE

One day later, with all these thoughts in mind, I was boarding a Chinook helicopter and leaving Camp Bastion behind.

* * *

The Chinook descended into the landing zone from which I would be driven to our outpost, and for the first time I took in the surroundings that would be home for the next six months.

Seen from above, the compound was little more than a big rectangle in the middle of the desert scrub, its walls comprised of wire cages filled deep with gravel and stones to protect against rocket attack. In the centre of the compound were the large tents with stark metal frame beds lined up inside – and, around them, a number of Hesco bastions. Inside several of these containers were our stores. In another sat our operations room, housing all the communications equipment we would be using. Outside one of the storage containers hung the solar shower packs which were all we would have for the next half year, and in another corner, the toilet facility – or, as it might more accurately be known, the hole in the ground.

This was everything. From here, 15 lads and I would base our operations, run our patrols and, if all things went well, maintain the district's fragile peace. There would be no luxuries. No frills. No nods towards anything other than bare, stripped-back functionality. It could not have been more distinct from Camp Bastion.

The troop sergeant whose tour was about to end was there to greet me as I arrived at the compound. After the briefest tour of the base, we spent some time in the ops room together, going through his notes and observations, looking at maps and charts of the area for which I was going to be responsible, and generally getting me up to speed on the task that awaited me. The guys we were here to take over from were Paras – and, though it's often said that there's a great rivalry between the Marines and the Parachute Regiment, there was no doubt that they'd done an exemplary job out here. As I sat with my predecessor, he ran through the plans for the hand-over, the checking of equipment, the routes we'd be patrolling, the areas where they'd last seen enemy activity.

"It won't be like your last tour," he said. "Not here. The neighbouring compound is three or four kilometres away, so you can't expect any company from the ranking officer there. No pow-wows at the end of a long day. Yes, you'll speak to them on the radio – you'll get your five minutes from everyone else, any points of note, what's happening where they are – but if you see them more than twice across the tour, you'll have seen them more than me. Maybe you'll bump into them on a patrol, but don't go counting on any more than that. You're on your own out here, Al. If you do get casualties – and you will – it's going to put a lot of stress on your guys. Even a niggling injury, something that means one of your lads needs a couple of days' rest, well, it's going to have a drastic effect on the effort the rest of your troop's going to have to put in." He paused. "You've barely half the lads I've had. We've had it rough, but it's going to be doubly difficult for you. Your lads are going to have to get used to it quickly. You're a long way from air support."

I knew all this from my pre-deployment briefings, of course, but the realities often become so much more tangible when you are standing there with your feet on the ground.

The troop sergeant looked out of the ops room at the tent where some of the lads were stirring. "Six months is a long tour out here. They've done well. But look, they missed Christmas with their families. They're due some R&R. You know how it gets towards the end of a deployment. Things get jumpy. You've just come through Camp Bastion. Nobody wants to go home in a bag, or have to be rushed to the field hospital there – not ever, but definitely not when the end's so near. Yes," he continued, "they're looking forward to going home."

Christmas already seemed such a long time ago, but actually it had only been a matter of weeks. Now, here I was, back in the searing heat of the Afghan desert, my father's death still preying on my thoughts, Johnny Cash's 'Ring of Fire' still playing on repeat in the back of my mind. I'd already known that communication with home would be strained – if Claire and I were able to speak for 15 minutes each week, it would have to be enough – but perhaps I hadn't fully appreciated until getting here what it would be like to be so cut off from other marines of my own rank and above. It is always a great release to have a few in close proximity. People who have been here before, lived it, experienced the same things you have and survived them, are so useful to decompress with at the end of an arduous day – but soon, there were going to be 15 lads here, few of whom had lived like this before. I could still remember the faces of the mothers, grandmothers and wives who had looked me in the eye at the Family Day on camp and asked me to make sure I'd keep their loved ones safe. There was no guarantee I could honour those promises, but I was going to do everything in my power to try.

The troop sergeant was still speaking. Together, we walked out of the ops room and into the implacable sun.

"Tomorrow," he said, "we're taking you out on patrol."

CHAPTER SIX

Helmand Province, Afghanistan, 2011

This was Afghanistan, but not as I'd known it.

Three years had passed since I'd last set foot on Afghan soil. All it took was a few hours out on patrol for me to understand that the war that had, even then, been going on for nearly seven years, had changed almost beyond recognition.

We stood over a blast crater out on the edge of one of the unit's regular patrols.

"This one got tripped," the troop sergeant began, meaning the IED that had been buried under the earth. Looking at what remained of the blast site, I recalled the images and stories I'd heard in the field hospital at Camp Bastion. Death can come suddenly, but injuries caused by something like this last an entire lifetime. I could already tell that this tour was going to be very different from my last.

"It won't be the only one you encounter. With any luck, you'll find them before they find you." He gestured towards the other lads on the patrol, two of whom were at the forefront with metal detectors in their hands. They'd become standard issue towards the end of my last tour, and now they were one of the principal weapons in our armoury. Locating an IED before you triggered it was the only way to guarantee its safe removal, and to avoid the chance of injuries like the ones I'd been shown. "But too many eyes on the ground..." the troop sergeant went on. "Well, that's bad too."

We went on a little further, the pace achingly slow with the metal detectors in hand to guide the way, and the troop sergeant pointed out the places where insurgents had lain in wait to take shots at them. "They'll know the kinds of routes you're going to patrol. They'll know when you're coming. That's why... good relations with the locals, that's vital. It isn't just winning hearts and minds. It's basic security as well."

I'd been on few foot patrols during my time in the Sangin valley in 2007-08, but that hadn't stopped me becoming a near-victim to a buried Soviet landmine. On foot, we were going to be so much more vulnerable to this kind of attack. But it didn't mean we could overlook more traditional engagements as well.

"The compound's going to come under fire," the troop sergeant explained. "You'd better get used to it."

Back at the compound, I debriefed again with the team leader. Long hours in the ops room would give me the best idea of the area's normal pattern of life. Through reams of photographs, maps and charts I could gain a distinct impression of who the locals were, who was helpful and who suspicious of the allied forces, but only by being out there would I get to properly understand the lay of the land. I reminded myself, there was still time before the rest of the lads arrived. I would still be able to acclimatise myself – not just to the heat and conditions, but to the very atmosphere of the place. Because no matter how dedicated and professional the lads who were leaving, both in terms of how they conducted themselves and how' they represented the area to me, there was no escaping one single fact – their eagerness to get home was written all over them. At the thought of family, friends and the comforts of a base in England compared to this compound in Helmand Province, they were clearly over the moon. Six months out here had taken its toll. They deserved the rest and recuperation that was about to come.

But where their story ended, ours was about to begin.

The lads from 42 Commando had arrived at Camp Bastion the day before I flew out. I'd watched them go through some heavy weapons training and spoken with Merf, my second in command, about how they were doing. One of them had only just joined the team a week before I flew out, and I was keen to see how he was integrating into the group, but I couldn't linger long before boarding the Chinook and heading for our location. Now, three days later, they too arrived for the beginning of their tour.

The Nad-e Ali District lay some distance south of the Sangin valley, where I'd been for my 2007 tour. This was farming land, crisscrossed by canals and nourished by the twin forks of the

Helmand river. On the other side of that river was the provincial capital of Lashkargah – but the command post where we were located, CP Omar, was out in the scrubland, as remote and difficult to reach as any posting I'd taken.

Three days after the lads arrived at CP Omar, the last of the troops we were relieving disappeared into the skies beyond our compound and we were alone, for the first time, in Afghanistan. The remoteness of our location was apparent from the start, but only as we ventured out on our first designated patrol did the oppressiveness of this new phase in the war become deathly apparent.

The war had changed in nature since I was last in Afghanistan, but it had changed in *feeling* as well. Part of our mission here was not so very different from that of 2007 – to draw and engage enemy fire, allowing the civilian population to put down its roots and rebuild – but more important than that was the push to win the hearts and minds of the population. Just as the Para troop sergeant had told me, this was not just for humanitarian reasons, it was strategic as well.

In 2007, it had been so much easier to know who was an enemy combatant and who was not. They were the ones with guns, popping up outside FOB Inkerman to loose bursts of small arms fire at us, or to send a Chinese rocket into our walls. In the intervening years, something had shifted. In 2011, the difference between an innocent civilian and an enemy insurgent was sometimes near-impossible to discern. The Taliban had begun using buried bombs and IEDs in the final stages of my previous tour, but now it was their primary form of attack. Nightly, they came out with hidden explosive devices to seed the roads and byways where coalition troops patrolled, and the effect was twofold. It provoked uncertainty and fear, making soldiers unsure of their every step, and it slowed us down, forcing us to scour the ground where we walked with metal detectors, and exposing us further to ambush by small arms fire. The Taliban had long realised they could not stand up to the UK, US and allied forces in a straight-up fight, so instead they hid among the civilian population, taking us out by stealth however they could.

It made the primary duty of our days – running our patrols – so much more difficult. In 2007, we'd used metal detectors only sporadically. I still remember all the runs I'd made to mark out a drop zone for a resupply or to collect the resupply itself, and sweeping the earth in front of us so that our vehicles weren't lost to some buried incendiary. Back then, when the Taliban relied on legacy mines salvaged from Afghanistan's war with the Soviet Union, hitting a buried device could be just as deadly – but it was so much more infrequent. Now that they had resorted to constructing their own improvised devices, the land around us was poisoned. Every hummock of earth, every tussock of grass, every place where the ground had been disrupted – and all the thousands of places where it had not – could be where death was lying.

Consequently, each patrol forced us out into that merciless sun two, three, four times longer than it might have done at a different stage of the war. Our lives became dictated by these patrols. Morning and evening were always the easiest times, because by the middle of the day, with the sun at its zenith, the temperature could quickly reach 40 degrees. And with heat like that there comes a kind of madness. Resilience will only take you so far, especially with 50kg of equipment on your back and laden down with body armour to protect against explosive attack.

Patrols were there to reinforce our presence to the local civilians – to provide the protection and confidence they needed to think that they could get on with their lives and start *building* again. But they were intended to draw insurgents out into the open as well. And part of that was getting to know the local leaders and people, stopping to talk to them, getting to know the feeling of the place. There is no knowledge in the world that can replace the gut instinct of a soldier on deployment – not when those instincts have been attuned over several campaigns. Only here, the feeling was a constant dread, a constant oppressiveness. The paranoia was with us from the tour's earliest days, every civilian we met was a possible killer – beneath every step we took, a possible explosive.

Returning to the compound after a long day's patrol always provided some comfort; there was a modicum of safety behind those walls. And yet – this was no fortress. There was no roof over our heads. We were open to whatever grenades or rockets might be fired at us during the night, with precious little cover. Half an hour from air support, all we'd have to repel assault on the compound was ourselves.

CHAPTER SIX

Just 16 men. I knew, from the start, that 16 men at CP Omar wasn't nearly enough. The team we'd replaced had numbered 25. This meant that each man had to pound nearly as many miles each day. It also meant that, when the time came for lads to be rotated out for R&R, we would be lucky if we had 12 marines stationed at the compound. My lads shouldn't have been out doing both morning and evening patrols on the same day – and yet, without enough to cycle around, that was exactly what I had to ask of them. Eight hours a day over the rough ground in desiccating heat, 50kg of equipment on their backs, their bodies enclosed in the equivalent of a medieval knight's armour – no, 16 men wasn't nearly enough. Every time somebody turned their ankle, every time somebody strained a muscle and needed some time to get back to full strength, the effect on the other lads was multiplied by a new order of magnitude. Even the smallest injuries have big knock-on effects when you're as undermanned as we were at CP Omar. But we sucked it up and made it work, because that's what we were here to do.

That night, before I turned in, I stood at the compound's back gate. Perhaps this was just another of those things we were going to have to bear, but the gate was unsecured – and beyond it lay all the dangers of Helmand. We'd have to put in a request for maintenance and do what we could to secure it ourselves, but the last troop must have taken the same measures, without success. Anything that required major engineering was virtually impossible out here. This far out, we were on our own.

Six months, I thought. At some points in life, six months can pass in the blink of an eye. Out here, I suspected, it was going to feel like an eternity. All we could do was take it one night at a time.

The tour was still young when the killing began.

We'd begun taking fire from insurgents in the first days, as I'd known we would. The change in team at CP Omar had not gone unnoticed, and it gave the insurgents a newfound confidence. Knowing that we were not yet as familiar with the land as the troops we'd replaced, they no doubt considered us easier targets. But we were trained well and, when my lads faced their first live engagements, they responded well, identifying and scattering the insurgents without immediate injury. I was proud of them for that, but it was going to get so much worse.

Today, it was quiet at CP Omar – even though, across the rest of the Nad-e Ali District, the activity was relentless. An operation had gone out to the areas bordering the Loy Mandeh, one of the major rivers that nourished the farmlands of Nad-e Ali and, one after another, compounds were being searched and cleared of both suspected insurgents and whatever caches they'd left behind. In the sweltering heat of the ops room at CP Omar, I listened as reports flew back and forth across the radio.

The voice on the other end belonged to Lieutenant Ollie Augustin. At 23 years old, he was on his first tour of Afghanistan. He'd completed his officer training the Christmas before we departed for Helmand Province and instantly won the respect and affection of the lads in J Company. Lieutenant Augustin might have been 14 years my junior, but he'd won my respect, too. He was easy to talk to and had a quiet authority about him, something that automatically put the other lads in the company at ease. What's more, he was hungry to do a good job out here – and that was why he was at the forefront of the operation in Loy Mandeh, leading a group of lads made up from both my location and his own.

Lieutenant Augustin had been based near the company HQ in the township of Shahzad. There they'd made their base at the local police station, tasked with boosting and training the local forces who would, one day, assume the primary role in the fight against the Taliban. Young and keen, he was one of the Royal Marines' brightest young prospects, destined for an even greater leadership role. I liked him immensely. When young officers like Ollie join a unit, it's often said that they have all the training but none of the experience – and that was why it was important that guys like me, troop sergeants who were over a decade into their careers, formed good working relationships with them. It had been that way with me and Lieutenant Augustin. He was the leader, so where he went I would follow – but I was the more experienced older head, and my experience was supposed to complement his authority.

We'd talked about me going out with them, but ultimately it was decided that I was of better use in the ops room at CP Omar. Nobody knew how long the operation was going to go on for, and while Lieutenant Augustin was out in the field, I would be responsible for activity at both our locations, giving advice and guidance to the corporal left behind at his base whenever it was required.

I was in that op room now, the air hot and fetid, despite the fact that the plate steel doors were open. In the heart of the compound, I could hear the lads flitting back and forth. Occasionally one of them would hang in the doorway, eager for a sitrep (a report, basically) on how the operation was going.

I was keeping close tabs on progress. Although the patrol was being spearheaded by the company command, Major McCully, it was typical of Lieutenant Augustin, his drive and talents, that he had assumed leadership of his sub-unit. Their task: to disrupt insurgent activity in Loy Mandeh and to supplement the "clear, hold, build" operation occurring in that area, eventually securing it from insurgent activity altogether. In that way, everything we were doing was designed to expand the influence of the new government of Afghanistan – one tiny district at a time.

As I listened now, Lieutenant Augustin and his lads had entered an Afghan compound, cleared it, but found nothing, no trace of insurgents, no cache of weapons. They stopped, forming a group in the middle of the compound, to debate their next move.

Then two lives ended and others were decimated forever.

The radios burst with white noise. Moments later, when the voices ghosted back in, I could hear the urgent voices from the ops room at Shahzad. Call-signs, questions, demands for information were barked back and forth.

In the door of my own ops room, one of my lads had appeared. "What's going on, boss?"

I shook my head. "There's been an incident."

It was all I could say. I still didn't know. The radio was being kept clear of everything but essential traffic, nobody wanting to jam up the net and delay the passage of any vital information – so, as desperate as we were for news, we observed the silences as best we could. Outside, the lads kept passing by, sticking their heads in, asking for the latest. The more they asked, the less I could say – and, the less I could say, the more they knew something was wrong.

There was nothing any of us could do. It had been over in an instant. When Lieutenant Augustin had gathered his troop to reflect before pushing onwards, one of the lads had knelt down. It was an action that tore families apart, that sent two of our own boys home in body bags, and another two in pieces. The act of kneeling had triggered an IED buried by whatever insurgents had bugged out in advance of the company's arrival. The explosion, driven upwards, had killed Lieutenant Augustin. It had killed Marine Sam Alexander MC as well. Sam had been the elder of the two. A decorated veteran already, he'd first been to Afghanistan in 2008-09 as part of Operation Herrick 9, and it was here that he'd proven himself to be the very best of men. Outgunned and with his machine gun out of ammunition, he'd charged down a group of insurgents with only his 9mm pistol, and all to draw fire away from a colleague lying injured in the field. What's more, it had worked – under fire from Marine Alexander, the insurgents had beaten a retreat – and, on his return to the UK, Sam had been awarded the Military Cross for gallantry.

Later that same year, he'd married his girlfriend Sophie and, barely nine months later, she'd given birth to a son. A son who would now never see his father again.

And all because somebody knelt in the wrong place.

It was the sheer randomness of it that terrified the most. A bullet in the back was more understandable than this. An ambush. A straight-up fight.

There was no way of sugar-coating it. In the morning, I asked the lads to gather outside the tents and delivered the news.

"The boss is dead," I said. "Sam died with him."

The silence in the compound was oppressive, but I could see the effect it was having on the lads. I knew the effect it was having on me as well. Ollie and Sam were so young, the lieutenant younger than I'd been when I marched to the recruiting station and signed up all those years ago. Now he was gone, never to go back home, never to see his family again, never to rise up and be the Royal Marine leader I knew he had the potential to become.

There was more. I had to tell them. It was good and right that everyone knew. *This is what we're up against, lads. This is what could happen to any one of us out here. If we stay strong and do everything right, well, it can* still *happen. This is Helmand.*

"It took Cassidy and JJ too. They're touch and go."

"Al?" one of the lads asked.

"I don't have any more detail." Well, I did, but I hesitated before saying it now. It brought to mind all those pictures I'd seen in the field hospital at Camp Bastion. "Cassidy lost his leg, lads."

I could see it on their faces. The realisation was dawning. Knowing intellectually that some terrible fate might befall you is not the same thing as *feeling* it, deep in the gut. The lads were feeling it now. So was I. And, as the bearer of the news, it was as if I was delivering the blow to them myself. I kept telling myself it was better this way. Better that they caught a glimpse of what their own futures could be.

I was still telling myself this when the very next day, more news buzzed over the radio. This time, it was the company commander, Major McCully himself. Another improvised explosive, this time hidden in a wall and detonated by remote control as his team passed by. He'd survive, I told the lads as we kitted up, but he'd be going home. He'd never be the same again. His career was over. He'd done nothing wrong. Neither had Lieutenant Augustin and Marine Alexander. There was so little they could have done to prevent what happened to them. All Afghanistan seemed to be, now, was a game of roulette.

So we booted up and went out through the compound gates, laden down in our body armour, metal detectors in hand, to take our own turn on the wheel – and do the very same thing that was picking off each of our friends and brothers, one by one.

There was a sombre mood at CP Omar in the days that followed. We went on our patrols, did our community work, followed what orders came down from on high – but all the time in the back of our heads was the knowledge that any day, any one of us could follow where Ollie and Sam had gone.

And it was then that I first realised: at least the lads had each other. At the end of the day, however gruelling it had been, whatever news we'd had to absorb, they had each other to cut loose with, to banter and vent and let off steam. I could hear them in the tents after dark, ranting and raving and railing against this blasted land – and every bit of it, every crude or ungraceful thing that was said, was helping them get it out of their systems. It helped them accommodate what had happened to Lieutenant Augustin and Marine Alexander.

I was glad for them, but for me, it was different. This was not like my last time in Afghanistan. At FOB Inkerman in 2007, I'd been one of a dozen and more marines of a similar rank. We'd been able to debrief together, to chew the fat and go over the events of the day, no matter how horrific. There is a cure in talking, it takes you out of yourself, lets you process things that have happened. Here, at CP Omar, all I had was the radio. For a few brief moments each night, I would connect with my contemporaries in the company's other locations to hear about any significant events from their own area. But visits by commanding officers were vanishingly rare. Later, the Royal Marines' padre would say that CP Omar – along with many other locations – was just too remote and dangerous for him to visit. So there was nothing for it, each night, but to try and shut it down on my own, to make sure the lads were OK, to think about the day ahead, and the day after that, and just get on with the job at hand.

It was all I really knew how to do.

* * *

July 2011, and beneath the military transport plane, English shores were materialising through layers of cloud.

I don't think I realised, even as the plane came into land and I began the long drive back to Taunton to reunite with Claire, how much I had been anticipating this period of R&R. On my past tours, I'd never overly cared about what leave I got and when. The first time I'd been in Helmand, I'd cared more about the lads I was with getting their R&R than I had my own. Now, as the hills and fields of Devon and Somerset rolled by, I began to understand how deeply *I* needed it as well. I cannot express it any more clearly than this: being in that compound, even surrounded by a multitude of lads whose company I valued and who I respected as deeply as I do all Royal Marines, was… lonely. It has taken me a long time to allow myself to put the word to it, but the experience of being the ranking officer, without anyone of my own experience and level to let off steam with at the end of a long patrol, after an attack, or after an engagement out in the field, had affected me more than I knew. But I had made it this far, relatively intact, and perhaps in these two weeks I could bleed off some of those feelings, tell Claire everything that was happening out there, and go back refreshed. By the time I got back to Helmand, there would still be three months of this tour left to survive. I needed to be at my best.

The two weeks I spent in England, though, were not entirely about rest and recuperation. Since my father's cremation on the eve of my departure for Afghanistan, my mother had kept his ashes in their urn at her house, a constant reminder of the husband she had lost. Now, six months later, it was time to say our final goodbyes.

Two days after I had returned to Taunton – days in which Claire and I enjoyed each other's company, and I tried not to describe the very worst of what was happening in Helmand – we got in the car and drove south, past the beautiful, rolling Blackdown Hills and towards the coastal town of Weymouth. I remembered the road into Weymouth well. To me, it is one of those things imprinted on you from childhood. A rush of feeling came over me as we pulled up in a familiar part of town, the boats bobbing together in the sun-drenched marina, and saw my mother, brother and sisters already waiting for us. My father was with them, too.

He was coming back home. This was the town where he'd been born. These were the streets and roads he had scrabbled around as a boy. This was the place he had brought us back to, time and again, for family holidays when we were young.

CHAPTER SIX

It is a day that will forever remain in my mind. We spent long hours looking around the area, my mother reminiscing about the places Dad had taken her to on their first tentative steps of the life they were about to spend together. That trip down memory lane brought us, at last, to the sweeping stones of Chesil Beach – and that was where my brother, my sisters, my mother and I said our final farewell to Dad. This was the place he had come to go fishing as a boy. We returned his ashes to it now.

Driving away from my father for the final time did not feel like a great sadness. The great sadnesses had already come. But it did make me realise how little time and presence of mind I'd had to properly accept the idea that he had gone. In Helmand my head was full. Every second seemed to be accounted for. I'd lost myself in the maelstrom of each day: the patrols the lads and I would be walking, security at the compound, the debriefs every time daytime paled toward dusk, the radio crackling out the casualties and fatalities we'd experienced across all our various locations. Out there, it was the deaths of young men like Lieutenant Augustin and Marine Sam Alexander that dominated the mind; there had hardly been a spare hour for all the manifold memories of my father to cascade past my eyes. I'd locked them down, like I always did – compartmentalising, as Claire called it, so that I could deal with it another day. Because out there, if the mind wandered, if you got lost in your own problems for too long – well, that could mean the death or injury of one of your colleagues. And even now, here in

Weymouth, I was thinking of them, what might be happening to them while I was gone.

And the IEDs. The constant feeling that any step could mean any one of us ended our tours just like Lieutenant Augustin and Sam Alexander. It got to the point where that the possibility of a buried device was at the very forefront of your mind. It was habit-forming, something you could not shake, enough to make you obsessive and compulsive.

I was about to find out how much it had been driving me.

"Al, are you... all right?"

I came out of my reverie. We were somewhere in Weymouth town centre, on our way to a restaurant to toast my father one last time. Claire's voice had not startled me, as such, but it had made me realise that I wasn't quite there, not in Weymouth under the English sun the way that the rest of my family were. As has so often happened, Claire pulled me back into the present.

"Why?" I asked.

But I knew before she explained it. She'd seen my eyes darting down, my gaze focusing on the ground beneath my feet with every step I took. I was here, in England, walking over paving stones that had lain undisturbed for decades, and cobbles that had been laid in the last century, perhaps even before... and I was looking for IEDs everywhere.

I put it out of my mind as we ate at the restaurant. For this I was eternally grateful, the food here in England outclassed the supplies we could get in our compound in Helmand Province.

CHAPTER SIX

But for the rest of my R&R, as Claire and I relaxed together, took walks, went out for drinks and generally tried to let off steam, I was deeply aware that two weeks were not nearly enough to shake off everything we were seeing and doing in Helmand. It wouldn't slough off me naturally, not any of it. But no matter how much I needed to, I didn't want to tell Claire about the feeling that ambushes were being pinpointed and planned for the patrols I was personally walking on – because, to the insurgents in our location, *I* was the prize scalp. I didn't want to tell her about the insecure lock on the back gate of the compound, nor how I had been ticking off each day as just another part of an inevitable countdown to losing one of my lads. I didn't want to tell her about the kinds of casualties they pieced back together at Camp Bastion – and how, even if you were spared death by IED blast, you could come back without the promise of a future and family to come.

So instead we enjoyed what little time together we had. And every morning, when I woke up beside her, it was another morning closer to my return.

CHAPTER SEVEN

The entirety of J Company was out in the field, called up from all our various locations.

For some weeks after my return I'd been trying to manage the staggering of our patrols better. Some of the lads at CP Omar had children back home – and, although they still had to patrol like the rest of us, I'd taken the decision to do what I could to make sure they didn't spend too long out there. After Lieutenant Augustin and Marine Alexander, the sudden, random nature of death in Helmand was emblazoned on my mind – and lads with children always took priority, in my eye. I'd done the same on my last tour of Afghanistan, when I'd made sure that anyone with children could get home for Christmas while the rest of us stayed behind. But with only 12 men remaining at CP Omar while the other lads were rotated out for their R&R allocation, somebody was going to have to take up the slack. So I'd done it myself. Even an occasional extra patrol was depleting, but it kept the lads sharp and at least it minimised the risk to marines who had children.

CHAPTER SEVEN

Before I'd finished my R&R, I'd paid a visit to the hospital where JJ was still recuperating from the blast that had killed Lieutenant Augustin and Marine Alexander. News on JJ and Cassidy had been thin on the ground back in Helmand, and it gave me some hope that they were both making steady progress. Cassidy had been moved to the rehab centre at Headly Court – and, although JJ remained in hospital, things were looking good for him as well. Sam and Ollie were gone, but any life saved is a victory of sorts, and I was grateful to see him. Sitting with JJ in his hospital room, I tried to assess how he was – not just physically, but mentally as well. Somehow, that seemed to matter most of all. Only when I felt he was in a good enough place to take it did I reach into my pack and produce a box of chocolate fingers.

"To replace the ones you lost in the blast," I grinned, looking down at his damaged arm.

JJ paused. Then, as he accepted the chocolate, his laughter rang out. It was what I'd needed to hear. I think it was what he needed as well.

Today, back in Helmand, we were out in force, with just skeleton crews left in our compounds while the entirety of J Company united in one single effort to drive whatever insurgents remained here further out of the district. Sometimes, a show of force worked wonders.

It was at times like this, when troops from different compounds came together – or perhaps overlapped on a patrol they were running – that we got to hear news from further afield. Secluded in our own remote base, news from other areas was often hard to come by, and, even though information flew across the radio waves at the end of each day, there was nothing like being in the company of other marines to hear the realities of being on the ground.

And what realities there were.

"It was a roadside bomb," one of the lads from another troop had said. The story that followed was almost too barbaric to comprehend. One of the lads from J Company had made the same mistake any one of us could: he'd set foot in the wrong place at the wrong time, and the earth had erupted in a geyser of shrapnel and explosives, decimating his leg. In the chaos of casevac that had followed, the severed leg had been left behind – only to be discovered, some time later, hanging from a roadside tree, black and leathered by the sun. The Taliban had left it there as a trophy.

It was an act of terror every bit as bad as it sounds. Not content with shredding the life of one of our lads, they'd used him to play on the minds of everyone around us. Stories spread like diseases in places like this. When they heard it, I could see the effect it had on my lads. More than once, I heard them talking: if they were captured, they feared they'd be skinned alive, beheaded, turned into trophies just like the lad who'd stepped on the roadside bomb. And the most problematic thing for me as their leader was that they were probably right. All we could really do was try to manage our fears. The random nature of what could happen to us we had to put out of our minds; there was only so much we could do to control the twists of fate.

It reminded me of another time when, suddenly, the radio in the ops room at CP Omar had erupted with the order to get out on patrol that very instant. I'd bundled out to the lads, ordered them to get suited and booted, and together we'd pounded the earth to reach our objective, setting up a checkpoint at a road junction to the north. The urgency of the order was intense enough that we took risks to get there, moving more quickly than we should have done, unable to scour the earth as exhaustively as we did on our ordinary patrols. When at last we got into position, more news poured over the short-wave radios. An army soldier, a Scots Guard, had left his compound alone and been taken by the Taliban. Why he'd done it, we didn't know. The fact is, we never would. But he was out there somewhere, and J Company was fanning out to help find him.

In fact, he was dead already. As we held our position, the ditches and fields were being scoured – until, finally, his remains were discovered, abandoned in a drainage ditch. I never saw that body, but I heard the stories. Another young man flagellated and mutilated before they snubbed out his life. That night, I had to gather the lads and deliver them an edict: never to wander off on their own. The bemused looks I got back told me that, of course, they already knew that. But if one young soldier could do it, so could anyone. We'd never know why. Maybe it's just that Helmand Province gets into your head...

Back in the Nad-e Ali District, we'd pushed north out of our location, sweeping through the Afghan compounds to the east of the canal that cut through this part of the land. Then, having reached our appointed location, we drew to a halt. Tasked with protecting the eastern flank of the operation, we held position and began to engage the locals in whatever chatter we could, capturing biometric data as we went. It was these biometrics that allowed us to build up a profile of each area, a basis from which we could begin to detect when things had shifted or changed in the civilian population. But hearts and minds were important, too, and winning the confidence of what locals we could was a central part of our mission in Afghanistan. Of course, in a nation where an enemy combatant could be hidden in plain sight – one moment a local farmer or labourer, the next an insurgent – getting to know who was who, and how they fitted into the district society, was about self-preservation as well. The most powerful weapon we had in this war wasn't the armoury we carried with us, it was knowledge.

I stood opposite an empty adobe house, propped up against one of the trees growing out of a drainage ditch – grateful, momentarily, for the modicum of shade it afforded. The lads around me were striking up what conversation they could with the locals, our translator flitting between us and assisting. Occasionally, something would skitter in the debris at my feet, then laughter would flurry up from somewhere further down the ditch. I paid it little mind: the children of Nad-e Ali were the same as everywhere else in the world, they just needed a little entertainment, and even I knew that throwing stones at foreign soldiers was good fun.

CHAPTER SEVEN

A few moments later, something else skittered on the ground at my feet. It barely caught my attention. Just more stones, I thought.

Then the world erupted.

I pitched forward, the blast at my back. Wheeling around, I was in time to see the second explosion. What I'd taken as stones thrown by kids were really grenades hurled by some insurgent, hidden in plain sight. The second grenade detonated in virtually the same instant as the first, peppering the tree I'd been propped against with shrapnel.

I stopped to breathe. It was only that tree that had saved my life.

It had saved the life of half a dozen civilians as well. They were scattering now. The ground close to where they'd been standing was blasted apart. If they'd been fractionally out of cover, their lives would have been smeared across the earth.

I looked around. In the adobe building across the road, there was movement. Whoever the insurgent was, that was where he'd been hiding. It was only the angle of the window, and the fact he hadn't wanted to be seen, that had prevented the grenade from landing where it might kill.

I was lucky to be alive.

And yet...

The explosion of the grenades was still ringing in my ears, the marines around me whirling into a defensive position, when from somewhere to our east somebody opened fire. As one, we turned. Just 200 metres away, a pair of insurgents had appeared with small arms, sending bursts in our direction. Taking cover, we returned fire, drove them off, but in those same moments more explosions broke the air and earth around us. Somebody, somewhere, had a grenade launcher and was zoning in on our position.

These were not locals out to get us. The locals, when they fought at all, did it because the Taliban coerced them into it, gave them 10 dollars, thrust a gun into their hands and instructed them to get out there and shoot. No, I knew that these were insurgents drafted in from somewhere else because as much as they wanted to kill Royal Marines, they were happy to kill local Afghans as well. To them, any locals speaking with a Royal Marine – or in fact any interloper from overseas – were collaborators, and that meant they deserved to die, too.

They'd taken their chance. In a wave of return fire, the insurgents scattered and my lads and I pulled ourselves back together, for the moment unharmed. But my mind flitted back to the first grenades that had been thrown. There was little doubt in my mind: they'd been directed at me. The insurgents knew who I was. They knew that I was the commander at my location. And it didn't help that I was at least half a foot taller than most of my lads. The insurgents, they knew me by *sight*.

It had been creeping up on me across the months. Every pot-shot taken was another sign of it. The way the lads went out on patrol without me and avoided a confrontation, and yet every time I joined them, there they were – waiting, as if they knew exactly where I would be and when. There was no denying that the Taliban had a list of high-profile targets – just as the allies themselves did. Theirs was not a war of open combat any longer, it was a bitter, attritional, directed war of terror – how to have the greatest impact with the smallest acts. And it buzzed within me, a tide of little voices at the back of my head, making themselves louder and more insistent each night when darkness fell over the compound and my thoughts turned to the unsecured compound gates: in Nad-e Ali, they knew who I was, and I was the one they wanted the most.

I don't think I shook that feeling until long after the end of my tour.

* * *

October 2011, and I stood at the gate of CP Omar as the armoured convoy hoved into view.

In a few days we would be bugging out, back to Camp Bastion and, finally, home. It couldn't come soon enough. When I looked at the lads, I didn't see the mix of fresh recruits and young marines whom I'd first met only a short time before deployment. I didn't see the boys whose mothers had asked me to make sure they came home in one piece. I saw tired and depleted men whose first experience of war had been purgatorial. When I looked back on my own first active deployment in Iraq and contrasted it with this, there was no comparison. The boys had been through hell on their first outing.

And yet they had made it. The armoured convoy coming into CP Omar was bringing with it a lieutenant from the

Prince of Wales Royal Regiment and, in a few days' time, our replacement team would follow. I was close to doing what I'd promised and bringing everyone home alive. And if the same could not be said for the whole of J Company or 42 Commando itself – across those months we'd lost seven of our number from different locations, some in the most horrific ways possible, and many more had been extracted with injuries that would completely transform their lives – I was still happy that my own lads had survived.

I spent the next day briefing the new officer on what he might expect in the coming months, sitting in the ops room going through the photographic index and biometric files we'd assembled: who was a local leader, who could be trusted, who it was best to avoid, and who might most easily be engaged in useful conversation. If there was a distinct sense of deja vu as I went through the process, that was only because it was exactly the same process I'd been through at the start of the tour with the troop sergeant I was relieving. Our conversations mirrored the ones I'd had then so closely that a Groundhog Day feeling washed over me. After all these months we'd given to surviving Helmand, the thought began to blossom inside me: had we effected any real change at all? Or were we leaving Nad-e Ali in the same volatile, pent-up, murderous state in which we'd found it?

The lads from the new troop arrived at CP Omar two days later, choppered out from Camp Bastion and travelling overland from the landing zone itself. Once they were acclimatised, we began their orientation, just as we ourselves had been oriented at the start of the tour. For three days we went out with them into the lanes, fields and compounds of the Nad-e Ali District. For three days, I effected what introductions I could. But three days under that baking sun could never be enough to make them properly understand what the district was going to do to them. Three days, however relentless, could not compare to 200. They too would experience the slow accumulation of dread, the constant gnawing feeling that each step could be their last, they too would listen to the radio chatter with its stories of friends gunned down or eviscerated from below, they too would come to know the relentlessness of being targeted and watched, and not being able to do a thing about it. I only hoped they all made it out – and that perhaps they'd make some progress along the way.

Returning from that last patrol, there was a sense of expectation, of celebration, among the lads in my own troop. As they stripped off their kits, some of them were whooping and hollering in delight that the end of the tour was nigh. Tomorrow we would be out of Nad-e Ali and, days later, back in the safety of the United Kingdom. But the other team, the one fanning out around us and preparing for their own six months in hell, were too close for comfort. I took some of the lads aside and urged them to exercise a little restraint.

"They've still got six months of this," I said. "They don't know who's going home or not. They don't know what's coming at them. So…" I didn't want to stop the lads from having their moment. Home was tantalisingly close, and the end of a first tour – especially one with the terrors of this one – is always an important milestone. But I gave them a pointed look. "Let's keep it to ourselves, shall we?"

Night came. Our last night in Helmand. The sky above CP Omar was blanketed in stars. The lads on the night watch were by the back gate, gazing out into empty desert. We did not expect an attack tonight; what insurgents were out there were no doubt busy seeding the lanes and fields with more explosive devices for the new troop to dig out, or die by, tomorrow.

I was readying myself to turn in when the news came out of the ops room that the Chinooks scheduled to come out for pick-up in the morning had been delayed.

In moments like this, the heart does sink, but it is one of the vagaries of military life that plans often change. CP Omar was as remote as I'd ever been stationed, so perhaps it was no surprise that extracting from here was not going to be as straightforward as all that.

My new instruction was clear: we were to spend the following day out on another patrol with the new troop. Another day of familiarising themselves with Nad-e Ali and learning from those who had gone before them would be invaluable.

But the lads were already finished. Mentally, they were already done.

In the ops room, I spoke to the officer who was taking over command of our location. "Look," I said, "you know what's happening here. I'm told we're taking you out again tomorrow. But…" I thought of the way the lads had whooped and hollered, high-fiving each other on reaching the end of this miserable tour. "Here's what's going to happen: you're going to lead the patrol. I'm coming out with you myself. My guys, they're going to stay back here. They're finished already. But I'll be there – I'll show you where we got shot at, where we've found weapons cached, where the IED craters are… But I'm not taking any of my lads. They got told that yesterday was their last – I'm not doing that to them."

The new commander was silent for a second. Then he nodded. "We've got six months of this," he uttered. "Sooner or later, we've got to do this on our own." He paused. "So, let's get on with it."

The morning came. Sun poured over the fields of Nad-e Ali, growing in intensity with each passing hour. Out on the road, as the new lads fanned out with the metal detectors and the rest of us kept watch for unexpected movements on the edges of our vision, the nerves took hold of me. They knotted and tied me inside. It is strange, the way that final days can take root in you, twisting you up into fantasies of catastrophe that may never happen. I had not known a day like it in what felt like months. There was silence beyond the walls of CP Omar. The lanes were empty. The local Afghan people were shuttered up inside. Something, it seemed, was changing out here – and no sooner had I come to this realisation than everything else from the last six months was resurgent inside me.

All I had to do was not listen to those voices. All I had to do was bottle it up for one more day. I threw in some changes of direction, trying to ascertain where the locals were disappearing to, what might have changed, and step by step, hour by hour, we walked a circuit around the district. The new troop asked me questions, and this at least pulled me out of the uneasiness I'd been feeling all day. When there are pragmatic things to accomplish, it is easier to shut that part of the brain down.

And yet the day ground on.

This was the last chance they had to target me specifically.

These were the last steps I would take, uncertain whether the ground beneath my feet was about to erupt.

This were my final hours under that heartless Afghan sun.

As CP Omar came back into sight at the end of the day, the knots loosened up inside me. The sight of the compound that had been home for six months – small and exposed as it seemed – was what I needed. When I tramped back through the gate, completely spent, I knew, finally, that it was over.

Soon, the transports would be coming to take us all home. For now, Helmand was a thing of the past.

As we debriefed at Camp Bastion and boarded the transports to come home, the lads thrilled again at successfully completing their first tour. But this was not the thrill of victory. Survival, yes. Victory, never. The lads had come through. They'd been blooded. They had performed admirably under circumstances so much worse, tenser, more barbaric, than the ones I'd been blooded in in Iraq all those years ago. But for what gain? The new troop officer and soldiers who'd come in to take over our location had found the area in no better a state than when we ourselves had come in at the start of the year – and we, I supposed, had found it no better than the previous soldiers had found it at the start of their own tour. Along the way, lives had been lost. Men had gone home with life-changing injuries. And yet the sense that something had been gained for their sacrifice was almost entirely absent.

This wasn't like 2007. The months I'd spent at Forward Operating Base Inkerman had been a different kind of trial. There'd been casualties, of course. There'd been fatalities. But at the end of that tour, we'd been able to look back at the Sangin valley and see exactly what the effects of our endurance and sacrifices had been. Sangin was on the road to rejuvenation and, if not thriving yet, had "thriving" in their sights. Its schools were operating again, its houses filling up with civilians eager to make the new peace last. And that was all because of us – drawing the fire and focus of the area's insurgents, refusing to let them re-establish their stranglehold on the area and its poppy fields. Men who'd been wounded, the friends and families of those who'd lain down their lives, could at least look at the way Afghanistan had profited from what we'd done. To suffer at war and make the world a better, safer place – at least that makes sense.

As we boarded the military transport plane at the end of our tour of 2011, I dug deep inside and tried to summon up the same sense of pride in a job well done. But in 2011 there was no rejuvenated Sangin. There were no schools reopening amid the fields and sun-bleached roads that we'd patrolled. We left the area no richer for our coming. We left it no safer. In the next months the patrols would go on, the same ground would be scoured for IEDs, the same insurgents would run the same ambushes and be beaten away time and time again. That was the war now, I supposed, the continuing stalemate of peacekeeper vs. insurgent, with the Taliban combatants growing ever more devious in the ways they tried to take us down.

I would go home, proud that all the lads from my location had survived, but knowing there was more than a healthy proportion of dumb luck involved in the achievement. Any one of us could have been ruined, the same as Lieutenant Augustin and Marine Alexander. When I looked back over those six months, all I really felt was a dull, abstract ache. We'd accomplished our survival, but not seeing – or even understanding – the fruits of our labour… well, that was the most difficult thing of all.

I looked down as the plane lifted from the air strip at Camp Bastion and took off into the skies above Afghanistan, grateful – for the time being – that I would not be coming back, but only too aware that I was taking a piece of Helmand back with me, a knotty little piece of it, still pulsing away at the back of my mind.

CHAPTER EIGHT

Taunton, England, 2012

And for a time, my war was over.

The feeling of coming home was not triumphant. In Afghanistan, the war went on. Somebody else was now walking the same patrols that we had walked. Somebody else was endlessly scouring the earth for any sign of IEDs, getting through each day one at a time. My tour of 2011 had been so different from my tour in 2007-08 that it almost felt as if we had been fighting two completely separate wars. Simply relieved to be back, I was happy for the peace of Taunton, and the extended time I got to spend with Claire.

I didn't see the lads from Helmand many times after the flight out of Camp Bastion. For those in 42 Commando who hadn't been out to Afghanistan before, there were the usual procedures to go through: the parades where they would be honoured for their service, presented with operational medals and more. But for me, the return to the UK represented another transition in my career. I was soon to learn that I'd been selected for promotion.

Having just returned from Helmand, I wasn't eager to return to 40 Commando – who would soon be redeployed – but another opportunity had presented itself. Another training role, this time with the army, helping to prepare guys about to go off to Afghanistan. Although the job would take me outside the Royal Marines for the first time, it was higher profile, more frenetic, and would allow me to use the experience I'd acquired across two different tours to better prepare our lads for the challenges they would face. At my time of life, it seemed the more worthwhile contribution to make. It would mean a move away from Taunton – I'd be based at the Shorncliffe Army Camp at Folkestone in Kent, more than 200 miles away – but at least it was closer than Helmand, and with what amounted to a regular day job, I'd be able to spend every weekend with Claire. Thinking back to the years I'd spent in the central training team at Lympestone, and all it had done for my relationship with Claire, this was what I wanted. Claire and I had been married for two years and, for big chunks of that, had been thousands of miles apart. Now I looked forward to some structure. Some normality. The marriage we had planned. The training job would give us all that – and, although it might on occasion take me back to Afghanistan, it would only be to the relative safety of Camp Bastion, where I'd deliver further training. It was the compromise our lives needed.

In this way, another year passed. For the most part, I was able to stop thinking about that little compound where I'd spent so much of the year before. For the most part, Claire didn't catch me staring guardedly at the ground, as if there might be IEDs buried beneath the simple paving stones and cobbles of Taunton's high street. Slowly, bit by bit, I began to feel like me again: no longer dogged by the incessant feeling that somebody out there, just beyond my line of sight, was planning to get me. I stopped checking that the back doors were locked. I did not go to sleep at night thinking about the rockets that might explode across our Taunton walls. There was Christmas at home, not in the middle of the desert with the radio crackling out threats of attack. There was a New Year, and a new beginning. And there was Claire.

* * *

A year later, weekends with Claire had become the fixture of my life. Long weeks on camp in Folkestone, the 200-mile drive home on a Friday night, waking up with Claire on Saturday morning to an empty weekend, when we could do whatever we wanted.

On that fateful morning in October 2012, we were lying in bed, skimming the surface of sleep, both of us dozing, half-awake, in that way so specific to Saturday mornings. I still can't remember what we had planned for the day. One of the joys of weekends is precisely having no plans, and because Claire and I could see each other so little during the week, slow mornings like these were something we treasured. Even so, neither of us thought anything of it when the knock came at the door. A knock at the door on a Saturday morning was not so unusual. It might have been the postman. A delivery for down the road. It did not have to mean that life was about to change.

It was Claire who got up. I rolled over, barely listening as she went down the stairs and opened the door. I heard voices, male and indistinguishable from where I was lying, but still, I thought nothing of it. The weekend was wide and open and stretching out in front of me. Perhaps, I thought, I would take Claire back to one of our favourite restaurants, perhaps even the one where I had proposed.

Moments later, Claire was back at the bottom of the stairs. "Al!" she called out. "Al, come down here…"

Later, Claire would tell me how she'd opened the front door in her dressing gown, thinking she would engage our local delivery person in some small talk. Instead, she was faced with four military police officers in plain clothes, and a pair of uniformed policemen from the local constabulary standing on either side.

Even as I lay in bed, I could hear that something was wrong. Something had changed in Claire's voice. It was not fear. It was a kind of… bewilderment. That is, perhaps, the closest I can get to describing it. The way she called out made me think it was fairly urgent, so in an instant I was up and out of bed, contorting myself into last night's shirt and trousers as I lurched to the top of the stairs.

I was halfway down when I saw the military police for the first time. They hadn't barged their way in, but they had arrayed themselves around the open door, with the first breath of autumn blowing in. I joined Claire in the doorway.

CHAPTER EIGHT

It was one of the military policemen who spoke first. "Colour Sgt Alexander Blackman?" he asked.

I nodded. "That's me."

"Colour Sgt Blackman, we're arresting you on suspicion of committing war crimes. You do not have to say anything, but it may harm your defence if you do not mention when questioned..."

The rest of it faded away. I was still trying to comprehend the first words he'd said. Was I really being arrested? And, more baffling still, was I really being arrested for... war crimes? I was still hesitating, letting it sink in, when one of the local constabulary spoke up. "We don't have to do this outside, not in full view of all of the neighbours. Mrs Blackman, might we come inside?"

Even then, with the idea of being arrested still so unreal, we did nothing to resist or push back. There seemed a common decency about the constable who'd spoken and Claire and I stepped back, welcoming all six police officers into the house. Perhaps it was the way the door fell shut behind them that made it seem more real. Somehow, it punctuated everything that had already been said.

"We have a warrant to search the premises," one of the military policemen explained, showing Claire and I their identifications and paperwork. "We have another to search your accommodation on camp in Folkestone, so we'll need your keys, too, Colour Sgt Blackman." He paused, as if waiting for us to say something. "Might we begin?"

Claire and I exchanged a look, each of us as bewildered as the other. "Of course," I began. "Feel free."

There was no panic. Panic does not come naturally to either Claire or me. If I was thinking anything as they fanned out into our home and began to rifle through everything we owned, it was only that this must have been some strange mistake, that it would be finished with soon, the whole affair explained as some accident or miscommunication. I was a Royal Marine. I'd spent the last year training soldiers in Folkestone. I hadn't, I was certain, done anything that warranted the military police going from room to room through our house, opening every cupboard and drawer, shining a torch into every intimate area.

And yet the search began.

They began in the front room first, keeping Claire and me in the kitchen until they were finished. Only then were we brought back into the front room while the officers went through our kitchen, cupboard by cupboard, drawer by drawer. I wasn't certain what they were hoping to find, nor how the charges they'd confronted me with related to the contents of our kitchen cupboards, but it soon became apparent that they were collecting every piece of electronic equipment they could find. They'd already asked for our mobile phones, which had gone securely into a zip-lock bag. Now, sequestered in the living room while police officers tramped upstairs and out back, there was little we could do but wait. With the kitchen now within bounds again, Claire got up and made a pot of tea. The officers stopped, momentarily, to drink before continuing their work.

Once the search was fully underway, one of the military policemen advised the local constabulary that they might think about removing the police officer who was standing sentry outside our front door.

"This isn't for the neighbours to gossip about," he said – and it was with some relief that Claire and I watched him go and deliver the news.

Moments later, the officer who'd been on our doorstep was inside and assisting in the search. At least, I thought, they didn't consider us flight risks. My nerves were growing, and I could tell, just by catching her eye, that Claire's confusion was turning to worry as well – but at least they could see what kind of people we were.

One of the military police officers appeared from up the stairs, brandishing an empty Blackberry phone box. "Where is it?" he asked.

I looked at him quizzically. "I upgraded to an iPhone. If it isn't up there, it might be down in my accommodation at Folkestone." When I could still sense his eyes on me, I added, "It isn't on my person. I'm sure it will turn up."

A little while later, after the search of our upstairs rooms had concluded, I stood in the bedroom that had just been turned upside down and began to put things back where they belonged. Opening the top drawer of my dresser, I saw the Blackberry staring back at me. How they'd missed it, I didn't know – but I took it back to the top of the stairs and, halfway down, held it out for one of the officers to take. "Is this what you're looking for?" I asked, and it disappeared into the evidence bag along with all the rest.

In the space of a couple of hours, the officers had assembled a collection of all our electronic equipment, every phone, tablet, laptop, every possible storage device in our home. Though they hadn't left a trail of chaos behind them – every step of this search had been conducted with respect – the traces of it were still all over the house. A set of drawers sat with each drawer still pulled open. All the boxes had been pulled out from under our bed. Claire's desk was denuded of the laptop that had sat upon it.

Finally, both military police and regular constabulary assembled in the living room where Claire and I waited.

"Colour Sgt Blackman," the lead officer said, "you'll have to come with us."

I got to my feet.

Outside, an unmarked police car was waiting. With an officer on either side, I was guided into the back seat, while Claire remained standing, alone, in the open doorway of our home. The last thing I remember, before the engine guttered to life and the police car wheeled away, was seeing her looking back at me, each of us certain that some terrible mistake was about to be revealed, each of us certain that, by the fall of night, we'd be eating dinner together, looking back on the most surreal day of our lives.

The car door opened, and I stepped out into the bracing air.

I hadn't been handcuffed. I was not grappled either side. I think – I *hope* – the policemen who were escorting me understood that I was not the kind of man who was going to make a scene, or worse still, try and fight his way out of this. But I cannot say that I was not, by now, feeling knotted inside. The uncertainty I had felt as I pulled on my clothes and came down the stairs, the bewilderment as the military police had moved like a wave through Claire's house, had given way to a certain unease. I looked up at the façade of the local police station, and it was the fact that I had no idea what was waiting for me inside that gave me pause.

Ever since I was a boy, I had believed in the "system". It is not something I had ever had to give much thought to, but I had always believed that laws and government and all of our institutions existed to make sure that the right thing happened at the right time. And my respect for the system had only become stronger the deeper I'd travelled into my military career. Consequently, as the military policemen escorted me inside the building and the desk sergeant took down my details, emptying out my pockets and finally leading me down a whitewashed corridor to a cell at the end, I still believed that all of this was about to be straightened out. Even as the cell door closed behind me and I heard the dull thud of the lock, I believed it was just a waiting game.

For some time, I waited alone. One hour turned into two, which soon turned into three and four. The police officers who came and went never treated me with anything less than respect, but somehow it didn't make the wait any less bearable. I had been in tight spots before, but these walls felt tighter every time I opened my eyes.

I thought about those two words: "war crimes".

I thought about Claire, and what she was doing now.

I thought about how both of us, separated by these walls, would be turning the same thoughts over in our minds.

And only as I lost myself in those thoughts did the cell door finally open.

A duty solicitor had been found and asked to come to the station. In the cell, he duly explained his role. In the absence of any family solicitor, or somebody I had opted to pay for, he was here to advise me and offer his counsel through the interview that was about to follow, and potentially whatever came next. I did not need convincing. After so long staring at the same four walls, I was keen to understand exactly what I was doing here.

Escorted by another officer, and with my duty solicitor in tow, I was taken out of the cell and led to a small interview room nearby. For a time, the solicitor and I sat in silence while we waited for the interviewing officers to arrive. I might have been advised to say nothing, but the greater part of me was prepared to speak openly and honestly in response to whatever questions the police officers needed to ask. Whatever the mistake was, I was certain I could help them clear it up, and soon. I didn't feel as if I had anything to hide.

The military police officers arrived and, taking their seats at the other side of the table, arranged a laptop on the surface between us. Moments later, one of them fired up the interview room's recording equipment and, for formality's sake, gave all our names for the audio record.

"Colour Sgt Blackman, you understand why you're here today," one of the officers began. I was uncertain how to respond – because, of course, there were still so many things I didn't understand. "You've been arrested on suspicion of perpetrating war crimes. We've a few things we need to ask you today, and your co-operation will be vital to making this process as painless as possible."

I was being interviewed under caution. My rights had been read to me. Again, my solicitor advised that, for practicality's sake, I could resist saying anything at all, if only to completely rule out the chance I might incriminate myself. But, as certain as I was that I was in the middle of some strange mistake, I nodded my agreement.

"Colour Sgt Blackman, you've been arrested today because evidence has emerged that suggests you committed acts that may amount to war crimes in September 2011."

September 2011. It was only a year ago. In September 2011, I had been with 42 Commando in the Nad-e Ali District of Helmand, approaching the end of that long, problematic tour. It had been some time since I'd dwelled on those months. I was, I suppose, one of the fortunate ones: even though I sometimes strayed back to it, I had been able to push much of it to the recesses of my mind and get on with my new job. Others were not so lucky. They'd come home missing arms or legs. They'd come home missing so much more – just like the men in those images we'd been shown in the hospital at Camp Bastion. And those were the ones who even came home at all. Right now, my time at CP Omar with 42 Commando seemed like a different era. I felt like a different person. And now my mind went reeling back.

"What evidence?" I ventured.

"Video footage has emerged of you on patrol in September 2011."

I said nothing. I froze. The idea that there could have been unofficial video footage of any part of my tour was a revelation to me. That is to say – it was not unheard of that young soldiers, especially those on their first tours of duty, might take illicit footage of their tours as mementos, or things they could share when they got back home, but it was frowned upon, and I'd had no idea that any of the lads in 42 Commando had followed this route. As early as my tour in 2007, online platforms like YouTube had been awash with videos uploaded by former soldiers, detailing the reality of work in a warzone.

Yet by 2011, the top brass had taken a firmer stance on such things, and by the time I returned to Helmand an edict had gone out forbidding the use of personal cameras on any operation. And with good reason: such use caused so many difficulties. Not only could it compromise security for our forces, but it made part of the official policy of the mission to Afghanistan, "to win the hearts and minds" of the Afghan people, so much more of a challenge. Video can distort. It isn't infallible. Sometimes, things seen out of context can look different from how they really were. Things can happen that are completely within the rules of engagement – and yet seen out of context and without the wider panorama of everything a soldier experiences in the field, they might inflame different passions at home.

I'd spent the first part of Helmand in 2011 making sure that none of our first-timers had recording devices on them. To be told I hadn't been successful was a blow. I'd always been of the opinion that if a soldier has time to turn on a camera and start shooting surreptitious footage, then that soldier is not doing his or her job properly. This isn't to say that cameras have no place in modern warfare. They absolutely do. Our patrols were always accompanied by a local interpreter, who would carry with him a proper SLR camera on which we could shoot high-quality images and video. It was a system that worked well. The locals would always feel more comfortable with an Afghan taking photographs, and we used it exhaustively to build up a data bank of local figures in the area. That way, when I had to hand over to another officer at the end of the tour, I'd be able to offer a proper debrief, the best possible head start on knowing who was who in the local area, who lived in which particular compound, who worked there. The photographs and filming we did was an invaluable part of the experience, it allowed me to greet locals by name, to build up fledgling relationships with them – anything to increase our security and theirs. But it was all officially done, and everything was transparent. The idea that other footage existed, while not altogether unsurprising, definitely unnerved me.

"We're going to show you this video now. It doesn't last long. And after that, we'd like to go through some of the specifics of what you've seen. Does that make sense?"

I nodded that yes, of course it did, and the officers proceeded to arrange the laptop on the table so that everyone present could see what was about to be shown. As they arranged the settings, one single image was frozen on the screen: a still-frame shot of a stubby cornfield, tussocks of green spread out under an empty, cobalt sky.

To somebody else, it might have looked like anywhere in the world. To me, it was characteristic of only one place, the outlying fields of the Nad-e Ali District, Helmand Province, Afghanistan.

I wouldn't discover until much later the provenance of that video. One of the lads we'd been on patrol with that day – who would later become known as "Marine B" – had joined us mid-tour after one of my other lads was shot in the leg and sent home, and he had secreted a tiny camera in his helmet in order to take personal footage. Some time after the tour was over, he'd shared the secret videos he'd taken of his time in Afghanistan with some friends and colleagues, including a reservist who was now back in his job at a local fire department. Nobody could have anticipated what would happen next. The reservist with whom my lad had shared the videos had bitterly fallen out with his wife, and the divorce that followed was problematic, to say the least. Accusations began flying back and forth, one of which was eventually serious enough for the police to become involved, and they seized the man's laptop. No inappropriate material was found, but in scouring the laptop to try and substantiate his ex-wife's allegations, the police found this snippet of video from our patrol in Helmand Province instead.

I watched it flicker on the screen.

I recognised the lads instantly, of course. You do not easily forget the faces and voices of people with whom you spent six of the most difficult, testing months of your life. But at first, that was all I recognised. I didn't know where or when this really was. The grasses, the skies, the lay of the landscape in the images, it was all the same to me. It could have been any one of a hundred days pacing the lanes and roads of Helmand Province.

The video lasted only seconds. Perhaps a minute. It cannot have been more. In the shaky images on the screen, I saw myself and three of the other lads from our compound in Helmand. At first we were diminutive specks in the distance, four figures approaching in a hurry through the stubs and rushes of a cornfield not yet knee high. The overriding noise buzzing from the speakers was the chopping of helicopter blades, but above that were the voices of whoever was filming the footage, and whoever else stood behind him.

The figures in the frame were coming quickly, growing bigger with every step. And there I was. My own face, looming up in the frame. Between two of the marines alongside me, there hung the body of a Taliban insurgent. Then, as the video neared its completion, we dropped the mortally wounded insurgent down into the longer grasses at the edge of the cornfield. Voices fired back and forth. I recognised my own voice among the others. We were uttering oaths. We were calling the man we had been carrying things that, here in the police station, sounded abusive and vile.

The video ended.

My mind was still reeling, trying to place this day in my mind. But it was not a memory that I could access easily, if at all. There had been so many long, exhausting days during my second tour of Helmand. Each day bled into the next – the tension and the monotony, the monotony and the tension – and nothing I had been watching screamed out at me.

I was still focusing on it when the questions began.

"Do you recognise yourself in the video, Colour Sgt Blackman?"

I did. Of course I did. That is to say – I recognised the physicality of the man who had been leading his lads in the video, carrying the insurgent to the much longer grasses at the edge of the field. What I found more difficult to recognise were the things we were saying. It didn't sound like me, but there is no doubt it was my voice – so I told the police officers that I did.

"For the record, the video we have all seen here today shows yourself, Colour Sgt Blackman, and three other Royal Marines from 42 Commando carrying a wounded enemy combatant out of this field and depositing him in the grasses at the edge of the field. Do you agree?"

I told them that I did.

"Why were you carrying him like that, Colour Sgt Blackman?"

I stopped. I looked at them quizzically. "Carrying him like… what?"

"So roughly, so inattentively… Would you characterise it as 'carrying', Colour Sgt Blackman? Because it seems to me, as an impartial observer of this video, that you and your fellow marines are dragging an injured man bodily out of that field."

At first, I didn't know what to say. The images that I had seen were not, I knew, pretty. They did not capture any of us in our best lights, and the choice language some of us had been using denigrated us further still. It did not represent us the way Royal Marines always strive to be represented, as the very best of the best. But we had been carrying the wounded insurgent in the way we had all been trained to do, across many years with the Royal Marines. I'd carried friends like that before. With two of my lads grasping the man's limbs, spreading his weight between them, we were able to provide enough support for his body that we could cross a distance swiftly and, at the same time, limit the risk of compounding the wounds he'd already suffered, or generating any new ones. That's all it was, just basic training, the kind designed to strike the right balance between getting help for an injured colleague and minimising the risk to yourself. In times like this, speed matters. An extra second in the field, recovering an injured comrade, means an extra second exposed to enemy fire.

But the things we were saying in the video, the curses and the insults, framed it so badly that I understood the question I was being asked.

"Why did you say those things?"

The question did not blindside me. I, too, was horrified by the language we were using. In the environs of this police station, with its air of formality and its pristine walls, the language was unacceptable, cruel and crude. It was the sort of language Claire had never heard me use. And yet, if I were to cast myself back a year to that tour of Helmand, the tour before it, or even my time in Iraq, it did not seem so very unusual. Throw a group of men together in circumstances that might, at any moment, end any of their lives, and sometimes the simple rules of civility melt away. It isn't that you want to be cruel. It isn't that you want to be rude or cause offence. But the tension can explode out of you in myriad ways, and releasing some of it by ranting and raving, goading and taunting each other, is something that men in combat situations have done throughout the centuries.

"Do you think it's appropriate?" one of them asked.

This time, I didn't answer.

One of the police officers reached out and slid the video back a few seconds. Still some distance from the edge of the field, the other marines and I had stopped to hoist the insurgent a little further up.

"What are you doing there?"

It was not as if I could remember the details, nor really the circumstances of the event. What I saw in the video was us stopping to get better purchase on the insurgent, a dead weight between our arms – risking extra seconds out in the open so that we could hoist him higher and get him to the cover of the long grasses at the edge of the field. What the police officers were seeing, however, seemed to be different. They were seeing us roughly manhandling him, treating him with complete disregard as we bounced him up and down and continued our charge across the cornfield.

The questioning went on for some time. I don't know how many times I saw the snippet of video that day. As I watched, and as I answered what questions I could, the memory of that day rose up from all the thousands of others I'd locked away. I began to recall the ill-fated expedition to the farm building, where command had thought an insurgent had cached an automatic rifle. I recalled the quick march back to our compound and how we'd hidden in the scrub at the edge of the road, awaiting further instructions. I remembered the sound of the Apache helicopter's rotor blades as it had charted its course overhead, before loosing the power of its chain gun and slicing the insurgent down.

There was little more I could say. By the time we were done, we seemed to have been through the video snippet frame by frame – and I still had so little idea where it had come from, how it had come into their possession and whether the "war crimes" they stipulated were based purely on the things they had seen and heard here, or on other evidence as well.

Back in the solitude of my cell, I reflected on everything I'd seen. It had taken some coaxing, but by now I could remember the detail of the day. I wondered if the other marines I'd been with and who had featured in the video had spent their days in police cells just like this one, scattered across the country, being asked the very same questions over and over and over again. Or perhaps, because I was the ranking officer that day, it was only me being asked to explain.

This time I did not have to wait that long. With the interviews and other formalities concluded and my duty solicitor released for the day, a police officer returned to the cell and led me out. For the moment, I was being released without charge – but I was left under no illusions that this was the last time I would be questioned.

The police officers took me back outside, where the afternoon was already paling toward the early autumn dusk, and drove me back to Claire. It was a nice courtesy extended to a fellow member of Her Majesty's armed services, but as I climbed into the back of the car, I was not feeling buoyed. A day that had begun in confusion and bewilderment was ending with an ominous sense that all was not right in the world, that the madness and ever-constricting tensions of Helmand were reaching out for me even now, beneath beautiful English skies.

Today was supposed to be the first day of a week's holiday Claire and I were taking, but tomorrow I would have to drive back to Folkestone and report to my chain of command, letting them know – if they didn't already – exactly what was going on. It might seem such a minor thing, but the fact that they had confiscated all my uniforms and been down to search my Folkestone accommodation had started to weigh on me. The chain of command down there deserved an explanation.

So did Claire. It had been a long day for me, shuffled between holding cell and interview room, but it would have been a long day for her as well, pacing up and down the halls of our empty home, rearranging everything that had been disarranged, unable to reach out or communicate with anyone given that all our devices had been taken away, wondering what on earth had happened to me and when she might hear any news. When I walked back through those doors, at least she would know where I was. And yet, as we crossed Taunton and drove closer and closer to home, I couldn't help but wonder whether I was about to create a whole range of other uncertainties, ones that could be so much worse.

CHAPTER NINE

Taunton, England, September 2012: Memories of Helmand Province

When the police dropped me off, I stalled momentarily before entering the house. I had been in so many life-threatening situations before that they had almost become normal. Helmand could do that to a man. But when sitting in a desert compound coming under rocket attack, I did not get the sinking feeling in the pit of my stomach that I got now. These sensations were entirely new.

So was the sensation I got next. That in the next few moments, I was going to relive it all for the benefit of the one person who loved me more than anything else in her world. Because the video I'd seen in the station had triggered in me recollections of that day in Helmand, and as I'd been travelling home I had been trying to draw all the disparate pieces of it back together.

Claire is one of the most principled and pragmatic people I know. When I finally walked in, there was no air of panic about her, only the quietly confused look of somebody who, even after all these hours, could fathom no earthly reason why her husband should have been taken away, and on such an unlikely charge. As I closed the door behind me, I tried to formulate the words I would use to explain. How to say: it really is a war crimes charge. How to explain that day in the desert to somebody who wasn't there – when, though I had been thinking of little else, it still seemed so distant from the man I was now. How to explain the disjunct between the man in the footage and the man I had always held myself to be, between the man who had said those words and the man who now took his coat and boots off and looked into the eyes of the woman he had married only three short years ago.

Perhaps Claire saw how withdrawn I was, or perhaps it was only that she saw her own confusion reflected in my eyes. She followed me into the sitting room.

"Al," she said. "What happened? What's going on?"

There have never been any secrets between me and Claire. It is one of the foundation stones of our relationship. I wholeheartedly believe that relationships like ours can only ever be based on honesty and trust. I had never told her a lie about my time in Iraq or Afghanistan before. It was a mark of how little I'd dwelled on that day in the desert that I hadn't told her about it in any of the phone calls I'd made home that tour, or on any day since. If I am being honest, there was a little piece of me now that hesitated to start explaining. I didn't know how to rationalise the footage I'd seen, and none of the memories I kept summoning up of that day matched the impression I had of myself, nor the one I understood everyone else to have.

There was a reason it had taken me so long to recognise what I was seeing in the shaky camera footage. That day is emblazoned on my mind now, so often have I relived it, but as I watched the footage for the first time, still wondering where it had come from and how it had ended up in a local Taunton police station, it was a while before the fragments started to piece together in my recollection. The fact was, I hadn't thought of the tasking that day since we returned to our compound before nightfall. I have sometimes wondered if this is strange, because of course the events of that day were far from ordinary. But there had been so many days. Six months is an eternity in Afghanistan. Six months of patrols. Six months of painstakingly mapping the earth beneath your feet with the metal detectors, searching for the IED that might suddenly end your life. Six months listening to the whispering of the locals, the unsettling feeling that they were picking me out in our remote location, all because I was its ranking officer. Six months like this and perhaps you lose sight of the sort of person you really are.

But there was no rationalising what I'd seen. What, I remembered now, I had done. The footage wasn't yet making sense to me. Some day soon, it would have to. And there was more, more about that day that was coming back to me, even now.

"Claire," I began, "I don't know if this… thing is going away." I paused. "There's something I have to tell you."

She was Claire, so I told her all of it.

We were still holding our defensive position in the undergrowth at the side of the road, scarcely 200 metres from our compound, when the tasking came through. With my seven lads in tow, I was to proceed to the fallen target's location, some 20 minutes north-west of where we now stood, and retrieve his weapon, if only to stop it from falling into enemy hands.

This was despite the lads having already been out on patrol all day, and despite our mistaken foray to the farm building where we kicked down the door and found nothing but a single-shot hunting rifle. So I hoped it would not be too arduous. That 20 minutes north-west might mean an hour in actuality, moving slowly and methodically to guard against IEDs buried in the ground, but in a couple of hours we could be back in the compound, rehydrated and ready to recuperate. The sun was beating down, still fierce as it passed its zenith, but we had received our orders. We moved out.

The grid references we had been given were only a guide. It is so difficult to be accurate about positioning from a helicopter, trying to correlate the charts in your hand with the landscape spread out beneath you – but, after an hour's methodical push through the blazing sun, we had, I felt certain, reached the edge of the field where the insurgent had been gunned down.

Somewhere up there, the Apache helicopter still flew. We could hear the turning of its blades, sometimes louder, sometimes softer, as it circled the surrounding area – because one thing was certain, the insurgent lying dead in that field had not been the only one to attack our neighbouring compound. A lone insurgent does not cause the kind of chaos we had heard over the radio. There were more of them out there – whether near or far, we did not yet know.

The edges of the field were deep with long, tangled grasses. Together we pushed through, keeping low to maintain some semblance of cover. For a time we waited there, scouring the field that opened up ahead. The corn that was growing here was low and stubby, but somehow it seemed to obscure everything ahead.

As we scanned the field, our radios crackled back and forth. The Apache, still doing its rounds, was louder now. I listened to its drone intensifying, then as it ebbed away.

First, a second insurgent had been sighted.

Then there was nothing.

Next, there were more insurgents out there.

Then there was silence.

"There," I said, and lifted my hand slowly to point.

The insurgent was lying in the very centre of the field. I could see so little of him from this angle, but I was certain it was him: the shape of a body, barely more than a few hummocks rising out of the uneven earth.

The radio crackled on, different grid references checked off as the search for his fellow insurgents continued.

I could see the outline of the fallen man's weapon lying next to him in the earth.

As a soldier, you are always nervous about going out into the open. Here, at the edge of the field, the grasses at least partially shielded us from sight – they might not stop automatic rifle fire, and if we were spotted we had little protection, but at least they gave us a modicum of cover. Out there, where the insurgent lay, there was nothing of that, only the stubs of corn growing irregularly. And still the radio crackled, other insurgents out there, and not one of them found...

The longer we were out here, the greater the risk of being exposed. The lads did not deserve that. They had been out for long enough already, and the sun was still beating down.

I turned to Jack, one of the lads accompanying me that day. I couldn't do this alone. "You're with me," I said. Then, turning to the rest of the patrol, I said, "Stay sharp, boys. We may be coming back at a run."

The quicker we got this done, the better.

Hoisting our packs onto our backs, Jack and I took off into the field.

In moments like these, there is so little you can do to protect yourself. The lads on the fringes of the field would do what they could if other insurgents were close by and happened upon us, but while we were out in the open, we were targets. We needed to move fast, but were hindered by the constant threat of IEDs, even in the field.

When we got to the insurgent, there was no doubt in my mind that he was dead. There he was, lying in a pool of his own blood and gore, the very earth steeped in the fluids that had pumped out of his body when the Apache's chain gun opened on him. Steeling myself – because you never truly get used to handling the dead – I prepared to turn him over, to check for whatever weapons remained.

The AK47 he'd been carrying was on the earth at his side. I picked it up.

"Keep your eyes open," I said to Jack.

Then, as he stood guard, I got to my knees and began searching the body. I did not want to; the amount of blood and viscera that had been thrust out of him by the force of the Apache's chain gun repelled me, and as marines we had been warned about the possibility of catching blood-borne infections from casualties in the field. But it was imperative that I did it. This was what we had come here for, why we were out here in the open, exposed, lingering – while out there the other insurgents could not be found – to retrieve whatever weapons he had. Not only the AK47 but everything else he had hidden on him – and take them out of circulation. Those were our orders.

I paused in the telling, looked at Claire. I still do not properly know what feelings and sensations ran through me when I put my hands on the insurgent's body. The revulsion is natural, of course, but more powerful than that is the sense of duty, and the urgency to just get the job done. I cannot lie, I was eager for us to be out of there. Out of that field, where shots might be taken at us from any direction. Out of that sun, which still seemed merciless.

"But the second I put my hands on him," I said, "he opened his eyes."

Until that moment I had not considered the possibility that there might have been life left in the insurgent's body. As we stood above him and secured his weapons, not a breath seemed to have come from his lips, nor the merest twitch in his body. Yet now his eyes were open. I cannot say that they looked directly into mine. They did not. There was not, as far as I could see, any lucidity in them. But the eyelids fluttered and came apart, and that meant that some corner of him still clung on.

I had no idea how. His body was a ruin. The chain gun that had raked through him was not designed for taking out enemy troops. It was designed for disabling tanks.

I steadied myself. I still had a job to do, and I was in no doubt that he would have other weapons on him. I gave Jack an excruciated look and, as gently as I could, rolled the insurgent over.

It was only when we turned him that I saw the true extent of the Apache's work. Its chain gun had opened him up, eviscerating his body. A great cavity had been carved into his back. What I took to be his lung was hanging outside his body, the earth and stubs of corn around him was covered in his viscera. Back down the track, as we'd listened to the Apache open fire on him, the radios had crackled back and forth with debate as to whether he had been hit or not. Well, he'd been hit. The bloody evidence of it was right in front of me, his body a patchwork of crimson and red.

I had promised myself I would be brutally honest with Claire, and even though I did not like to admit it, I kept to my promise and told her what my immediate reaction was. I was... crestfallen. Frustrated. Angry. Not because the insurgent was alive, but because it changed everything. Moments ago, I had been contemplating turning around and getting out of the open, then joining the rest of the lads on a hurried march back to the security of our compound. Now, with our radios still alive with chatter about where the other insurgents might be, I was contemplating something else entirely. How to get this man, critically injured by our own ordnance, out of this field and to a military hospital.

I took my radio and sent a message up the chain of the command.

"He isn't dead."

The voice crackled back, "Are you sure?"

I took a breath. "He opened his eyes. I'm pretty sure."

The radio controller acknowledged it, but the rest was up to me. Somehow, we would have to clear a landing zone, call in a casevac helicopter and have him loaded aboard.

I looked back at the insurgent. His eyes were closed again now. Before I could even consider calling in an evacuation, I would have to search him, so I got to my knees. As I patted what was left of his body down, I unearthed further magazines for his AK47, as well as a grenade. It was the grenade that gave us most reason to pause. There had been so many attacks by grenade in the past weeks as we walked our peacekeeping patrols between the local settlements and farms. I suppose we would never know if this man had been among those responsible, but it was good to have one more AK47 and its ammunition, and one more grenade off the streets.

"What now?" Jack asked me.

Now, I thought. *Now... I don't know.*

They'd blasted so much shrapnel through him that the cornfield we were standing in was littered with it. There may even have been IEDs hidden around us. Any of those things could frustrate a helicopter using the field as a landing zone – and, besides, it was so exposed here that we could not simply camp out while we waited for a chopper to come in. At this distance it would take at least half an hour for anything to reach us. And the other insurgents were still out there.

I called over two of the other guys.

"Right lads," I said. "Get him over to the edge of the field, to the other lads, as quick as you can."

All new recruits are shown how to transport a fallen colleague quickly and safely, and we put that into practice now. Shneb and Jim, the lads I'd called up, used the "two-man drag method" to move the insurgent. With one man on each side of him, they hooked their arms under his armpits and heaved him to the cover at the side of the field. There's no doubt about it – it isn't pretty, and it isn't comfortable – but it's the fastest way to move someone a short distance, and it was how we'd all been trained.

It was not gentle. It never is. It was quick and it was rough, but it was competent and safe – and in no short order, we reached the others. Here we lay him down. Under my instructions, one of the lads began to go through the medical processes in which we were all trained, dressing what wounds we could, attempting to stabilise him, trying to make sure what airways he still had were clear. By now, there seemed to be no movement whatsoever. And the minutes were cascading by…

I'd heard the rest of it on the video footage they showed me in the police station. The dark things the lads were saying. The way we joked about finishing what the gunner in the Apache helicopter had started and getting out of there. When you are in the military, sometimes the only sort of humour you know is gallows humour. In the quiet of that police station it had seemed so brutal to me. Out there, in those fields, on those patrols, in our base under rocket fire, I thought so little of it.

By now, the Apache that had done this was disappearing, the noise of its rotors rapidly fading away. After it had gone, the silence at the edge of that field was deafening. An Apache hanging above instils a certain kind of confidence in you. You feel more secure, more sheltered, knowing that any insurgents in the area will think twice about springing an ambush on you and, with extra sets of eyes in the air, you are as confident as you can be that nobody will be able to approach unannounced. In its absence, all that remained was the pervading sense that, with insurgents still out there and one dying at our feet, we were out here on our own.

There was nothing to be gained waiting in this location any longer. If we were ever going to get out of here, we'd need to find a place where a casevac helicopter could land. That meant locating a landing zone. It meant clearing it of shrapnel, scouring it for IEDs, securing the location so that, whatever happened, the incoming helicopter was protected from attack. Yet, when I looked back at the insurgent, the lads clustered around him administering what medical aid they could, it all seemed so pointless. There were so many holes in him. Shrapnel had cut through him in so many places that what medical aid we were administering was never going to have any effect.

I looked at the skies, open and vast and blue. Any casevac helicopter would take a full half hour to get here. I couldn't even call one in before I'd found a landing zone and cleared it. My mind began to reel through the possibilities: where we might go, how we might get there, how long we would have to last out here, while the radio still crackled with the news that the other insurgents hadn't been accounted for.

I had not remembered, even as I listened to the voices on the recording the police had shown me, the things the lads and I had said as we waited there in the scrub at the edge of the field. Hearing them, as plainly as I had, had been difficult, and I cannot claim that I am proud of the things that were said. No, I cannot clearly remember the words we barked back and forth, but I can very clearly remember the way we were feeling. Many long hours out under that incandescent sun, trussed up in body armour. Five months of touring the hell that was Helmand. The way we'd lost friends and colleagues in Ollie Augustin and Sam Alexander. The day in, day out threat that every step you take on patrol might be your last. Stones thrown by children that could suddenly be grenades, the constant voices in the back of my head, telling me that they were out here for me alone, singling me out, planning their ambushes for the patrols I myself was on, and all because I was the commander in the area. These things are ever-present in your mind when you're out there, and that's what it had been like for me. Even when you're not thinking about them, they're there, colouring your subconscious, directing your every move. You hold it together, because that's what your job is, that's what you've been trained to do.

But the fact of the matter was: I was scared. This is not an easy thing to confess, and in lots of ways I did not even confess it to myself. But some of the lads I was with were 18 years my junior. One in particular was deployed a few weeks after the rest of the group, as he had to wait for his 18th birthday before he could go to war. It was their first active deployment. There were other insurgents somewhere out there, and yet here we stood, hidden by nothing but long grasses, attending to the body of a mortally wounded insurgent who, only a couple of hours ago, had been launching an attack on our neighbouring compound. How long we had to be out here, I didn't know. The day was already growing old.

Frustration was boiling over. Anyone seeing our faces would immediately know how little we wanted to be there, how desperately we wanted to be back in our compound where we ought to have been – not safe, perhaps, from sudden attack, but at least in a defensible position and out of immediate threat.

I looked back at the insurgent. What scant signs of life there had been now seemed vanishingly rare. I watched him for the longest time, the lads increasingly jumpy around me. A thought that had been growing in me began to solidify. There was no way this insurgent was making it back to any military hospital alive. There never had been. The chain gun on the Apache helicopter wasn't a weapon that anything as frail as a human body – devoid of armour, just flesh and blood and bones – could ever survive. It was a wonder he had lasted this long. He was lying there, inert in the scrub, and his life – which had been ebbing away since long before we found him – seemed already gone.

And here we were, out in the open, unable to do anything for the ruin of a man the Apache had taken apart, listening to the radio buzz with reports of other insurgents still out there.

At last, I gave voice to the thoughts that had been growing in the back of my mind. "He's passed." I said it a couple of times. "He's dead, lads."

In that moment, I was sure that any last breath in his body had dwindled away. I took to the radio, reported it back up the command chain, and waited.

Then waited some more.

Back in our sitting room in Taunton, I looked at Claire.

"And then I shot him," I said.

The Apache had been gone some minutes before I did it. In my recollection we can hear the cut and turn of its rotor blades fading to silence. Then, nothing. Only the wind moving through the scrub in which we stood, the curses and muttered exclamations of the lads I was with.

I shot him.

Some things happen in an instant. Some things have happened before you really understand them at all. So it was here, on that day in Helmand.

The sitting room in Taunton was silent as a confessional and, I suppose, in some respects, that was what it had become. Over the last 12 hours I'd found myself cast back a year and more, plucked out of the place that had become my one true home and planted back again in the scrublands beyond CP Omar. It had left me disoriented. It had left me unnerved. But most of all, it had left me confused – because the things I had seen in the video, the things we had all said, I could hardly marry with the man I had been this morning, lying in bed with my wife in the comfort of our country home. There was a disassociation in my head.

Hindsight is the strangest thing. Sometimes it helps you make sense of things, but as I sat there looking at Claire, waiting for her to tell me what she thought of everything I'd said and done, that was not my experience. I could make little sense of it and, in many ways, I still can't. If Claire had asked me then, or at any time since, why I did what I did that day, I would not have been able to tell her. I recognised my voice. I recognised my form. But

I did not recognise myself. I recalled it as if it were somebody else, some other Alexander Blackman, stranded in some foreign field, scared beyond sense and acting in ways that, for the rest of his days, he would not fully understand.

Was I drawing a line under the events of the day? Was I putting a full stop on the merciless hours away from the base? At the end of a long tour where friends had died, was I taking out my frustration on this mortally wounded insurgent, whose comrades – perhaps even the man himself – had killed and maimed so many British soldiers? I still do not know if there is any one answer that fits. The only way I can fathom it at all is to say that, for a brief moment, madness took hold of me. And there in the sitting room with Claire, the idea that I did not understand my own actions seemed to push me towards madness again. It is a strange, unnerving thing not to understand your own self. The only thing I do know is that I believed, in my head and my heart, that there was no way this insurgent would make it back to a field hospital alive. Whether I had lifted my weapon or not, the outcome of that day would have been no different. So why did I do it? I have no answer to that.

"I knew I'd done something stupid almost straight away," I said, while Claire still listened. "It came over me like a cloud. Something had shifted in me. Something had changed. And... I tried to shrug it off. We were there 20 seconds and then I said something, anything, to get rid of the moment."

I'd needed to say something, anything, to conclude what I'd just done. And so I looked at the lads and muttered words that would come back to haunt me: *Shuffle off this mortal coil*, I'd said, quoting Shakespeare – even though I can't remember seeing or reading Shakespeare in my life. "It was just something to cut through the tension. I just came out with it. I don't know why. It was poor judgement, Claire." The fact of the matter is, everything I remembered about that day was poor. These were the poorest judgements I'd ever made in either my professional or private life, and moments later I said as much to the lads: the mistake was mine to own.

"But then it was over. We did everything we had to do." We had to biometrically enrol him. Take fingerprints. Take samples of DNA, as we had to do with every insurgent we killed and whose body we could recover. "Then we bugged out. Extracted ourselves from the location, got back to base, deserviced our kit and just collapsed. By morning, we were back on patrol again. The same old fears, the same old dangers, just a different day. It was another month and more before the tour was over, before we all came home. Claire, I haven't thought about it until this day."

There it was. I'd told her all of it.

The truth was, I didn't know how Claire was going to react. I hadn't had the time to process it myself. The arrest and the video I'd seen in the police station had dredged the memory up from somewhere deep inside and, as I spilled it all out to her, I was still trying to make sense of it myself. It was only as I stopped that I wondered, what might this mean to her? What might it mean for *us*?

CHAPTER NINE

That was when Claire did one of those incredible things that has always made me thank my lucky stars that she entered my life. She had listened to every last thing, this description of a man she must not have recognised as her husband, and done it all with the kind of quiet strength I had observed in her since the day we met.

And she told me she had my back. That I was her husband. That, whatever I'd done when I was in Helmand, it was not her place to judge me. That she trusted me implicitly, that whatever my judgement had been that day, whatever decisions I had made, I was still me, Alexander Blackman, the man who ruined his Jack Daniels by mixing it with Coke, the man who'd asked her to be his wife so flippantly on his 34th birthday, only a few miles from where we now sat.

There is such a thing as unconditional love.

As we sat there that night, neither one of us knew what was coming next. For the longest time, I prowled the house, conflicted, bewildered, uncertain of myself and my own actions – but confident that whatever happened next, I could get through it, because Claire was going to be at my side.

CHAPTER TEN

Bulford Camp and Colchester Military Prison, October 2012

The night was paling to darkness by the time I'd told Claire everything about that day. I could already feel the dull ache of fatigue creeping up on me. But the day wasn't finished yet. The thinking and wondering, the endless questions, the second-guessing of myself and everyone else, might have been over for a time – but now I had work to do.

One of the very last things the military police had said to me before releasing me from the station was that they had been in touch with the hierarchy back at camp, and that I would have to report in to my commanders at the earliest opportunity. They'd taken my phone, taken all my uniforms, but it was imperative that I got down there as quickly as possible to report in, to provide some kind of explanation for what had just happened, and why military police had got hold of my accommodation keys and searched the premises there.

CHAPTER TEN

It was a Saturday evening, the start of the week Claire and I had planned together, but all that would have to wait.

Promising to update Claire the moment I knew anything further, I got in the car and contemplated the long drive from Taunton down to Shorncliffe Army Camp in Folkestone. As I drove, the adrenaline of the day still coursed through me. It wasn't just sitting in that police cell and interview room that had unnerved me, it was the feeling of being transported back, 12 months and 4,500 miles, to Helmand Province. As the hedgerows and farms, the service stations and laybys of Somerset and Wiltshire flickered by, I tried not to think about that video – but somehow it kept overl§aying itself on the landscape through which I drove, dominating my thoughts.

At least, by concentrating on the road, I could focus on something else. That is the way I have always trained myself to be, able to shut one side of my brain off while dealing with the other. Action helped me push the worry to the back of my mind, but every now and again – when I was not being vigilant enough – it flurried up. It was those two words – *war crimes* – that I struggled to get my head around. I was losing what little faith I'd had that all of this chaos was going to evaporate in a puff of smoke.

It was late when I reached Folkestone, too late to report to my commanding officers, but at least I would be here for when the camp woke up the following morning. For now, I went to my accommodation. The military police had already been here. Though it had all been done with the precision and respect with which we try to treat each other in all corners of the armed services, I could see the signs of their search everywhere I looked.

I wanted to call Claire, but they'd taken my phone, so instead I went out into the camp and called her from one of the public phones. Reassuring her that I was fine, that I'd get it straightened out with my commanding officers just as soon as I could, I returned to my accommodation and lay down in the bed that must have been searched only hours before. What they were hoping to find, I could hardly guess.

It was a long time that night before sleep stole up on me and dragged me under. The night was long and vast, as I turned over Helmand in my mind.

In the morning, I reported in.

My commanding officers knew, of course, that a search had been conducted of my accommodation. What they didn't know was what had happened in Taunton the preceding day, nor what crimes I was being accused of. The truth was, at that point in time, I hardly understood it myself. The video they'd shown me in the police station did not represent me or my lads in the best light, nor the light in which I knew we had conducted ourselves across the remaining six months of that hellish tour, but the police had not yet made clear the specifics of the "war crimes" they had arrested me for. And I did not yet know what steps the military authorities would take next, nor even if there would be any steps at all. What would happen, how it would happen, *when* it would happen – all of these were unknowns.

My commanding officers at Folkestone understood. This was unfamiliar territory for all of us, but they had always been happy with my work at the training centre and, given my record, were happy for me to continue in post while whatever this was worked itself out around us. I welcomed the normality. Sorted out with new uniforms, I returned to work, because 4,000 miles away, in Afghanistan, the war went on, and there were always more soldiers who needed to be prepared for their own journeys into theatre.

Six weeks passed.

I cannot say that I ever put the arrest to one side. The words "war crimes" have a visceral effect on a man, and for six weeks – although I was able to compartmentalise and focus on the job in hand – they kept rearing up, like unwelcome intruders, at the back of my mind.

Six weeks later, the world changed again.

I had been delivering lectures at the training centre that morning. My work was focused on how the British armed forces could effectively partner with the Afghan army and police force – a difficult subject, because there had recently been a number of attacks on coalition forces by insurgents who had infiltrated the new Afghan forces. With my lecture finished, I left the lecture hall and returned to the team house on camp. I'd gone there to check the schedules and see what was coming next, but as I stepped through the door and saw a trio of military police waiting in the reception area, something deep within me became knotted and hard. It was not out of the ordinary for military police to attend camp to deliver lectures of their own, but as I moved past them and climbed the stairs to the camp offices, part of me already knew what was coming.

I'd been upstairs 10 minutes, nominally sorting through paperwork and considering the training I would deliver in the days to come, when the military police appeared again. This time, they were ready. They stood in front of me, three abreast, and I steeled myself for what was about to come.

"Colour Sgt Blackman," the lead ventured, "we are arresting you on suspicion of murder..."

I don't remember hearing the rest. If I'd been thrown and confused by the mention of war crimes on my first arrest, the word "murder" hit me harder. There was so little ambiguity in the word, so little room for misunderstanding. The shock piled into me with the force of a rocket and, though the military police read me my rights as they gathered around to escort me out of the room, if I heard any of it it was only in a fleeting, distant kind of way, the words washing over me like waves.

"What happens next?" They were my own words, though I barely recognised them.

"We're going to take you to Bulford Camp, Colour Sgt Blackman, for processing and questioning."

CHAPTER TEN

I was dimly aware of them putting me in handcuffs, locking my wrists in place against the heavy steel bar. Then, with one military policeman leading and the two others behind, I found myself taken back down through the team house where I had worked for so long, out into the sunshine and the unmarked military police vehicle waiting to take me away. As they opened the door and shepherded me inside, I looked back and asked that somebody get word to Claire, that somebody tell her what had happened and where I was being taken. In all the confusion and uncertainty at what was to come, this seemed the most important thing. The last thing I heard before the door closed and the engines gunned to life was them promising me that somebody would send word. Then, the sights and sounds of Folkestone were blurring past as I sat flanked by one military policeman in the back of the car, another in the front craning around to push a video recorder in my face, as we made our way to whatever lay ahead.

It must have been two or three hours later – I had no way of telling, save for the way afternoon started paling into dusk – when we approached Bulford Military Camp on Salisbury Plain.

Bulford Camp has been here for a century and more, its permanent barracks a feature on the landscape since long before the second world war – but, although I'd passed it innumerable times, shuttling back and forth between Taunton and Folkestone, I'd never entered it before; as a Royal Marine, I had never had cause to visit. But the camp has also been home to the Bulford Military Court Centre since 2006, and I was here under its auspices. As the unmarked police car ground to a halt and the military police asked me to step quietly out of the vehicle, the gravity of it was not lost on me. The sinking feeling that had hit me with the word "murder" had not gone away during the long, empty silences of the journey. Something in it even intensified as I was led across the forecourt and into the centre.

I was still numb as I was taken through the motions of being booked in and taken to the stark, concrete cell where I was to be held in anticipation of questioning. The desk sergeant had already confiscated everything I had on my person – my military ID, my wallet, shoes and belt, all of it documented and sealed away pending any release I might get further down the line – and, with scarcely another word, I was deposited in the cell, with only my reeling thoughts and the strip light to keep me company.

They'd asked if I wanted a lawyer, so now all there was to do was wait. Without a watch, without any way of knowing the routines and rituals of this place, the minutes seemed to drag laboriously by. One hour turned to the next, which seemed to stretch on forever. Sometimes, I became aware of voices outside the cell door, of other cells being opened and closed along the row where I was being housed, but apart from that there was nothing. Nothing to indicate how long I would be here, nothing to indicate what might happen next. I braced myself against it.

CHAPTER TEN

I was used to the long hours of limbo that you can face on a deployment. But this was different, somehow. The walls seemed so incredibly close.

I lay back on the thin mattress overlaying the cell's concrete bed and closed my eyes. I thought about that day in Helmand. I thought about the video they'd shown me in Taunton police station. I thought about that single, deafening word: murder, and what it meant. But most of all, I thought about Claire, and whether she knew, even now, where I was.

An interminable time later, the cell door opened and I was led out to the lobby of the Military Police HQ where, for the first time, I met the lawyer who had been appointed to me.

Permitted a few quiet moments together, I explained the evidence they'd shown me that first day in Taunton police station, when they'd arrested me for "war crimes" and released me without charge. After explaining the process we would now have to go through and the legalities of my arrest and imprisonment, we prepared to be interviewed.

"They haven't shown me anything else," she explained. She'd already told me that they could keep me here for a week without charge, but that at that point, they had to make a decision one way or another: either charge me with the crime for which I'd been arrested, or let me go as they had done before. "You don't have to answer any of their questions. The right to remain silent is real. For this first interview, I advise you to say 'no comment'. Let's just go in there and see what they have to say."

Soon, guards came to escort us out of the lobby and out into the brisk air of Bulford Camp. It was good to feel the fresh air on my face – I supposed I'd been here less than a day, but I'd had no way of gauging the passing of the hours and it seemed so much longer. But it was short-lived. The suites where we'd be interviewed were on the other side of camp, and I was duly escorted to the back of an estate car and transported across.

The interview suite was simple and stark, with recording equipment, a single desk, and chairs spread around. I waited, my lawyer at my side, as the military police sat opposite us and began formal proceedings.

After preliminary questions, the military police directed me to a screen where they played the same footage I had seen in Taunton. On the flickering screen, myself and three of my lads came into view as we charged toward the camera, carrying the mortally wounded insurgent between us. In the background, the lads spat curses and the rotor blades of the Apache helicopter made a maelstrom of the air.

The questions came thick and fast:

Why were you holding him like that?

Why aren't you taking more care?

What would you have done if it had been one of your guys?

I resisted the urge to tell them that, if it had been one of my own lads injured in that field, I'd have flung him over my shoulder and pounded across all the miles that lay between us and our compound. I'd have taken every risk, shouldered him bodily myself, to get him to a safe location from where he could get a casevac back to a military hospital. I'd have taken every chance, because he was one of *my* lads. I'd met their mothers, I'd sent them out on patrol, I'd lived day and night with them as my charges, there in our compound where the back gates all but fluttered open at night. The man we were carrying had spent the last five months bent on killing us – but, even so, we were carrying him the way we'd been trained to carry casualties, ever since we were new recruits.

What did you mean when you said that?

I listened to our voices from the computer's tinny speakers. Here, in this utilitarian office so far from the tensions and relentlessness of Helmand, the things the lads were barking out seemed so mordant and black. But it was not like that in the desert, not where the radios crackled with news of other insurgents, not after so many hours spent baking under that 40-degree heat.

Why didn't you administer more first aid there and then?

These questions and more blitzed at me. In this way, an hour passed. The first hour faded into a second, as the questions turned round and round. Then, when at last the questions seemed exhausted, they began again. Soon, it seemed, I had seen the same video of us in the cornfield half a dozen times. It got so that I could anticipate every roar of the Apache's rotor blades as it hovered somewhere above.

Then, at last: "I think we're finished here, Colour Sgt Blackman."

Moments later, I was back in the transport being ferried across the camp and locked back in my cell. In its silence, I waited. I tried to think about Claire, but even that brought me so little consolation.

And the day turned inexorably into night.

The next day, the knock came at the cell door again and I went out into the lobby area. Again, there was my lawyer to meet me. Again: the car out to Bulford Camp's interview suite. Under its dull strip light, I sat and listened to the same questions. I answered them each with the same "No comment," listening as my interviewers turned circles around me, asking me over and again to relive that long-ago day. I have to admit, the details had paled to me now. When I thought about it at all, it all merged into the same barren hellscape of Helmand. I thought of it and remembered the grenade thrown at me, skittering off into a drainage ditch that directed the blast away from my body and legs. I thought of those nights, uncertain if some local marauders would force their way through the loose back gate of our compound. I thought of body parts, hung in the trees to taunt us. But the details of that day seemed imprinted on me more by the video snippets I'd seen than they did in the vaults of my memory.

Then they showed me something new.

Until the second day, I hadn't understood that more snippets of video existed. I'd listened to the same questions about the way we'd carried the wounded insurgent out of the field and, today, I anticipated more of the same. But instead, the military police loaded fresh footage onto the computer screen and I saw the long grasses and rushes at the edge of the cornfield from a new angle.

The snippets of video they showed me were all from that same fateful day in Helmand. Though they were all taken from the same hour of my life, they were not a continuous record.

The marine who had shot this footage had stopped his camera at intervals to save its battery, so that the videos I saw did not construct the full story of what had happened that day.

Nevertheless, what they did capture made my stomach sink further.

On the computer screen, I watched as I shot the mortally wounded insurgent.

Seeing it for the first time was like wading through a dream. A voice that was hardly recognisable as my own, curses and utterances that I cannot believe I truly felt. I tried to put myself in the mind of the man on the screen, forced myself to acknowledge that the man was me, and listened as the litany of questions from the military policemen began. *What did you mean?* one of them asked, but I didn't know. *What were you thinking when you said that? What did you do next?* Under my lawyer's advice, I answered "No comment" to each, but inside I too was wondering what had been going through the mind of that man, what had triggered him to say those things. Helmand was 4,000 miles away, but the gulf between the person I was here and the person I'd been in those few seconds seemed, to me, vaster still.

"No comment," I answered, and they played the video again.

Over the next days, the pattern repeated itself. Over and again, I was woken from the cell where I was waiting, sleeping or just generally trying to keep my darkest thoughts at bay, and taken to a car for transportation to one of the camp's interview suites. Sometimes, as I was loaded into the vehicle, I would catch sight of other prisoners being unloaded and returned to their cells – and it was then that I first understood I was not the only Royal Marine to have been arrested in the investigation. Faces I had not seen in a year, not since the days after we returned from the hellish environment in Helmand, appeared fleetingly at the edges of my vision, themselves being escorted to and from the cells. I came to understand that five of us had been arrested: myself, and four of the lads I was responsible for, four of the lads I'd brought home safely from that taxing tour, now in cells charged with murder, and all because of that impulsive, tormented afternoon we'd spent in the field. As I was ferried back and forth, always being asked the same questions, always being shown the same footage and asked to revisit, in my mind, those long months in Helmand Province, it was this that began to weigh on me most of all: I'd brought those boys home safely, returned them to their families and loved ones, and now they were staring down the barrel of this, an altogether different kind of trauma, and all because of something I myself had done. As their commanding officer, the sense of having let them down was immeasurably large.

Perhaps it was the fourth, fifth or sixth day of questioning, but it soon became apparent that the investigation was locked into a holding pattern. The same questions being asked, the same questions being – on the advice of my lawyer – rebutted, while I turned over and over the events in Helmand Province. Something had to change and, with the authorities only able to hold us for a week without either formally charging us with the crimes for which we'd been arrested or releasing us without charge, my lawyer challenged my interviewers: it was time that they made up their minds.

Withdrawing from the interview room, they deliberated their next move while my solicitor and I sat in the oppressive silence. It was 15 interminable minutes later when the door opened again and the military police resumed their seats across the interview desk.

They had come to formally charge me with the murder of an unnamed insurgent in Helmand Province, Afghanistan.

CHAPTER ELEVEN

My devastation complete, I was returned to my cell, all hope that this might soon be over vanishing in the instant they showed me my charge sheet. The emptiness inside me was everything. A chasm seemed to yawn open, somewhere in the pit of my stomach, and drag me down, down into its darknesses. I tried to sleep, but sleep did not come. All I had was the deadening knowledge that I'd ruined my life. More than that – that I'd ruined Claire's. And more than that still, that everything I'd done across 16 years of exemplary service no longer meant anything, that the long years I'd spent representing my country across the world, fighting for democracy and peace in Iraq and Afghanistan, training up countless other Royal Marines to serve their country with the same honour to which I myself had always aspired, was all just dust.

Some time later, I was finally able to speak to Claire.

In a closeted portion of the hallway beyond my cell, open enough that I could be seen but secluded enough to give a modicum of privacy, I cradled the telephone receiver to my face and listened to her voice.

My solicitors had maintained contact with Claire through-out, even though I could not. She knew, without me having to tell her, that I had been charged, and what that was doing to me. For now, though, just hearing her voice again was enough. After the long hours of solitude in my cell, punctuated only by my interrogations, it was the kind of restorative I needed – not to feel OK again, because in that moment I was not sure if I would ever feel OK, but to feel something closer to *myself*, somewhere nearer to the Alexander Blackman I could be proud of, the man I recognised.

Even so, it took only moments before it came frothing out of me. Once I started speaking, I couldn't stop. It was like a valve had been opened, or as if some volcano had erupted. I needed to purge myself of everything I was feeling. The regret, the hopelessness, the terror that I'd squandered not just my life, not just the lives and livelihoods of the lads who'd been out with me at CP Omar, but the life of Claire herself.

"I've ruined everything," I said. "Everything we had planned, Claire. Everything we wanted. Claire, I've ruined our lives..." In the midst of it all, she was trying to console me – but, in the torrent still spilling out of me, I could barely hear. I pulled myself together. There was something I needed to say. "Claire, if you want to... forget about this, forget about *me*, if you want to move on and get on with your life, not waste

even more years on me, if you don't want to stick it out, I'll..."
I hesitated, knowing that I had to go on. "...understand. I
wouldn't hold it against you."

I'd been thinking about it in the cell before I'd come out
here and, with trembling fingers, dialled Claire's number.
Claire hadn't asked for this. She hadn't signed up for a life with
a man charged with murder, a man who might be separated
from her for yet more years to come – and just as our thoughts
were beginning to turn towards the future. What right did I
have to ask her to stay by my side as I was pulled inexorably
into this system? The responsibility stopped with me. If I loved
her at all – and I did, with every fibre of my being – I had to be
willing to let her walk away.

My words had petered out, and into the great silence that
followed came Claire's voice. "Al," she said. "Listen to yourself.
You're not making any sense. If you love me enough to tell me
to go, well, maybe I love you enough to tell you here I am, that
I'm not going anywhere. And to tell you I never want to hear
you say those things again. Al, I'm *here*. Where I always am. It's
going to be OK..."

The words calmed me. It was the effect of Claire's voice,
but it was the effect of the things she was saying to me as well.
I'd been untethered for too long, spinning adrift in my own
mind as I lay there in the solitude of my cell. In a few short
moments, Claire had anchored me. I felt centred for the first
time in days.

"I'm not going anywhere," she had said, and it gave me strength enough to lift my head up as I was led back to my cell.

I wasn't going anywhere, but neither was Claire.

The day after we were charged, arrangements were made for our transportation up to Colchester Military Prison, where we would await our first formal hearing in front of a judge. Taken from our cells, all five of the marines who had been charged with murder were loaded into two minibuses, and the long drive began.

It was the first time I'd seen the lads this close since our return from Helmand Province. I hadn't entirely forgotten that sense of being responsible for them – and, indeed, it had been resurgent in me ever since I'd caught fleeting glimpses of them being shuttled around Burford Camp – but it came back to me, stronger now, as strong as it had been on those long, lonely nights in Helmand.

These were my boys – and I had let them down.

The drive to Colchester was long and, realising we wouldn't get there until fall of night – when the dining times in the prison would already have passed – the Royal Marines who were escorting us pulled into a service station and, facing us through the partition at the back of the van, made us a pact. "We're all going to go in there, lads, and get some food. And because you're Royal Marines, there isn't going to be any problem with that, is there?"

The lads had largely been silent throughout the journey but, as one, they turned to our escorts and nodded in agreement.

"And, after we've had a feed, we're going to get straight back in here and be off, OK?"

Afterwards, when our bellies were filled and we were back in the van, the fading lights of London's satellite towns and the M25 flickering past, it wasn't the food that filled me with something like sustenance. It was the respect we'd been shown by the Royal Marines transporting us, even though we'd been charged with wartime murder. It was the fact that they still held us in high enough esteem to know that we wouldn't try anything funny if they afforded us a tiny flicker of freedom. It was the fact that, to them, we were still Royal Marines.

We arrived in Colchester after dark. By the time we were processed and booked in, dressed in simple military fatigues and escorted to our new cell on the custody wing where all prisoners awaiting trial were housed, it was already approaching lights out, and there was silence all along the hall.

For a week we lived according to the routines of Colchester prison. Housed together in a six-man cell, with one of the beds remaining empty, we decided early on that we were not going to discuss the case, nor the events of that day in Helmand that had tarnished us all. I wanted to play this straight, by the book, and avoiding any suggestion that we might have colluded on what we were going to say seemed of critical importance, even at this early stage. I'd gone over those hours in Helmand so many times already – and though, as I've said, I knew we hadn't represented ourselves well in the things we'd said and the dark banter we'd indulged in that day, I also knew that I had nothing to hide. And so we made the promise to each other that we would not talk about that day, nor the trials that now awaited us. We would keep our heads down, be good and compliant, and remember that, even now, we were still Royal Marines. Here at Colchester prison, we would represent ourselves as such.

Every morning, the lights would come on at 6am. By 7am, when the doors were unlocked, we were expected to be showered, dressed and ready to be marched down to the dining area for breakfast. Here, overseen by guards, we would feed ourselves and clean up, before being marched back to our wing. After another hour of cleaning – our cells, the corridor outside, the other communal areas – we were told what was happening that day. For us there would be no formal training, so perhaps we would visit the prison library, spend time in the prison gymnasium, or commune in the television and table tennis room where prisoners spent their days. Between times, the hours were empty and dull – but I was determined to be as model a prisoner here as the model soldier I had aspired to be throughout my 16 years of service.

In spite of all of this, it was difficult not to remember that, only a year ago, I had been the troop sergeant responsible for these lads in an altogether different kind of prison. The responsibility weighed on me keenly at night. When I closed my eyes, it wasn't just thoughts of Claire and how I'd squandered her life that played on me, it was the thought of what I'd done to these boys too, so much younger than me – some of them, at a stretch, young enough to be children of my own. The weight of that was incredible.

After a week living by rote according to the routines of the prison, we were led out of our cells and taken to a courtroom where, for the first time, we were put in front of a judge. A date had yet to be set for the beginning of our trial, but here the court would come to its first conclusion – whether or not each of us could be released from prison pending trial, or whether we would have to spend the next months under lock and key while cases for the prosecution and defence were constructed.

It took only minutes for me to understand that the prosecution were determined we should stay inside – and that I, in particular, should not be eligible for bail. They argued that I was a flight risk, capable enough to avoid the long arm of the law by disappearing overseas and out of the jurisdiction of the UK. They argued that, because of the way I'd been trained, I was a danger to other potential witnesses – though who those witnesses might have been, they could not say – and that I even represented a danger to my fellow defendants. It was my first taste of real vilification, but I tried to breathe through it, tried not to let it affect the way I'd been thinking.

Soon, our own lawyers started arguing the case for our release. "After Colour Sgt Blackman was first arrested for this crime, he continued to work delivering training at Folkestone in Kent, scarcely a 10-minute ride from the Channel Tunnel. I would suggest that, were Colour Sgt Blackman a flight risk, he might have been anywhere in Europe, or beyond, by now – and yet he remained on camp, working diligently under the supervision of his commanding officers. And as for posing a danger to his fellow defendants, well, might the court be reminded that Colour Sgt Blackman has spent the last week incarcerated at Colchester Military Prison in the same cell as those self-same defendants – and as yet, none of them has come to harm. He has been courteous and polite to all staff, has engaged in a range of prisoner activities, and conducted himself with the gravitas expected of all Royal Marines…"

Some of it buoyed me up. Some of it dragged me down. And I was still in a haze, dogged by the prospect of what was to come, when the judge announced that they would not be keeping us on remand. Instead, each of us would be released back into the custody of the Royal Marines.

The next day, the sky was grey, the rain churning somewhere up above Taunton, when I stepped out of the military transport and looked up at a simple brick building.

I'd been released from prison, but I hadn't been sent home. Not yet. The building at which I'd been deposited wasn't the home I shared with Claire – whose absence I was still feeling keenly – but a civilian mental health unit attached to the hospital here. Soon after the judge's decision, I'd been taken aside and told of the caveat to my release. The wardens at Colchester had detected something in me, some capacity for self-harm, some aspect of depression, that troubled them – and, consequently, one of the conditions of my release was that I should first spend a week being appraised and treated here. Only then would I be placed back in the custody of the Royal Marines and, for the first time in what felt like an age, be with Claire again.

Checking in to the facility, I tried to reflect on the weeks that had brought me here. Had it really been only two months since that fateful knock on the door? A lifetime seemed to have passed. Life, I began to think, is like a military deployment – long periods of limbo where nothing happens, where days and weeks flow by with barely a ripple breaking the surface, only to be punctuated by short, rapid bursts of kinetic activity. After Bulford Camp and Colchester, after listening to the lawyers for the prosecution decry me as being callous and evil, a threat to the same boys I'd been sworn to in Afghanistan and for whom I'd have done anything, I was coming out of one of those moments now. The shell shock of it, I supposed, was real.

The mental health facility was supposed to afford me the time and space to decompress, to normalise after what had been – in spite of Helmand Province – the most abnormal weeks of my life. Yet no sooner had I checked in than a nascent fear put its roots down in me. Perhaps all this was doing was prolonging that sense of abnormality, stretching it out into a longer, more defining time. Something inside me craved not the time to decompress and work the depression through, but the strict regularity of the routines by which I had lived most of my life. I craved being back on camp, contributing to something bigger than myself – not being stuck here, focusing only on me.

The accommodation here was simple and spartan, but I supposed that even this was a luxury compared to the cells I had been kept in, and the cells in which I might yet be incarcerated. I tried to settle in. Just as I had done in prison, I did everything that I could to be compliant, treating the doctors and other professionals with the respect and courtesy I have always believed they deserved. But I was coiled, more coiled than I had ever known I could be. I existed there in those rooms and yet I was somewhere else as well. Physically I was here in Taunton, but mentally I was thousands of miles away – a year in the past, when we'd marched out to that cornfield in Helmand, or a year in the future, into whatever dark places my imagination took me.

But there was still hope. There was fresh air through my windows. There were the restorative smells of home. My legal team, who had already begun marshalling the defence they would present on my behalf, spoke confidently about the unique circumstances of the event and the ways in which they hoped to exonerate my lads and me of wrongdoing. With every day that passed, the prospect of getting back to Folkestone and re-engaging with life on camp came nearer into view. And then, on my second day at the facility, the door opened. I looked up, and a familiar face looked down into mine. I'd been away from her for much longer before, there had been thousands of miles between us – but, somehow, the distances of the last few days seemed vaster still.

There was Claire.

CHAPTER TWELVE

Bulford Camp, Military Court Centre, October – November 2013

Christmas Day, 2012: Claire and I celebrated together, surrounded by family, uncertain if, by this time next year, I'd be with them or not.

I'd stayed in the mental health facility at Taunton for nearly a week, but I'd known from a very early point that it wasn't a place I wanted to be, or a place that was benefiting me. The depression I'd felt after my arrest was real – it had taken me and pulled me under and I'd known, in a way I'd never known before, that I was not impervious to its assault – but my release from prison, the faith my legal team had in me and reuniting with Claire all combined to lift me out of it.

There, in the mental health facility, surrounded by people with much greater mental health concerns than my own – many of whom had been sectioned and could not expect to be released for some time – I thought of all the friends and colleagues I'd known who'd come back from Afghanistan with full-blown

PTSD. Perhaps it was my habit of compartmentalising that had helped me avoid those avenues, but whatever tensions I'd carried in Helmand hadn't been with me since I got back to Claire and the routine of military life here in the UK. Even so, seeing at that facility the things a mind could do to itself frightened me in a way that other things hadn't. The horrors we inflict on ourselves felt so viscerally real. And although the process of talking with the therapists, decompressing and being visited by Claire every day helped to lift whatever malaise I'd slipped into, I was eager to be out of there and back in the routines of life as quickly as possible. Like many military servicemen, I knew it was the routines that would save me.

According to the conditions of my release, I was compelled to spend my weeks not at home, but in camp accommodation at Lympstone, where I would continue to work approaching trial. If the irony of a man charged with murder being asked to train other Royal Marines in heavy weaponry was noticed by anyone in the court system, no one remarked upon it. Certainly, no civilian in my position would have been permitted near the 40mm grenade launchers or 50-calibre machine guns that I was routinely using to train young lads so that they themselves could be sent out to Afghanistan – but I found comfort in the work. The routine put me back in a safe space. The structures I had been used to for my entire adult life brought me as close to normality as I could get – and, although there was not a day that went by when I wasn't anticipating the trial to come, nor turning over those fleeting moments in Helmand and contemplating what had made me do and say the things I did, it was easy to get lost in the task directly in front of me. I enjoyed the feeling that at least day to day, I was doing some good for the Royal Marines, who had always been so good to me.

When Christmas 2012 had given way to New Year, the conditions under which I'd been released were slowly being relaxed. Rather than reporting in to my commanding officers every morning and night so that they knew where I was at all times – effectively ensuring I hadn't done as the prosecution suggested and taken flight – things had developed so that I was allowed to call in from a landline phone to prove where I was and at what time. And, after a period of being compelled to sleep at camp during the weeks, I was finally allowed to live at home in Taunton with Claire, where I still felt I belonged, as long as I obeyed the rules of curfew and was contactable by phone at all times.

One month bled into the next. Winter became spring and started turning inexorably into summer. I cannot say there were not nights when I woke up, turned to Claire in bed and thought, again, about the way I had risked everything, squandered the life we wanted to live together, but whenever we met our legal team, every three or four weeks, I came away with a renewed feeling of positivity. I would sit in an anteroom of the officer's mess at the training centre in Lympstone with them, Claire having driven down to be by my side, and as we'd go through the various parts of the case and the defence they were preparing for me, the feeling that we would get through this, that by next Christmas Claire and I would again be looking to the future, was real.

Even so, in our Taunton home at the weekend, with summer at its height, Claire and I decided that we wouldn't get too far ahead of ourselves.

One day at a time. It was the defining principle of our lives.

By the time the early summer sun was turning fields of Somerset to full colour, my legal team contacted us with the news we had been waiting for: my trial would begin in November 2013. By that time, charges against two of the lads in my troop had been dropped, leaving only three of us to stand in the dock and answer the charges against us. Perhaps it sounds strange, but it filled my sails to know that two of the lads I'd taken out there and brought home safely would not be found culpable for my own momentary lapse of judgement. Too many people were already being put through the wringer for those fleeting minutes in Helmand Province. At least two more families could be spared the full glare of whatever was to come.

The knowledge that the trial was coming gave us something to focus on. But, if I began to see it as the chance I needed to draw a line under this worst year of my life and reacquire my good name, I was always aware that an unfavourable outcome would blow open my world. As the months had ticked by, the idea that I'd done damage to the reputation of the Royal Marines had been growing on me, and the fear that I'd brought

42 Commando into disrepute only grew as the trial approached. More urgently still, I was desperate that my service record should not be reduced to a few scant seconds of action that I still did not properly understand myself. I'd served in the Royal Marines for 16 years. I'd been through Iraq and Afghanistan with them, training countless others to do the same, and in my final tour of Helmand I'd endured the six most hellish months of my life. A conviction would inevitably mean a dishonourable discharge, the kind of stain on a service record that a veteran never really comes to terms with. As well as everything else, I *needed* my good service acknowledged. I'd built my sense of self around it my entire adult life. It was who I was, it was *why* I was, and if it all boiled down to nothing, well, I was not quite certain how my life would look.

* * *

My trial began on 23 October 2013.

We'd driven into Bulford Camp under unseasonably clear skies the day before, our car laden down with pots and pans, crockery and cutlery, suitcases filled with clothes, blankets and bedspreads and duvets and more. The Military Court Centre had decided that me and the other two marines on trial would not be held as prisoners while the court was in session, so instead of being in a cell on camp, we had been allotted a house in the camp's married quarters. Because we'd be here for two weeks, we'd brought our lives with us – but, as Claire and I unloaded and set up our temporary home, there was precious little sense of "settling in". My legal team remained confident that the charges against us would not be upheld by the military court and that, in two weeks' time, I would walk out of here an exonerated man, but even so, there was no denying the feeling that had been simmering inside me as the date grew closer. *One step at a time,* Claire and I had said. *One step at a time.* But the next step I was taking was into a court where a board made up of my superiors in the Royal Marines and navy would determine my future – whether I walked free, or lost it all. I was on the edge of something final in my life.

Military courts in the UK differ from civilian courts in certain important respects. Many offences, including ones that are specific to military personnel – like insubordination, malingering or communicating with an enemy without the proper authority – can be handled by commanding officers through a summary hearing. This simple, stripped-back way of delivering justice can be short and swift, allowing an engine as big as the military to react more quickly than it might otherwise. But more serious offences, such as the one we were accused of, are decided at trial by court martial. These are presided over by a judge advocate, with the decisions of the court being decided by a "board" of between five and seven "members of the court" – directly analogous to the juries in a civilian trial. Unlike a jury, however, the board has an extra role: where a guilty verdict has been handed down, its members join the judge advocate in debating the sentencing for the crime.

214

CHAPTER TWELVE

Stepping into the courtroom at the Military Court Centre on Bulford Camp, I took in the place where the next years of my life – perhaps my entire life – would be decided. The room itself was not vast, it had pitched white ceilings and an elevated pine platform at the front, from which the judge advocate would oversee proceedings. To one side were the stalls where the seven-strong board would sit, deliberating all the evidence, and in front of that banks of pine tables and chairs where the teams for both prosecution and defence would be based. To the rear was the public gallery and benches where members of the press would sit, taking notes. But my fellow defendants and I would see none of it. Instead, we would be sequestered behind a partition screen and be visible only to the judge advocate and the board. Only from here, hidden from the rest of the court, would we listen to the evidence presented against us, hear our lawyers' cross-examination of the witnesses for the prosecution and ultimately deliver our own testimonies.

The case had received some interest from the mainstream media when our arrests were announced, but over the last year that had petered away. Now that the trial was beginning in earnest, the attention was acute. The judge had imposed an anonymity order on us when we were first awarded bail more than a year ago, and although it still held, it was difficult not to feel the clamour of the press for more details. Perhaps the anonymity order lent the whole thing a greater sense of spectacle, on top of the photographs and audio snippets that would, at the conclusion of the trial, be released to the press. The full video clips were still under embargo – nominally for fear they might incite attacks against Royal Marines, or otherwise radicalise those who viewed them – but the information released was enough for the newspapers to go into overdrive, speculating on what might happen to "Marine A", as I had become widely known, and his fellow defendants.

The "Marine A" moniker had dogged me across the year, even though nobody – even at Lympstone, where I spent all those months working – knew that the stories in the press referred to me. In one sense, I had been grateful for the anonymity: it let me live that year in relative isolation, not compelled to talk about or defend my position everywhere I turned. But in another, and as the coverage of the trial grew exponentially across its duration, I came to understand that it shrouded the truth about who and what I was.

"Marine A" was a voiceless, nameless figure, a silhouette at the head of a news item, a man without a family, a history, a life. A man synonymous with a few moments in Helmand Province, without any of the context of the arduous months that had led up to that point. "Marine A" wasn't really a human being, he was a cypher, two-dimensional, consisting of only a few brief facts and a few briefly narrated events. Being hidden by the anonymity order meant, by definition, that nobody could know about my service history, that nobody could know about my character and personality, that nobody could see me as a rounded human being, with strengths and frailties, hopes and hates, people I loved and people I looked after, just like everyone else. And although I understood its importance in not prejudicing the trial and allowing justice to take its correct course, something inside me wanted to shed it, to tell the world that I wasn't "Marine A", I was Alexander Blackman. In the light of everything that was debated in court, that seemed to *matter*.

On 23 October, the trial began in earnest.

It is a strange thing to sit hidden behind a partition while unseen lawyers call witnesses, bombard them with questions, cross-examine and interrogate them – all while trying to build up an image of you as a cold and calculating killer. Because, as the first day turned into the next, and then the next, what began as an administrative procedure soon changed in tone – when the board were shown the video snippets from that day in Helmand, and the sequence of events we were all agreed upon was presented in intimate detail to the court. Experts were called to attest to what was said on the video. The pilot of the Apache helicopter that had been called in to gun down the insurgent was summoned to describe what they had seen and done that day, how they'd spent a long time determining that this was the insurgent they were searching for, how they'd confirmed that he was armed, and how the decision had been taken to open the chain gun on him. Others were called to attest to what the conditions had been like in Helmand at that time (though none who had been there on the day in question) – as, gradually, a picture was built up of the context in which my lads and I had been sent out to recover the insurgent and his weapons.

At the end of each day, back in the married quarters, I tried to take stock of the evidence presented against me and the case the prosecution were building, hour upon hour. Claire and I had resolved to keep ourselves secluded from the media coverage of the trial as much as possible, to focus only on the things we could personally affect, but it was difficult to ignore completely. Fragments of the news coverage always seemed to find their way to us. And though some of them had bought into the image the prosecution were building of me, there were rays of light as well. Writers who argued that nobody was qualified to understand, not unless they had been out there as well, columnists who, echoing the views of the readers they spoke to, empathised with a group of young men sent to a remote corner of Helmand, who had heard their friends and colleagues perish, and who had been faced with an impossible task at the end of the most difficult tour of their lives. I found what succour I could in those reports, and the way my legal team debriefed us at the end of each day was enough to keep the hope alive that, by the time another week was through, this nightmare would be over.

It was not until the second week of the trial that, with my defence team now presenting their case, I was called to testify myself. Still shrouded from public view, lawyers who knew me better than anyone else in the court except for Claire, still had to refer to me as Marine A, and my fellow defendants as Marines B and C – but at least, for the first time, I would be able to present the facts of that day in my own voice. That seemed important to me. It still does. Stripped of my name and voice, it felt as if I'd surrendered the story of my own life to the journalists who wrote about me every morning and the prosecutors who took apart everything I'd done and said to build up their own narrative and ascribe motivations. I wanted people to hear me, plain and simple. I didn't plan to make excuses. I wanted to own the things I'd said and done, and yet to make people *understand*. So, although I was experiencing a great deal of anxiety as I took to the stand for the first time, it was coupled with a kind of relief. For the first time in more than a year, I could speak for myself.

Of the three defendants, I was the first to take the stand. I preferred it that way. At least I would be blazing the trail for my lads to follow; from the cross-examination of me, they would be able to gauge the attitude the prosecution team was taking.

It was my defence team who opened the questioning. They'd already outlined the sort of things they would ask and how they would lead the courtroom through the events of that day from my own perspective, so for this, at least, I was prepared. By this point it had been two years since I last set foot in Helmand so, although the video had prompted my recollections, I cannot claim that I was infallible. I could picture what had happened, but in the long months since, I'd worked the worst of Helmand out of my mind, and recalling the exact details of what I'd been thinking was taxing.

Yet none of it was as taxing as when the defence announced they had no more questions and the prosecution were invited to begin their cross-examination.

What had started out as a cold assembling of the facts surrounding that day in Helmand had transformed, or so it seemed, into an evisceration of my character. Perhaps I should not have been surprised. I was the patrol commander in charge and the responsibility for what had happened stopped with me. I had always owned that. And yet, when the counsel for the prosecution spoke about me, I did not recognise myself. When they said that I had led the lads from my troop as if we were an execution squad, deliberately roaming around our location in search of insurgents we could kill – and all for the benefit of our own egos – I did not see myself reflected in their words. When they insisted we were racially motivated, I could understand where they had got that impression – some of the phrases caught on the video footage played to the court represented us badly. But in the heat of the battlefield, when nerves are on edge and bodies depleted, terrible things can and do get said, only we knew, in our hearts, that the expletives and epithets we spat out that day were borne of frustration – out of fear and exhaustion, not real hate.

As Royal Marines, it was our job not to let hatred and resentment fester inside us. It was our job to follow orders – and we had gone out into that field to do as we were asked. Nothing that had happened afterwards had been premeditated, none of it had been part of any grand design. The dark humour and crude – even offensive – banter we'd shared had not, on all the honour I've always considered myself to have, been born out of a bloodthirsty desire to kill, nor out of any deep-seated xenophobia in any of us. Just as doctors, nurses and surgeons often develop a mordant sense of humour – something to offset the gravity of the decisions they must make each day, and the horrible human frailty with which they're faced – soldiers develop their own coping mechanisms, too. What gets said at moments like those, when we felt our lives were in danger every second, might seem horrific if repeated on the streets of Taunton – but, in Helmand, it was very different. You need to bite back. You need to give vent. You need some sort of release.

Listening to it again in the courtroom, I felt ashamed, but I didn't hear hatred in those words, I just heard a group of lads giving release to pent-up frustrations that, had they been kept within, would have made them less effective soldiers and put them even further at risk.

I tried to represent the day as I had lived it – and had continued to live it, over and again, in the many months since. But how to capture the feeling of six whole months of hell in a few short sentences? Sometimes I think it would take a lifetime to explain it. Sometimes I have thought that if you were not there in Helmand, you could never understand. What I had done that day had been an error of judgement. I accepted that. I had never made that kind of error before, and I hadn't made one since – but, in my heart, I knew I had not murdered a man. There was no design in it. There was a group of marines, tired and bloodied after five months of Helmand, exhausted after a whole day under the implacable Afghan sun, listening to the chatter of other combatants across the radio and facing yet more hours out in the field so that they could evacuate a man whose body had already been eviscerated by our own boys. I'd told every officer listening in a 30-mile radius that he was already dead, that his injuries were too severe for him to possibly survive. Nothing I did that day had changed who lived or died. What I had done had been a pointless, foolish act of madness, but surely it was not murder?

Was what I had done that day a release of all the pressures I'd been feeling? Was I drawing a line under the events, as daylight turned towards evening? I did not know then and I still do not know now. But as the prosecution continued, orating at length about intentions I knew did not tally with the Royal Marine I'd been for 16 years, painting me in such a light that it seemed I even relished the killing I had done on behalf of Her Majesty's government, that I had perhaps even basked in adding another bullet hole to the monstrous wounds the Apache helicopter had already inflicted, I tried to hold onto that kernel at the heart of myself, the core that was good and right and would have done anything – *anything* – for the lads I had out there with me.

There were moments when my frustration threatened to boil over. I kept it bottled up, as I knew I must. But picture, for a moment, the way the prosecution took every word I had said and twisted it to some other purpose. When I'd expressed my belief that the insurgent was already dead, or that there was no way he could possibly recover from his wounds, it was actually an order to my lads to finish the job; though I'd proclaimed to everyone within a 30-mile radius that the insurgent was already gone, what I actually meant was that we should execute a man who would otherwise be saved. This, I quickly realised, was the prosecution's strategy: every word I uttered, every breath that I took or look that I gave, would be recast in a dark and mysterious light. In future days, I would look back and fear that I hadn't been eloquent enough when I tried to make clear to the board that the uncomfortable things I'd said were just me roaring into the void, the last six months rearing up inside me. Being packaged off to Helmand only days after saying my last farewell to my father. The Family Day, and how responsible I'd felt for the unblooded lads I was taking into the worst theatre on earth. That visit to the hospital at Camp Bastion, where I'd suddenly known the specific kind of hell I was leading young men into. And six months of life at CP Omar, where the radios burst with news of colleagues eviscerated by IEDs, where the trees were strung up with the body parts of our fellows in arms, where we patrolled in the 40-degree heat as laden down as medieval knights in armour, and where every step might be our last. And where, at the end of each day, I went to sleep at night uncertain if the gates of our compound were truly secure, without anyone of my rank with whom I could consider the events of the day, just vent, or find some sort of... equilibrium.

I mean none of this to excuse the error of judgement I made at the edge of that cornfield. But in that courtroom, as the prosecution turned every flurry of dark banter into evidence of a xenophobic hit squad mentality, I wanted the board, made up of three Royal Marine and four navy personnel, to *understand*.

At the end of the day, back in our married quarters, I tried to block out the things the prosecution had said and the image they were trying to evoke – of a loose cannon, a Royal Marine without any moral compass, somebody who'd gone "off the reservation" and begun acting out his own fantasies rather than approaching his tour in the ordered, structured and responsible way in which all Royal Marines are taught to do. Somebody who had taken the training the Royal Marines had given him and turned it to his own ulterior purpose. Whatever had happened in that cornfield – whatever had taken hold of me in those moments while the insurgent lay, already dying, among us – I was not the racially motivated monster, galvanising a group of young lads to follow his example, that they were seeking to portray.

I just needed Claire to remind me of it as the trial moved toward its conclusion.

The prosecution had been fierce but, even as the final arguments were made and the board retired to deliberate their judgement, the defence team remained confident that our case was robust enough that the verdict would finally allow me to go home with an untarnished service record. As for me, I only hoped my voice would be heard. I'd kept my frustrations to myself, I'd tried to listen with respect to every attack the prosecution made, even while I sought to rebuff them. I knew, in my heart, that I was not the reprehensible person they'd tried to paint me as, and I could only hope that between the testimony I'd given and my unblemished history until that day in Helmand, the board could see it too.

There would be no verdict on the night the trial came to its conclusion. In some ways, it was another frustration. This limbo had gone on for so long, and the greater part of me just wanted to *know* again, to be able to look to the future. But I was grateful, too, for one more night.

In the morning, the board reconvened to continue its deliberations while, in full dress uniform, I waited in the Military Court Centre. Some hours later, my legal team came to notify me that a verdict had been reached. Until that moment, I'd managed to keep the worst of my nerves at bay. I'd lain awake the night before, listening to Claire sleep, and tried to empty my mind of everything: of Helmand, of the military court, of the picture the prosecution had painted of me. When sleep had come, it had been empty and dreamless – but, as I stood to follow the clerks out to my place in the courtroom, still hidden behind the partition, whatever fleeting moments of peace I'd been able to achieve seemed a long time ago.

In the courtroom, all was silent. My fellow defendants took their seats beside me, but I cannot say that we shared any words; each of us was lost in our own worlds, imagined futures and the imagined past. They'd given good accounts of themselves in their testimonies, and in lots of ways I still burned for them. Their careers were so much younger than mine, they still had so many years to give, and in my heart I knew they did not deserve to be here. I was their commander, in Helmand or not. I still felt it as, holding ourselves rigidly, we waited for the judge advocate to bring the court to session.

Finally, the moment came.

"Will the court rise."

At the judge advocate's direction, my fellow marines and I stood. Still shrouded from the view of the rest of the court, I tried to hold myself up high and faced the judge advocate directly. But no amount of effort could conceal the anxiety I was feeling. I'd spent so much time being buoyed up by my defence team. I believed I had given a good account of myself. Yet the knowledge that everything – as I saw it, the sum total of all 16 years I had spent with the Royal Marines – boiled down to these next few moments unnerved me in a way I cannot easily express.

It was not like the fear of going into combat, because there you have your training to fall back on, and no matter how perilous the situation, there is always something you can do, some choice you can make, to try and make things better. In a combat situation, you are rarely truly helpless. But here, listening to the sound of my own breath, feeling the starch of my dress uniform collar chafe against my throat while my heart hammered in my chest, there was not a single thing I could do. The die had already been cast.

Into the silence of the courtroom, the voice of the judge advocate resonated. I listened as he invited the head of the board to step forward and announce the verdicts which he and his fellows had reached.

"To the charge of murder, we find Marine A…"

The moment between one word and the next seemed to last an eternity.

"…guilty," the spokesperson concluded.

There are moments in life that will never leave you. They are imprinted on you forever. They become a fundamental part of your being. I'd had moments like that before. Lying in a drainage ditch with Craig Capewell, grinning madly as he kicked a rocket away and uttered, "I think we're fucked here, Al." But never had a moment piled into me with the force of this. Time seemed out of sync. I looked up, unable to see Claire. All I could see was the sheer white of the partition – the partition that cloaked me, that kept me separate, that isolated me, here, on the stand.

There were still voices rising up in the courtroom. They came to me through the miasma.

"To the charge of murder, we find Marine C innocent."

If I detected the sweet release in the figure standing beside me, it was only on the very edges of my perception.

The voice sounded again.

"To the charge of murder, we find Marine B... innocent."

Now the tension palpably lifted from the lads beside me. Something in it brought me momentarily back into the room. The burden I believed I'd put on them was, in two short sentences, gone. I'd done what I'd promised their families on the Family Day at Bickleigh Barracks on the eve of our deployment: I'd brought them home in one piece and, more than that, I hadn't burdened them with my inscrutable actions that day. The responsibility I owed them was done.

But the walls of the courtroom were still closing in. The partition that blocked me from view of anyone but the judge advocate and the board seemed suffocatingly near. I was both in the room and not, my mind spinning at a million miles a minute. Until that moment, I'd always thought that the idea of the earth opening up and swallowing a person whole was just a writerly image. Now I felt myself being dragged down, the courtroom a swirling vortex around me.

Somewhere up there – though I could only vaguely hear it, such were the thoughts cartwheeling through my mind – the judge advocate had asked the chairman of the board to retake his seat, thanked him for the board's verdicts, and begun to make an address. My fellow marines were being led down by guards, out through a side door, while the judge announced that I would be remanded in custody pending a sentencing hearing to take place at some future date. But the last words that rang in my ears as other guards came to take me away swam up through the white noise in the courtroom and imprinted themselves upon me: I was a convicted murderer, and my sentence would be no less than life.

There was a room at the back of the courthouse, a guard posted at its window in case I made a sudden bid to escape. There I stood, yet more guards at the door, awaiting the arrival of my legal team. As I waited, I took off my dress uniform, one piece at a time. It was like the shedding of a skin. For 16 years, a Royal Marine – and now I was nothing more than a convict. I changed back into my regular military garb, but even that would not be mine for long. Another skin would have to be shed. Now that I was convicted, I would begin the transition from the military prison to a civilian institution. No longer Sgt Alexander Blackman, now I was just Al, an inmate.

It was minutes before my legal team arrived. The anger was evident on their faces: though they reined it in, they were incandescent with the decision of the board. I let their words wash over me. I wasn't sure if I could string a sentence together anyway. All their talk – that this was only the beginning of a process, just a step on a journey, that we still had avenues of appeal, reasons to contest the verdict – none of it mattered to me. I was grateful for everything they'd done, but I was looking inward again now, and I had no use for their positivity, no matter how genuine they were and how much they wanted to help.

There was only one person I wanted to see.

Some time later, while my legal team still busied themselves around me, Claire was ushered into the waiting room. As a courtesy, for which I remain thankful, the guards and my legal team allowed us a few brief moments together. I knew I had to make them count. The transports were already being organised for my return to Colchester Military Prison and however many years of incarceration awaited me.

I didn't know what to say. I have never been a man of many words, but now they all failed me. In the middle of it all, I told her that I was sorry. I must have said it a dozen times. I was saying it, still, as the guards came to take me away.

I would see Claire one more time before I left Bulford Camp. I'd been transferred to the same holding cells in which I'd been held after my second arrest, and they permitted her to visit me there. In the barren, empty cell, I held her hand and looked into her eyes.

"I meant what I said," I uttered.

Claire wasn't sure what I was referring to – and, once again, I knew that I had to lay it all on the line.

"Back then, the last time they brought me here. When I said… I wouldn't hate you, if you wanted to call it quits. That if this happened, you could walk away, get on with your life, find a new way to live. It isn't right, Claire. You shouldn't have to do this… not for me." I hesitated, uncertain if I should go on. "I'd never hold it against you."

CHAPTER TWELVE

Claire's hand tightened on mine. "You won't have to. Because I'd never do it, Al. Oh, and Al —" She seemed serious now, and something in her tone brought me around, brought me back to my senses. "—I never want to hear about it again, do you hear? I never want to hear you offer anything as stupid again. I'm here, aren't I?" She stopped, her hand gripping mine more tightly than ever before, and more tightly than it would for so many years to come. "And I'm not going anywhere."

CHAPTER THIRTEEN

Before dark that day, the guards came to collect me from the custody wing at Bulford Camp. I was still reeling when they put me in the caged back of a transit van for transportation back to Colchester, where I would await sentencing before being transitioned into the civilian system. I sat in the back as the two military police escorts readied themselves for the journey.

I was waiting there still when one of the army personnel from the Military Court Centre emerged and, on seeing the two military policemen about to close me into the darkness of the back of the van, inveigled his way between them.

"Isn't anyone going to sit with him?" he asked.

I watched the two military police share a dismissive look. Finally, one of them explained: "He's a convicted murderer. We'll be sitting up front."

They were about to close the door again when the stranger said, "Wait there," and disappeared back into the Military Court Centre. Minutes later, he re-emerged with a pack slung over his shoulder. Throwing it through the open door, he climbed up into the cage beside me and looked back at the military police. "I'm due up in Colchester anyway. If you won't ride with him, I will." He paused. "He's facing life in prison. What cost a little compassion, even if they did convict him?"

The military police only seemed to shrug, indifferent to his decision, before closing the door and leaving us in the dark. But I can still remember the sensation of having him there with me as the transit van began to rumble, thrusting us around the cage. It mattered so much that this man, a perfect stranger, did not automatically want to shun me because of what had happened in Helmand. It distracted me, lifted me, made me feel a little more human to have company on that journey into the dark. Little things can make such an enormous difference – and though we scarcely spoke as the van lumbered on, just his presence was enough to stop me disappearing into the black hole of my imagination.

Intermittently, he would hand me his mobile phone. The screen would flicker with images from Sky News. My own name would buzz out at me. Talking heads spoke of how I'd brought the service into disrepute, how I'd tarnished the name of the Royal Marines and the British armed forces, how it was evildoers like me who perpetuated the cycle of revenge and recrimination in the theatres of the Middle East. But somehow I found the strength to bear it all – and, to this day, I believe it was because of a random act of kindness by a man I would never see again.

I was going to need more of that to get me through.

Colchester Prison was, at least, familiar – but familiarity was my only comfort, that first night. The last time I had been here, the prison officers had observed me lost in a depression, and so it was now. Rather than be left alone in a cell, I was taken to one of the observation suites where prisoners at risk of committing suicide were housed. I do not know that my thoughts had ever turned that way, but it was true that I could not bring myself out of the crevasse in which I was stuck. My conviction, my mandatory life sentence, the idea of Claire alone on the outside and yet still standing beside me – all of it was enough to put me in a stupor as they led me down.

In the observation suite, I tried to sleep. Perhaps sleep would not have come to me that night anyway, but here it was impossible. Strip lights glared. Through a one-way mirror, I could sense the eyes of the prison officials on me. If I turned so that they could not see my face, or if they could not see my hands above the bedcovers, a guard would speak over the intercom and wake me, if only to make sure that I was still alive. I awoke, if I had slept at all, with eyes heavy from exhaustion, tormented by the knowledge that the next night I would have to do it all over again.

One day bled into the next. Part of me was sleepwalking through the days, and it wasn't only because of those harried nights on suicide watch where I was unable to get an hour of unbroken sleep. The only thing certain about those days was the uncertainty itself. At some point, soon, I'd be sentenced, but until that happened, Colchester Prison became a kind of purgatory where I was waiting – just *waiting* – for whatever came next.

I think my body came to terms with it before my mind. The rhythms of prison life, the rules and regulations by which the days are ordered, are not, in some ways, so very different from those of the armed services. But the weeks between visits became eternities. Claire would come. Guys I knew from the Royal Marines would come. And if my mother couldn't yet come and see me, it was only because of the difficulties she had in travelling so far. But those weekly visits were hardly enough to soothe the transition to this new form of life, not with the words of the prosecution and the judge advocate still spiralling through my mind. The only thing that brought me any comfort at all was the idea that my two fellow defendants were out there now, enjoying the freedom I no longer had. It was a small victory, I supposed, but little things can make such a big difference – and, in those days, it mattered intensely.

And one week turned into the next...

Christmas 2013 was approaching.

Six years ago, I'd woken on Christmas Day to carols being sung in the desert, spent my day listening to the shriek of a mortar attack on FOB Inkerman.

Two years ago, I'd come home from Helmand to recover some sense of normality.

One year ago, I'd emerged from the mental health facility in Taunton, under bail for murder, picked myself up and tried to get on with life.

But this year there would be no release. It would be my first Christmas in prison.

I am not in the habit of feeling sorry for myself, but the magnitude of what it is to live in institutions like this was still working its way into my subconscious. Perhaps a part of me had yet to reach acceptance. Perhaps a part of me still railed against it – and, powerless to do anything further, turned in on itself. I woke that morning to the silence of my cell and considered all the years ahead.

Even inside prison, I was not immune to what was being said about me in the outside world. On 5 December 2013, the anonymity order placed upon me at the start of the investigation had been formally lifted – and now every news outlet could report my conviction by name, dig into my background and tell my story from the beginning. Some of the more condemning voices continued to preach about what a terrible human being I was. Even figures high up in the military were keen to denounce the evil I'd wreaked. No less a figure than General Sir Nicholas Houghton, then the chief of defence staff of the British armed forces, had come out and said that there should be no special pleading for me at my upcoming sentencing hearing, that "murder is murder" and that the circumstances in Helmand were irrelevant to my case.

Yet, in the weeks before Christmas, as my sentencing hearing approached, not all the voices in the media wanted me thrown to the wolves. My conviction had led to a range of responses, but a Change.org petition asking for leniency had been signed by tens of thousands of supporters, thanks in part to being picked up and championed by the *Daily Telegraph*. Meanwhile, in the *Daily Mail*, Colonel Richard Kemp – the ex-chairman of the Cobra Intelligence Committee, who had himself been deployed into Afghanistan early in the war – argued that General Houghton was misguided. Colonel Kemp believed that the court was under pressure to make an example of me – to show that the deeply unpopular war in Afghanistan was being dealt with satisfactorily at last, and that the national conscience of the United Kingdom could finally be soothed. Colonel Kemp feared I was becoming a scapegoat for all the perceived wrongs of war, and urged his readers to understand that what had happened in Helmand was hardly comparable to a gang killing on the streets of London.

As the voices fought back and forth in the press, I was faced with the uncomfortable fact that the time I had for influencing my future was already over. Now, one day at a time, all I could do was wait.

My sentencing hearing had been set for 6 December 2013, a month after my conviction and a day after my name had been released to the public. For the final time, I was escorted by military police back to Bulford Camp and, in the Military Court

Centre, stood in my full dress uniform – still, for a little while longer, a Royal Marine.

The judge advocate began.

His summary of the case was measured but brutal. We had, he told me, handled the insurgent with so little care that it was tantamount to deliberately inflicting even deeper injuries as we carried him from the cornfield. "The tone and calmness of your voice," he continued, "were chilling." It seemed, in the judge's eyes, that I was barely a soldier, I was the insurgent's executor, without mercy.

I let the words envelop me. It was hard to recognise myself in the way the court depicted me, but this was their finding and I tried to bear it. But standing there, with my own character and motivations being dictated to me, I felt suddenly exposed. There I stood, for the first time without the obscurity of a partition, with all the court's eyes on me. But it wasn't *me* he was describing. I clung onto that. When he spoke of the rough, uncaring way we carried the insurgent out of the field, he barely acknowledged the fear hanging over us, that yet more insurgents were unaccounted for – and that we were all exposed. When he spoke about my tone of voice, as if I was a cold and calculating killer without any human emotion at all, he was not there with me, in Helmand, five months deep with all the tensions of that time piled up on me.

"You," he said, "have betrayed your corps and all British service personnel."

Those words bit deep into me.

"You abused your position of trust."

But my corps were my brothers. I'd trained and fought alongside them for 16 years. I'd have given my life for any one of those lads I'd been with out there. To be branded a traitor for a terrible error of judgement – I wore those words like a wound.

The judge advocate's words continued to cascade over me.

"By law," he went on, "the sentence for murder is imprisonment for life and, by virtue of the Armed Forces Act 2006 s217, that is the sentence we must pass on you. There is no discretion to do otherwise. You will remain subject to that sentence for the rest of your life... We are therefore required by law to set a minimum term – and, having balanced all of these matters, we have determined that the minimum term you must serve, before you are eligible for the parole board to start considering whether you should be released on licence, will be 10 years."

Ten years.

If the words "life sentence" had destroyed me, these two words only compounded the blow. Ten years felt like a lifetime. Ten years ago I hadn't known Claire. I had been returning from my first tour of Iraq, having seen a live warzone for the first time. In 10 years, the world had changed – and so it would change again. By the time I had any chance of seeing freedom again, I would be 50 years old. What world would I recognise? How could I ask Claire to wait for me all that time – not knowing, even then, if they would ever let me out?

But the judge advocate wasn't yet finished. In fact, he had saved the most soul-destroying blow for last. Looking down at me from the head of the courtroom, he intoned, "As an inevitable consequence of life imprisonment, you will also be reduced to the ranks and dismissed with disgrace from Her Majesty's service."

As it sunk in, I found myself compelled to stand. On this, the protocol was clear. Before I was taken from the courtroom, I was obliged to lift my hand and salute the board, as if to thank them for the life sentence they had just handed me. As I held the salute, I felt out of step, out of time with the rest of the world. This would, I realised, be my last act as a Royal Marine, saluting the men who had discharged me.

I was not expecting what happened next. In a move that I believe is unprecedented, the board lifted their arms and returned my salute. Something deep inside me began to quake. They should not have done it, I knew they should not have done it – and yet they had felt that they must. For a flickering moment, each of us saluted the other.

Then, no longer a Royal Marine, I was led out of the courtroom.

Returned to Colchester Military Prison while the process of transitioning me into the civilian prison system began, I found myself taking off my military fatigues for the final time. After everything else, perhaps this seems an insignificant moment, but for me it had deep meaning. Until the sentencing hearing,

I had worn standard military fatigues in prison, signifying that I remained a member of Her Majesty's armed forces. Now, dressed in a simple prison boiler suit, I was a civilian again, for the first time since I'd worked on the dairy farm as a young man. Nothing had changed, and yet everything was different.

After two weeks, the time came for me to leave Colchester. This, I understood, was where my real prison journey would begin. For a night, I was transferred to the civilian prison in nearby Chelmsford, where I was taken directly to the hospital wing. There, once again, I slept in an observation cell, constantly scrutinised through the mirrored glass. The following morning, bundled back into a prison wagon, I sat in the darkness, unable to see anything more than a sliver of the world outside. We travelled north 150 miles to the prison that would be my home for the first two years of my sentence, Her Majesty's Prison Lincoln.

The journey there was one of the most uncomfortable of my life. I seemed to spend the full 150 miles in the brace position, lest I be slammed against the walls every time the wagon slowed down or made an unexpected lane change. When we finally arrived, the prison hung stark above us, a vast Victorian brick edifice against the Lincolnshire skyline. Inside, the echoing halls put me absurdly in mind of the old BBC comedy series Porridge, with its arched doors leading into the cells, its long landings, its air of 19th-century austerity.

Across the first days, I tried to keep myself to myself. I had no battle plan. I kept my head down when I collected my meals, which I took back to my cell to eat alone. Sometimes, I made the trip to the prison library and borrowed books, which I took back to my cell and spent the long hours poring through. The prison gym, which would later be a regular haunt of mine, I visited only rarely, and I had precious little contact with the other inmates. All I really knew how to do was keep putting one foot in front of the other.

Two weeks later, I was sitting there, content in my own silence, when somebody rapped their knuckles on my door. I'd been eager to keep myself to myself a little longer, but I'd always known I couldn't seclude myself for long. Sooner or later, I was going to have to integrate myself into the fabric of prison society – and I did not want to get off on the wrong foot. Consequently, I called out for whoever it was to come in – and in walked a prisoner I had caught glimpses of a number of times from a cell across the landing from my own.

After introducing himself he said, "It's all right, mate. I've told everyone who you are."

I did not show it, but something knotted itself up inside me. I'd had a conversation with members of Her Majesty's prison security at Colchester before I was transferred, and they'd advised me, in no uncertain terms, to spend my time at Colchester growing a beard, letting my hair grow long, contriving a cover story as to why I'd been locked up in prison. Their thinking had been that the prison system was full of extremists and that any one of them might have relished taking the opportunity to assault me in retaliation for the murder of the insurgent. I'd told them, in equally uncertain terms, that I did not intend to hide. It was not in my nature to lie – and besides, my face was already so well known that any fabrication I concocted was bound to unravel at some point, and I did not want to deal with the repercussions of that when it did. I would rather, I'd thought, be secure in myself and deal with whatever came my way. But now, as the inmate looked down at me, I wondered if it had been the right course of action.

"Oh yes?" I ventured.

"Yeah, you're that marine fellow, aren't you? See, you've been so quiet up here, not getting involved with anyone, it'd got some of the others talking about you, what you might have done. They had you down as a sex offender, see, you being so eager to keep yourself to yourself. But I told them, that isn't it at all. He's the marine…"

The logic of it unnerved me, but I supposed I ought to be grateful. I would rather be known as a convicted murderer, still fighting for my name, than let anyone think such a despicable and unforgivable thing about me. I might have been dismissed from the Royal Marines, but I still intended to comport myself within its values. I'd just learned an important lesson about life in prison, one that would benefit me throughout my stay – everyone was there because of some transgression they'd made against society, but it didn't mean they were bad people, not necessarily. My neighbour had approached me because he was looking out for a new inmate, and hadn't wanted me to get tarred with the wrong brush at such an early juncture. I was going to have to get out there myself. However long this lasted, somehow I was going to have to make it work.

I still had hope it might not last long.

As aghast as they had been at the board's guilty verdict, my legal team remained confident – or at least conveyed a confidence – that there were strong grounds to challenge the conviction, and in particular the sentence that had been handed down. Personally, I found it difficult to imagine their confidence was anything more than lawyerly bluster. Every night, alone in my cell, I wrestled with the prospect of the years ahead, and though I clung to the idea of an appeal somehow changing my circumstances, in my heart I felt it was a vain hope. The board had found me guilty, and the words of the judge advocate at my sentencing hearing still tolled, over and over again, in my mind. Perhaps it was only the blackness that came upon me throughout those long nights, but I had precious little faith that we could change an outcome as rigid as this.

Even so, what little hope I had, Claire tried to keep alive. In the outside world, she was exposed as she had never been before. Known publicly, now, as the wife of a convicted murderer, the infamous "Marine A", she held herself together with the dignity and grace-under-fire that I have always admired in my wife. Newspapers hounded her for interviews, the BBC came to Taunton to interview her for a documentary chronicling my case – and, throughout it all, she was the same strong, impassioned woman I had met all those years ago. I needed and loved her for it.

"There's an awful lot of politics, international politics, tied up with this case," she said. "But for me, at the end of the day, this is about one man and his life, and for something not to happen because of politics just seems wrong. Bottom line – Al is no risk to society."

It was hearing things like this that kept hope alive.

On 10 April 2014, four months after I'd entered this fresh hell, the court of appeal convened. My legal team were appealing against both my conviction and the length of sentence, their first principle being that my case was so unique that any sentencing guidelines were not fit for purpose – the precedents simply did not exist. Jeff Blackett, the judge advocate in my original court martial, had argued that I had to be dealt with severely in order to show the international community that battlefield crimes committed by British troops would not be tolerated. But my legal team were going to argue that the length of my prison term was manifestly excessive – more in keeping with a civilian murder – and had not properly taken the context and tensions of the battlefield into account. As to how those tensions had affected me, my legal team intended to submit new evidence from a mental health professional who had assessed me in prison, via a detailed interview, to determine how the environment in Helmand had changed and challenged me.

We would also attack the conviction on technical grounds, arguing that it was inherently unsafe because the seven-person board at the court martial could have convicted me on a "simple majority", not the majority verdict of 10 or 11 out of 12 that was necessary for a guilty verdict in a civilian trial. As such, my legal team submitted, there was no evidence that the original prosecutors had ever satisfied the "criminal standard of proof" – and that I had been unfairly denied these procedural safeguards by the very nature of the court martial process itself.

After hearing arguments from my legal team and their robust rebuttals by a prosecuting QC, the court accepted that the sentence I had been given did, perhaps, err towards the draconian. The evidence they had seen made them confident that the remoteness of our outpost and the lack of contact I'd had with superior officers had left me in a fragile mental state, and that the original court martial should have given this "greater weight" when determining the length of my sentence. Instead, they had made the point that "thousands of other service personnel have experienced the same or similar stresses" and yet not acted in the same way. It was "self-evident," the appeal court said, "that armed forces sent to a foreign and hostile land to combat an insurgency will be placed under much greater stress than armed forces sent to fight a regular army," and they agreed with my legal team that I had had so little contact with my commanding officers that nobody had assessed the effect the conditions in Helmand were having upon me.

And yet, when the court reconvened six weeks later to present its decision, they upheld my conviction for murder – and, despite the new arguments presented concerning my mental state at the time of the incident, reduced the minimum term of my sentence by only two years.

On the evening after the appeal's findings were released, I stood in the hall at Lincoln Prison, cradling the receiver to my ear as I spoke with Claire. My family had already issued their brief statement to the press through our legal team. Our disappointment at the appeal judge's decision was already a matter of record. We were, we said, considering further appeals. What they were, at that moment, I did not know. All I really knew was that this felt like the end of the road.

"Eight years is the same as 10," I said to Claire. I did not mean to sound ungrateful, I was glad that the minimum term of my sentence had been reduced. And yet... whether I was here a minimum of eight years or a minimum of 10, my future still looked the same. Claire's future, bonded to a man who could never really be her husband or treat her as his wife, still looked the same.

She told me it wasn't over yet. There were still avenues to explore. Other appeals we could submit. But the feeling that swept over me, as we said goodbye and promised we would speak again the next day, was not the hope she was trying to instil in me. It was that our best efforts had now failed twice. It was that – even though it was now three years since I had lain awake at night at CP Omar – Helmand was here with me in my cell, and would colour the rest of my life.

It was hopeless. In my heart, I still did not understand what it had done to me, why I had pulled that trigger. And if I could not understand it myself, how on earth could anyone, no matter how legally proficient, begin to understand it instead? How could they know the desolation of Nad-e Ali? How could they feel the 40-degree heat sapping them of life, or hear their comrades dying over the radio, or close their eyes at night to see images raking across the backs of their eyes, the body parts of their friends strung up in the trees? How could they possibly know what it had felt like to stand on the edge of that cornfield, your enemy already near death at your feet, while the radio buzzed with news of other insurgents out there? And how could they begin to imagine what that might do to a man?

The thought had been creeping up on me ever since the moment of my sentencing, when I had stood up to salute the officers as if thanking them for my lifetime behind bars – they were never going to see. No matter how hard we worked or how much belief we had, no appeal was ever going to work. The establishment needed me to be the scumbag they were painting me as. It was important to them that the evil of Helmand had a human face. With a human face, it could be bound up and locked away, and eventually forgotten about. Better that, perhaps, than confront the reality of a war like the one we were waging in Afghanistan, the impossibility of winning hearts and minds in a land where any stranger might be your killer, the endless grind with nothing to accomplish and no tangible success. Better that than face up to what a war like that could do to good men sent out and sacrificed. I'd known paranoia before, out there in Helmand where it seemed the Taliban had me personally in their sights, but I was certain I was not being paranoid now. No – the establishment needed me exactly where I was, and no matter what appeal we attempted next, this was where I was going to stay.

CHAPTER FOURTEEN

I'd become accustomed to the idea that at least eight years stretched ahead of me. Eight years, my universe entire. And the pragmatist in me had, like so many prisoners, decided to put the time to good use. In that first year I began studying for an A-level equivalence course, before moving on to begin a BA honours degree in combined social sciences with the Open University. Something to occupy the corner of my mind that had always been engaged in learning ever since I'd signed up with the Royal Marines. It was a panacea, but it could never occupy all my time. I built my weeks around the visits I got from Claire. Sometimes, other family members would accompany her on the long trips up to Lincoln, and the stories I got from them, the glimpses of the outside world, meant everything to me, even while they were a constant reminder of the life that in a parallel universe I would have been living.

Hope springs eternal, but the reality is that after our first appeal led to only a minor adjustment in sentencing, what hope I had been harbouring was gone. So the news Claire brought me one weekend, when we sat in the meeting hall together and I thanked the fates that she hadn't taken me up on my offer to call our relationship quits, was entirely unexpected.

At the time of my second arrest, when the investigation into what had happened in Helmand was only just beginning, the counter-terrorism police had advised us that we should close down all our social media accounts, ensuring that we had as minimal a digital footprint as possible. Claire and I had always been relatively private people – it wasn't as if we were in the habit of constantly sharing our lives with the world online – so this hadn't been difficult for us, but even so, we understood the gravity of the step. The incendiary nature of our case might have left us open to attack – online, certainly, but perhaps even in real life. As a consequence, neither Claire nor I had been active online since a year before my conviction – and, although Claire's friends often filtered to us the talk about my case on social media, it was not something we made an effort to keep on top of. Public perception was the one thing we couldn't sway. Instead, we had resolved to survive this together, the two of us in the eye of a storm.

But Claire's friends had recently made her aware of a Facebook group that had started some months before and grown exponentially since the time of my conviction. There had been other Facebook groups founded by people who wished me well, but the "Justice For Marine A" group seemed to have risen up out of the pack, and by the time Claire stumbled across it, it already had in excess of 100,000 members. In time, that membership would nearly double. The scale of it was humbling: I had always taken heart from hearing of people who championed understanding and compassion in respect to my experiences in Helmand, but to know that somebody else – somebody who neither Claire nor I knew – was marshalling support like this filled me with renewed hope. The words of the judge advocate and many others had been so damning of me – but the fact that these views weren't universally held gave me a second strength.

Claire had reached out to the administrator of the Justice For Marine A group. Jonathan Davies was himself a former Royal Marine, and had had his service cut short due to injury. Perhaps his own experiences left him perfectly poised to understand what we'd been through in Helmand, but it was another aspect of his career that had drawn him to my case. While in the Marines, he had himself been a member of the Royal Marines Police Troop. Following my case, he had become increasingly incredulous at what he saw as the injustice of my arrest, and later conviction. Adamant that when he had been in the military police himself, he would never have been able to investigate or arrest somebody under the circumstances in which we'd been serving, he had set up the Facebook group as a way of demonstrating the wide-ranging support he believed would be out there. So far, it was working. The 100,000 people who had already joined and "liked" the group came from all walks of life, many with an attachment to the military in some regard – perhaps via a family member who was out in Afghanistan, serving in similar conditions to the ones that had laid me low – but others who weren't attached to the military at all, and whose hearts went out to me in the posts they left on the page.

When Claire sat in the prison visiting room and told me all this, it was as though a wall cracked inside me, letting the light shine through. Perhaps I was not so damned after all.

Claire had gone further, as I had always known she would. Keen to thank Jonathan for all the unsolicited support he was giving, she had arranged to meet him. Soon afterwards, Jonathan had zoomed over from his Bristol home to Taunton, and over coffee Claire had heard about his own experiences with the Royal Marines. She'd seen how incensed he was at the investigation and arrest, and how – in the words of so many members of the group – I was being thought of not as a human being suffering under extraordinary conditions, but as a symbol of everything perceived to be wrong about the war in Afghanistan.

It hadn't taken long for Claire to realise that Jonathan's intentions were pure, that setting up the group and working tirelessly to get the message out there was done from a position of empathy and pure altruism. What was more, she *liked* him. Perhaps it was down to the years we'd spent together – or perhaps it was one of the things that drew her to me in the first place – but, as another marine, she found him likeable, impassioned and easy to speak with. She left reassured that she could trust him and all he was doing for me, and as she told me everything, I realised what this meant – not only for me, but for Claire herself. She'd always been surrounded by supportive family and friends, but in Jonathan she had one of our first real *allies* in the upcoming campaign for my release.

The Justice For Marine A group gave me fresh reason to hope. The fact that there was a groundswell of support for me from everyday people on the street buoyed me no end as I continued to live life by the prison routine of work and study, visits to the gym and to the prison library. But, some time later, another chance communication with Claire was to transform everything.

Claire did her best to avoid the constant opinion pieces that were written about me. Life might have changed irrevocably for her, but she still had a life to lead. There was still her work. There were still her ambitions. There were still family and friends to support and be supported by – and, although I knew that her life was different now, I still wanted her to *live* it and experience the things that, together, we had always taken for granted. As a consequence, it was important for her to ignore the things still being said about me. There was already too much negativity in the world.

On occasion, however, a friend would send her a cutting or a link to some article, hoping that it might cheer her when her spirits were low. And, in April 2015 – 16 months into my sentence, and a whole year since our first appeal – an envelope landed at our Taunton home, carrying a cutting from the *Daily Express* newspaper. At the head of the page was a headshot of the best-selling novelist and political commentator Frederick Forsyth, and below that the headline: "Courts should feel ashamed for their treatment of a British hero."

> *"Twenty-one years ago we, the British, took a young man and allowed him to become a Royal Marine, a member of one of the world's most elite military units. Over two years, we turned Alex Blackman into a superb fighting machine. Then we sent him to every filthy, dangerous hellhole we could think of. A tour of the killing fields of South Armagh, two tours in even more lethal Iraq – then two tours, one after the other, in ultra-dangerous Helmand, Afghanistan. Finally, four years ago, exhausted, drained, stressed out by battle fatigue, in 50-degree temperatures, in a terrorist-surrounded field in the wilds of Helmand, he made a mistake."*

Frederick's writing was filled with righteous anger. Claire and I had always tried to manage our own feelings over what was going on. There was so little use in us remonstrating and raging against the system – and, although I didn't agree with my conviction, I honoured and respected the processes by which that conviction was reached. But Mr Forsyth's words meant everything to Claire and, later, they would mean everything to me as well. It was the unquestioned understanding that meant the most. The judge advocate and board at my trial had, of course, listed some mitigating factors in their final account of the matter, but it seemed to me that they had dismissed them just as readily. Here was a complete stranger, wielding what influence he had in an impassioned plea to *understand*.

He went on:

"There are simply too many people, many in the Marine Corps, who believe there was something not right about his prosecution and court martial. Frankly, it smells to high heaven. We British imprison men who are dangerous to the people of Britain. Sgt Blackman was only ever remotely dangerous to Britain's diehard enemies and it seems he has paid a savage price for a mistake in an Afghan field four years ago when surrounded by fanatics trying to kill him and his men."

At the end, he signed off:

"I have a gut feeling there is more to come on this affair."

And Claire knew, then, that she had found yet another ally in the outside world.

Soon after she received the article, Claire got in touch with Freddie via his publisher, thanking him for his support. Thinking nothing of it – only that she wanted to show our gratitude to such a high-profile voice for speaking out – she ploughed through the next few days at work, made the long drive to visit me at Lincoln and prepared to go on in that manner for the long months and years to come.

But everything changed when Frederick himself replied to Claire with a simple message: he thought that they should meet.

A date was arranged and, some days later, Claire opened the door to our Taunton home to find Frederick Forsyth on the doorstep, his gleaming Suzuki Swift along with his driver parked at the kerb.

Freddie was as avuncular and impassioned as he'd been in his article. Over successive pots of coffee, Freddie trying desperately to resist the urge for a cigarette, he listened to Claire's experience and found himself swept up, again, in what he perceived to be the injustices of my court martial and conviction.

Freddie's own military experience was limited to his national service in the late 1950s when he served with the Royal Air Force, flying the de Havilland Vampire fighter jet – but his subsequent journalistic career had seen him devoted to the military and many of its causes. In 1985 he'd narrated a BBC documentary series, Soldiers, which chronicled the history of men in battle all the way from antiquity up to the recent war in the Falkland Islands. Following the reportage on my own court martial, he'd felt the undeniable need to weigh in. Some gut instinct told him that he had to. As Freddie would later write, what had stirred him was simple incredulity that, although I'd given 16 years of my life to the Royal Marines, gone into

257

hell for them on numerous tours and endured the very worst of Helmand on that final tour, the moment their loyalty was needed in return, they'd looked the other way.

"He gave the senior officer corps of the Royal Marines his total loyalty," he would write later that same year. "But what support did the top brass give to their sergeant in his hour of need? They could have ensured he got a first-class defence in court... but they have just turned to face the wall, consigning the man who laid his life on the line for his country more times than anyone else in that courtroom had had hot dinners to be thrown to the wolves."

What happened to loyalty? he asked Claire, still filled with fire. What happened to honour? Nobody, neither Freddie nor Claire, was there to make excuses for the terrible error of judgement I'd made on that fateful day, but to Freddie the court martial and its result could not be ignored. All 15 men at CP Omar had been at the limit of exhaustion, reduced by battle fatigue, combat stress and sleeplessness. For a few short seconds, I had snapped – and, to the court, all that seemed to have mattered was those seconds – not the months and years that surrounded them, giving them their context.

Claire was able to show Freddie some of the other support already out there. The Justice for Marine A Facebook group was continuing to grow, accruing more messages of support with every week that passed. The public sentiment, it seemed, was out there, waiting to be harnessed. But to make anyone stand up and take note, to transform the direction of our lives, it was going to take something more gargantuan yet.

"We're going to need a campaign."

The response to Freddie's *Daily Express* column had been immense, but Freddie had something else in mind. The *Daily Mail*, he was canny enough to understand, was the paper best known for campaigning – and their coverage of my court martial and conviction had been one of the most sympathetic out there. Freddie told Claire that he planned to put in a call and see what he might stir up. But there was more. Freddie had a barrister on his team, a solo practitioner called Jonathan Goldberg QC who worked out of North Square Chambers in London, and he intended to ask him if he and his juniors might dive back into the facts surrounding my case. Perhaps, Freddie reasoned, there was a route back into overturning the conviction. My first appeal might not have yielded much, but there was still the Criminal Cases Review Commission (CCRC) to think of – and, much further down the line, the European Court of Human Rights.

"Goldberg was against me once," Freddie explained, with his skill as a raconteur already in full evidence. "I had a financial advisor who took me for a ride. I lost a lot of money. But when I sued him, he had the most brilliant barrister fighting his corner. Jonathan Goldberg. He won as well. I lost everything. But after the verdict was delivered, I approached Goldberg myself. Somebody that talented, even if he'd been ranged up against me, was worth their weight in gold. I had to have him on my side – and he has been ever since. If anyone can find a way back into Al's case, it's Jonathan."

As Freddie took his leave, leaping back into the Suzuki Swift and disappearing in a flash up the country road, Claire took stock of everything that had just happened, and when she visited me in prison later that same week, there was a flicker of new hope in her eyes. Just a crack, to let the light shine in. We were both steadfast in our understanding that this might mean nothing at all – but for now, it was enough.

CHAPTER FIFTEEN

In the spring of 2015, Jonathan Goldberg QC visited me in prison with his two juniors at his side. Though they had already trawled through the paperwork on my case, teasing at every angle to ascertain whether my first legal team had covered every base or whether there were legal grounds to find my conviction unsafe, what they were really here for was to hear the story of Helmand in my own words. It had been told so often it had solidified into a few broad brushstrokes in my mind, but as we began I made a new resolution: I would paint it in the most brutally honest light I could, not shying away even from those aspects that I still didn't understand, the unpalatable things I'd said and done.

I was already 18 months into my sentence and staring down the barrel of a further seven years before there was even any hope of being released. There was no point in playing games, no point in pretending that things had been better than they were out there in the desert. Better that I paint myself in the worst possible light – then, perhaps, if they found something that had been overlooked, it would raise no false hopes.

For two hours I recounted not only that day in Helmand, but everything that had preceded it and everything that had gone after. Two hours later, spent and exhausted, we turned to how my first legal team had conducted the process and framed their advice. Jonathan Goldberg listened intently, his juniors making transcripts of our conversation as they went.

"The English legal system," I was eventually told, "is like the Ritz... It's open to anyone as long as they can afford it."

What they meant was that you get what you pay for, and the legal advice we'd been given was not, perhaps, as full as it might have been. This is not to say that my first legal team had done everything wrong – indeed, Jonathan Goldberg admired much of what they'd done and would have done precisely the same. "But there are other aspects," he began, "where we might have conducted ourselves differently. The mental health analysis, for instance."

What really stuck in the craw was that my first legal team had only commissioned a psychological assessment for the appeal, not for the court martial itself.

"We're going to get a mental health specialist here to see you. Professor Greenberg's written the book on mental health in the military."

The idea of exploring a mental health defence did not sit easily with me. I knew too many people who'd come home from Afghanistan with full-blown PTSD, or developed other mental health disorders while coming to terms with their service and the bodily injuries they'd experienced. My mind flickered back, instinctively, to those early nights on suicide watch in prison, or being despatched to the mental health facility in Taunton. I'd felt the same back then: I did not want to dishonour the experiences of my fellow veterans by being seen to use mental health as an excuse for what had happened. Too many servicemen and women suffer with mental illnesses, and I did not want to detract from their struggles. I wanted honesty, as brutal as I'd given to Jonathan Goldberg.

They understood that from the first. It became our overriding principle. We would be open to whatever diagnosis we discovered, for better or for worse, but we would not seek to exploit something that wasn't there. My fellow veterans deserved better.

An appointment was made and Professor Neil Greenberg came to interview me in prison some weeks later. Professor Greenberg had himself served in the UK armed forces for 23 years, during which he'd helped develop its approach to traumatic stress and had been awarded the Gilbert Blane Medal for his contribution. It was, in part, thanks to Professor Greenberg that the UK armed forces have a policy of "trauma risk management" or "TRiM", a method of preventing second-ary PTSD and other combat-stress-related disorders before they can take root. At the time we met, he was also the president of the UK Psychological Trauma Society and the Royal College of Psychiatrists' expert on the health of armed forces veterans.

Nobody, Jonathan Goldberg had explained, was better poised to diagnose a mental health condition, if one existed. If he found nothing, we would discount it as an avenue of approach and focus on other ways to challenge my conviction. But Jonathan Goldberg had also impressed upon me the fact that most people with a mental health disorder don't *know* they're ill. Some people recognise symptoms in themselves, especially those with chronic illnesses like depression – but people like me, with no personal experience of mental health disorders, often fail to recognise that they're ill until it's too late. Consequently, there was a possibility that although I'd always believed myself immune to the ravages of mental ill health, I had been affected by something I didn't understand. Only a thorough psychological assessment would be able to say – and I would have to be open to the findings, whatever they were.

The prospect daunted me. I have never been a man to wear his heart on his sleeve, but nor have I been one to actively repress my feelings. I am not ashamed to remember the way tears wracked my body after my father passed away before our departure to Helmand. I am not ashamed to admit the new uneasiness and fear I felt upon seeing some of the injuries the medics at Camp Bastion were confronting. I had never thought that acknowledging emotion made a man, or a Royal Marine, weaker than he might be. But, if I am being brutally honest with myself, I had never truly considered the possibility that my experiences at war might have an impact on me mentally. I'd been conditioned, from the first, to accept the dangers war presented to my body. That was the deal you made when you signed up, to put your body in harm's way, and all for the greater good. The idea that war slowly corrodes the mind might seem obvious, but when you are in the thick of battle, it is the last thing you consider.

In Helmand, every day had been about making it to the fall of night. Every night had been about surviving until the break of day. Mine and Claire's mantra – to keep focusing on what was directly in front of us, to take one step at a time – might have applied equally well out there. There, you just got on with the task in hand. You patrolled and cleared and patrolled and cleared the area once more. And, if little bits of your psychology were being chipped away each day, well, at first you hardly noticed. Disorders like PTSD do not always come in an instant. Just as often, they accumulate, growing incrementally worse each day – until, finally, something snaps.

I resolved to be as brutally honest with Professor Greenberg as I had been with Jonathan Goldberg QC. I wouldn't glorify anything, seeking a diagnosis that just wasn't there, but neither would I sugar-coat anything, nor pretend that everything had been all right when it wasn't. Honesty was the only way I could be sure they would come to the correct diagnosis – and that consequently, whatever happened next was genuine. Because the fact was that as much as I wanted freedom and the restoration of my reputation with the Royal

Marines, I didn't want it disingenuously. I didn't want to lie or cheat my way back to my life with Claire. I wanted it pure and unvarnished. The whole truth, and nothing but the truth.

And so I told Professor Greenberg everything, from going into that tour underprepared and still reeling from my father's death, right through to the moment when I shot the insurgent at the edge of the cornfield. That was all I could do. Professor Greenberg probed deeper, asked a litany of questions about my intentions, feelings, the hopes and ambitions and survival tactics of that tour – and then he retreated to make his diagnosis.

My future was in somebody else's hands, once again.

In fact, my future was in the hands of tens of thousands of people. Jonathan Goldberg QC had been correct when he said that the legal system in the UK was only really open to those who could afford it, and the costs of mounting a new defence with a new team far outweighed what Claire and I were able to finance alone, especially given that I had been dishonourably discharged and therefore stripped of all pay. Without any funds, we were left in search of a miracle.

Freddie Forsyth had come good on one promise – to introduce us to his personal legal team – and he came good on another as well. Thanks to his intervention with the *Daily Mail*, a public campaign began in the summer of 2015 designed not only to garner moral support for the new defence we were hoping to mount, but to pay for it as well. The *Daily Mail* established a legal fund to be administered by Freddie himself, Major General John Holmes – formerly the head of UK Special Forces – and another celebrity supporter, the lyricist Sir Tim Rice. Galvanising their readers to see me not as the pariah the court martial had painted me as, they ran interviews with both myself and Claire, framed the killing of the insurgent in the context of that hellish tour of Helmand and the friends we had lost, and treated me as a human being, in peril, for the first time.

Claire and I remained true to our first maxim, to take nothing for granted, and always assume the worst. But we soon realised that the public support that we'd already seen, especially via Jonathan's Justice For Marine A online presence, was broader than either of us had hoped. Though only a fraction of it reached me in prison, and Claire could filter only so much of it to me when she came to visit, Freddie's article had prompted others to come out of the woodwork and begin expressing their support. This is not to say that people condoned what I had done in Helmand, only that more of them understood the nuances of the situation. Freddie Forsyth himself never wavered, remaining vocal in his support throughout. On one BBC programme, he argued that the Ministry of Defence was trying to "pile every single thing that went wrong" in Helmand onto me – and though he did not completely reflect my own view on what the ministry was doing, it took moments like this to remind me that, in spite of the legal record and what my dishonourable discharge inferred, I was not personally responsible for the torments of that tour.

"They sent 15 men to the most dangerous square mile in the world for five and a half months unvisited, unrelieved, underresourced, and then when one man at the extremity of exhaustion made a mistake, they are saying it was all his fault," Freddie argued.

Words like these gave me strength to keep believing in myself, whether they came from Freddie, the MP Richard Drax or Colonel Oliver Lee, my own commanding officer at the time of the shooting, who had resigned in protest over my treatment.

But even more moving and humbling were the letters that, thanks to the visibility the *Daily Mail* had given my story, began to tumble through the door at our Taunton home. The *Daily Mail*'s campaign had begun in full earnest, and within days they had been inundated not just with contributions to the legal fund but with letters, notes and postcards, many inscribed with handwritten messages of solidarity and support.

Many had come from veterans of the last century's wars, those who knew what it was like in combat environments and whose hearts went out to me. "I have always said you were a much better bootneck and man than those trying so readily to condemn you," one old marine wrote. "PS. I am an old git now, served from 1961-70. I still keep in touch with my old association and the lads send you all the very best."

"My father, who is now 94 and no idiot," wrote another, "had the distinction of fighting the Japanese on a hand-to-hand basis in the Far East. He told me yesterday that it was pure hell with the constant stress of attending to his men by day and by night where the enemy was constantly set upon killing them. The Japanese were not interested in taking prisoners, rather as the Taliban are not interested today."

But among the letters from veterans and those with family members in the armed forces came countless others from people with no attachment to the military whatsoever. "Thank you for putting your life on the line," wrote one. "Chin up!" Pensioners had written, donating £5 from their weekly pensions; other prisoners had written, donating what little money they still had, or just filling pages with best wishes. Some local associations or clubs had got together to send cheques for £100, £200, £500. More often, individuals had reached into their pockets at the end of the week and sent along a single £10 note, or whatever they could spare. Daily the parcels of letters arrived from the *Daily Mail*, cascading onto the doormat. Claire could not show me the letters during our visits, but she did recount their contents across the table in the visiting hall at Lincoln Prison. The effect on me was stirring. Ten thousand and more missives from beyond the prison walls, and not one of them took the same view of me as the judge advocate and board had done.

> *"My eight-year-old daughter wanted to know why I was crying. I explained your case and, although I do my best to shield her, I believe she should know injustice and respect. You fought for us and now we need to fight for you. Sir, you are a hero. God bless you and*

know this, we thank you from the bottom of our hearts and feel deep
sorrow at the way you have been treated."

Letters like this were enough to make me feel alive again. "This is just a very small effort to drop in a very large ocean," read one. But every tiny droplet counted. Somehow, by the time the *Daily Mail* stopped accepting donations – returning some, and donating a surplus to charities chosen by the administrators – those tiny droplets had amounted to more than £800,000.

There are moments in life that will forever humble you. They come out of nowhere and reinforce the belief you have that the world is full of good, decent people living good, decent lives, who only want to make the world a better place in what little ways they can. This was one of them, and perhaps the most restorative, redemptive moment of my journey so far.

Out there were countless thousands of people who understood, who wished me well, who were willing to reach into their pockets and donate whatever they could, just so that I had one last chance at coming home. The British people will never cease to amaze me for their generosity of spirit and their dogged belief in doing the right thing. But people from much further afield – in fact, from all over the world – had contributed as well, and the idea that people in far-flung corners of the world cared enough about me to reach out like this was almost overwhelming.

That £800,000 was a treasure chest for us. It meant that Jonathan Goldberg QC and his team could champion our cause into the future and do whatever they needed to do in an attempt to overturn my conviction. But even more important than that was the *belief* I felt coming to me from all corners of the globe. From veterans and civilians, from pensioners with so little to give, from everyday families in cities, towns and villages from one side of the world to another. The money everyone had donated would carry us so far, but the kindness and faith will stay with me forever.

CHAPTER SIXTEEN

Professor Neil Greenberg's diagnosis came back.

Towards the end of my time in Helmand, I had been affected by what is known as an "adjustment disorder".

When my new legal team conferred the news to me at one of our scheduled visits, I did not know what to think. I had known people with adjustment disorders before. It is not full-blown PTSD, but it is the first step on the road to that devastating condition. And it was the first time I saw that if I'd stayed in that environment much longer, I too could have degenerated to the point where I had a lasting post-traumatic stress disorder. I'd seen the way it debilitated people. I'd seen the way it can colour a life. At once, I felt fortunate that my time in Helmand had come to an end. Then I began to consider its implications.

I'd never truly understood what I'd done in Helmand. After 16 years of dogged, resolute service, in a few short moments I'd transformed the complexion of my career. But now, as the diagnosis sunk in, little bits of me lit up... and I believe I began to understand. Adjustment disorders are characterised by unusual and excessive reactions to stress or events. People react severely to provocations they would ordinarily have handled in a more ordered or disciplined fashion. The decision-making process can be impaired as the sufferer struggles to normalise his or her responses.

I cannot say I was not relieved. I hadn't been anticipating an actual diagnosis, and in my heart I had not wanted one: part of me still rejected the idea that I had been mentally ill in Helmand, as if there was something to feel ashamed of, or even to fear. But even so, I was glad of the sense of understanding it gave me. It was as if there was a locked chest inside me, and in it the secret of why I'd behaved as I had that day in the cornfield. Now, thanks to Professor Greenberg, I'd been allowed a glimpse inside. It wasn't pretty. Inside there was Helmand Province and all the memories that I had bundled up and locked away. But inside there was also a realisation – my response was not just to the normal stresses of deployment, as they'd said at my sentencing hearing, there had been something more preying on me, building within me day on day. If I'd gone on longer, it might have frothed up and erupted out of me as full-blown PTSD. It was just good fortune that I'd come home, settled back into normal life, and let the adjustment disorder naturally ebb away.

Later that night, when I spoke with Claire, we allowed ourselves a moment of relief – but we did not let ourselves get lost in it for too long. There was always the chance that it made no difference, that it was just a footnote to be appended to the mountain of paperwork my case had already created.

But for the first time there was light shining in from the future – and, although I went to bed that night still struggling to conflate the idea of my adjustment disorder with the Royal Marine I thought I'd been, for now that was enough.

* * *

By early 2016, while Jonathan Goldberg and his team were still awaiting the results of the paperwork they had submitted to the Criminal Cases Review Commission, I had been transferred from Lincoln to Erlestoke Prison in Wiltshire. Whereas Lincoln had been a category B prison, Erlestoke was category C, meaning that its security conditions were not quite as stringent as at Lincoln: its prisoners could be trusted, just a little bit more, not to try and escape. Its principal advantage for me was that it made Claire's life so much easier, cutting the distance she had to travel to visit me by as much as 150 miles. This, more than anything else, made imprisonment more bearable. I had always hated with a passion how much Claire had to configure her life around those long drives.

In September of the year before, a debate had been held in Westminster in response to an online petition that garnered more than 100,000 signatures, all demanding my release. The debate, led by the MP Richard Drax, was followed a month later by a public show of support on the streets of Westminster. Drax had said, "War is a filthy, horrible, frightening business – and every man has his breaking point, even the best. Sgt Blackman was, and is, no cold-blooded killer, just a man pushed to the very edge. A man sent to do a filthy job with his hands tied behind his back. A man who is now no threat to anyone. A man who is now paying a terrible price for a misjudgement."

But not everyone shared the sentiment. The Ministry of Defence itself banned serving soldiers from attending the Westminster rally to support me, deeming it a political protest and not simply a show of support for a fellow Royal Marine.

Inculcated into the rhythms of prison life – still studying for my BA in combined social sciences and making use of the prison gym as much as I could – I tried not to think too much about the report Jonathan Goldberg QC had submitted to the CCRC. In it they'd raised six points of order which, together, built up an argument that my conviction for murder was legally unsound – and that, if the board had been presented with appropriate evidence regarding my mental breakdown, it might have drawn a different conclusion. But brooding on it overly, as tempting as it was, would not help me now.

The letters which continued to pour in from the *Daily Mail* provided me with a new reason to get through the weeks, and there was no denying that the feeling of support I got from every corner of society was the kind of sustenance I needed in the long, often empty hours in prison. But Claire and I needed to remind ourselves of the reality. Anyone, whether they had an expert team of lawyers or not, could submit their case for review with the CCRC. As a consequence, the CCRC was inundated with requests from prisoners, lawyers and families to reopen old convictions and test them, and only a tiny fraction – somewhere between 4% and 5% – would ever be sent upwards to the appeals court.

Soon after the paperwork was submitted, and perhaps due to the debate that had raged in Westminster about the support the armed forces owed its servicemen and women, the CCRC indicated that my case would be given high priority. Even so, Jonathan Goldberg's team advised me that it might take six months before it came back with a response – and in the meantime, there was nothing more we could do. So, burying any hopes and dreams, Claire and I returned to the limbo of life, trying not to get carried away, telling ourselves, over and over again, that all we had done was take one step closer.

In the end, we didn't have to wait six months.

We waited 12.

As Christmas 2016 approached, it is fair to say that although my mind still drifted to the CCRC and the hope of a promising outcome, the possibility had also been lost in the unknowns of that year. The wheels moved so slowly that, perhaps as a mechanism of self-preservation, I had blotted it out. For three years I had lived the rhythm of this life, and if the minimum of five – and potentially many more – that stretched in front of me was reducing day after day, the magnitude of it still seemed as vast as the world. Now, I was on the eve of my third Christmas away from Claire, and the uncertainty felt as if it had lasted forever.

The anniversary of the submission of our paperwork to the CCRB dawned, 12 December 2016. On that same day, on a routine call with my legal team, the news came through – the CCRC had finally been able to deliberate my case and, although they didn't agree with three out of the six points Goldberg's team had raised, any one of the remaining three was enough for them to recommend another hearing in the appeals court. Principal among these points was the lack of mental health evidence presented at the original trial, and the fact that the board had been unable to consider a conviction of manslaughter, rather than murder.

It was the news we had waited for the entire year.

That night, over a buzzing telephone line, I tried to explain it to Claire. Three-quarters of all the cases referred to the appeals court resulted in some favourable outcome for the appellant. This did not necessarily mean the complete overturn of a conviction, but it was enough to fill my sails with fresh belief.

I needed Claire to talk me down. It felt like momentum was with us, but momentum means so little in a court of law. The same, rightfully so, goes for public opinion. I forced myself to look back three years to my original trial, and to how my first legal team had been confident of my exoneration. The impact of them being wrong had been brutal. I did not want to let that happen again. So I resolved to keep my head down, to think only of the next day, and then the next. *One step at a time*, just like Claire had always said.

Talk flurried up about the chance I might be granted bail and released for Christmas, pending the result of my appeal in the New Year. For the briefest moment, I let myself believe that I might wake up alongside Claire on Christmas morning, or make the long drive from Taunton down to Brighton to spend it with my mother. But it was a dream. No bail was awarded, and on Christmas Day I collected my meal from the hot plate and retired with it to my cell, trying to keep the upcoming appeal out of my mind.

New Year came. Weekly, Claire and I sat in the visiting hall and tried to keep this out of our minds. But soon a date was set for the appeal hearing. By April, my future would be set in stone.

The news of the upcoming appeal had made headlines across the UK, and as a result the deluge of letters Claire was still receiving had changed in nature. The fresh hope given to me also gave, or so it seemed, fresh hope to the tens of thousands of supporters I had out there. Yet, while Claire braved the hordes of reporters and supporters gathered outside London's Royal Courts of Justice, I would see nothing of it – nothing except the glimpses of veterans gathered on the steps, well-wishers carrying placards, and police keeping order on the television news. Because I would not be present in the courtroom for the appeal. Instead, I would be in a small cubicle at Erlestoke Prison, my supervisor at my shoulder, watching my legal representatives and the judges on a split television screen. Of the gallery and well-wishers, of my family and fellow marines, I could see nothing, only the eyes of the people whose arguments would decide my fate.

As the appeal got under way, Mr Goldberg recounted the details of my time in Helmand, building up a picture of our location that I had always wondered if I'd painted vividly enough in the testimony I'd given at my original trial. He spoke about the austere environment, the daily skirmishes, the death waiting for us beneath the crust of the earth. "Official statistics show that there was an explosion by IED every 16 hours on average throughout the six months of the tour." The most common injuries were to the lower limbs and genitalia.

"It hardly needs a psychiatrist to point out that the conditions under which Blackman was serving at CP Omar were ripe for mental illness or breakdown," Goldberg added; but, in fact, he was able to call three independent mental health experts to attest to just that. "It's a recognised fact of all mental illness that a lot of those who are mentally ill do not recognise any symptoms in themselves, and so it is with Blackman. His nature is to be very reserved. He's a John Wayne character."

It is not how I would have described myself, but it pointed to something I now understood to be at the very heart of my character, and central to my time in Helmand. Without any "padre", as Mr Goldberg termed it, to speak with, nobody of my rank to confide in, I'd turned inward – and those same instincts to be reserved and put on a macho front, not wanting to show any sign of weakness in front of my lads, had finally snapped. A statement from Colonel Oliver Lee supported Mr Goldberg's argument that, left to our own devices in Helmand, we had been failed by our officers. Lee, who had resigned his post with 45 Commando in protest at my treatment in September 2015, argued that the leadership and oversight of my commanders had been shockingly bad – and the fact that I was visited by my commanding officer only twice during my six months at CP Omar seemed enough to persuade the court that something fundamental had gone awry.

The first expert witness was Professor Neil Greenberg. "He was a husk of his former self," said Greenberg, and the sense of me teetering on the edge of a major psychiatric event was compounded when Claire herself attested to me searching the ground for IEDs when I'd been on leave from the tour.

The counter-arguments, argued by the articulate and fiercely intelligent Richard Whittam QC, mirrored those of my original trial. They argued that my actions had been cold and calculated, that my judgements were rational and in keeping with the kind of man I'd become. But when it came to refuting the combined mental health analyses, they had little to offer – no analysis of their own, and no independent witness to call.

The appeal process itself lasted three days. On the final day, the session ended late, and it was decided that the ruling would not be made that day. In the morning, when we returned, the five senior judges who had gathered to hear the appeal were ready to make their ruling.

It was clear, the lord chief justice Lord Thomas said, that there were discrepancies in the original court martial. It was clear that vital pieces of evidence – things that ought reasonably to have been taken into account – had been overlooked, or glossed over. The evidence presented at appeal, first by Professor Neil Greenberg and backed up by two other mental health professionals, made it incontrovertibly clear that no matter how I held myself and failed to understand it at the time, I was operating under the influence of an adjustment disorder. In light of all these considerations, the court had come to a decision. My conviction for the murder of the mortally wounded insurgent was unfit. In its place, the court would charge me with manslaughter on the grounds of diminished responsibility.

In London, the celebrations of my supporters were about to begin, but in my tiny cubicle at Erlestoke Prison, my work was not yet finished. The court broke for a few minutes, to allow my legal team and me to talk through the implications. In that cubicle, I was still reeling – uncertain whether to be elated or not. My insides, which had moments ago been knotted, were unravelling fast. And yet the clock was ticking, and I was faced with perhaps the biggest decision of my life. Whether to accept the charge and await a new sentencing hearing, or to challenge it again and ask Mr Goldberg to steer the court towards permitting a full retrial, based on all the facts and evidence now present.

A corner of me still burned to be exonerated entirely, but after three years my faith in the concept of justice was eroded. I wasn't sure I could put Claire through another two years of trial. The British public had already taken me in and shepherded me through this appeal process, reaching into their pockets to help me, a complete stranger, with my defence, and I was not sure I could in all conscience go back to them, cap in hand. The fight was still in me, but greater than that was the love and debt I felt I owed Claire for all she had done. Standing here, on the precipice, I did not want to march further into hell with her. I wanted to wake up in Taunton and live our life together.

And then Mr Goldberg addressed me. "You don't have to decide straight away, Mr Blackman. I can see you on the screen in court. If you want to accept a manslaughter charge, give me a thumbs-up. If not, we'll push for a retrial."

Minutes later, the courtroom had reassembled. Ten minutes was all I had to make the biggest decision of my life – so I fell back on my old training, and the way I had, when in my right mind, always made my decisions.

I relied on my gut.

I wanted this to be over. I wanted to be home with Claire, to get on with the rest of our lives, to build something together as we'd always planned.

I lifted my thumb, and Mr Goldberg accepted the judgement on my behalf.

Sometimes, all it takes is one moment to shed one skin and don another.

I was no longer a convicted murderer.

Two days later, I returned to the cubicle at Erlestoke and, with the camera trained on me once more, stared out over the courtroom. I'd lain awake the night before, trying to battle back the hope that the upcoming sentencing hearing might bring positive news – but here, watching as the faces assembled on screen, the anxiety knotted up inside me once again.

I was knotted still as the lord chief justice began to recount the case. Before my deployment, he ventured, I had been an exemplary soldier, but the cauldron of Helmand Province had bubbled with "quite exceptional stressors" that had chipped away at me, disrupting my ability to form rational judgements. "There can be little doubt," he said, "that the appellant was angry and vengeful and had a considerable degree of hatred for the wounded insurgent. On prior deployments, similar emotions had been controlled by him." But here, he accepted, things had changed. "The appellant's decision to kill was probably impulsive, and the adjustment disorder had led to an abnormality of mental functioning that substantially impaired his ability to exercise self-control."

In some ways, it was everything I needed to hear. Some of the stain was being scoured from my skin, even as I faced up to the frightening reality that, towards the end of my time in

Helmand, I had not been in my right mind. The things we had said about life in Helmand were held to be true. Here was the acknowledgement I needed that those six months really had been a hell on earth – and that the hell they had wreaked on me, too, was not in my imagination.

The judge continued. Taking all the fresh evidence into account, it had been decided that my sentence would be reduced from a life term to a sentence of seven years, with half of that to be served in prison and half to be served on licence in the outside world. It took me a moment to compute properly, but by this point I had already served nearly three and a half years, including the time I had spent on remand after being charged. The reality of the new conclusion came to me slowly, as if by degrees.

After spending three and a half years of my life imprisoned, I would be going home in less than a month.

It wasn't until later that the other great implication dawned on me. With my conviction for murder overturned, the dishonourable discharge I'd been given was also to be overturned. Though I would never again wear the uniform of the Royal Marines, my discharge would become an administrative one, and the stain on my service record would be scrubbed clean. The 16 years I had given to serving in Her Majesty's armed forces no longer counted for nothing.

I was no longer Marine A. I was Sergeant Alexander Blackman, of the Royal Marines, and as I left the conference room and returned to my cell, that meant more than almost anything in the world.

I was going back home.

* * *

Midnight approached on 26 April 2017.

At Erlestoke – silence, punctuated by the patrolling footsteps and occasional shouts of a prison at night. In my cell I sat alone. Sleep would not be coming to me tonight, not for a few hours at least. There I was, propped on the end of the bed I would never sleep in again, my bag – with all its simple possessions – at my feet. For three and a half years I'd breathed in the air of this and other prisons. Tonight, all that would change.

I'd been given a rough date for my release in the days after the appeal. Some time after that, the prison administration had taken me aside and, leading me through the procedures, asked me a pointed question. "How would you like to be released, Al?" they'd enquired.

Implicitly, I understood the need to ask. The media frenzy had not abated since the appeal reached its climax, and it seemed as if the entire British media – those who supported me, and the voices who still questioned my release – wanted to know how and when I would walk free from Erlestoke Prison. Ordinarily, prisoners here would be taken from their cells and into the prison reception, where they would be handed back their belongings, fill out exit paperwork and then be shown out of the front gate by an official. They might be given the train fare back home. Somebody might be waiting to pick them up and welcome them back to the world. But for me, it seemed clear that the world would be waiting – and that was a prospect that neither the prison, nor I, wanted to face.

I didn't need long to think. In spite of everything, the prison service had treated me well and with respect. I had worked hard to fit into its routines and demands and they, in turn, had treated me as a human being and handled the vicissitudes of my particular case with great professionalism. Perhaps it is something my military service drummed into me, but I have always had a great respect for systems that work. So I did not want to put the leadership at Erlestoke through any unnecessary aggravation. Whatever made my release easiest for them, I explained, was what I would do.

That was why I hadn't known until 24 hours before that tonight, I would be leaving my life in prison and being returned to what I was increasingly thinking of as the "real world".

The lights had been out across Erlestoke for two hours when, on the stroke of midnight, I heard footsteps approaching my cell. A guard had come to take me away. In dutiful silence, I followed him down and out of the wing. In the prison reception, I was processed out. I signed my name on what seemed a dozen sheets of paper. I was given back the few scant possessions I'd carried with me when they took me down, out of the courtroom at Bulford Camp all those years before.

CHAPTER SIXTEEN

Then, shaking the hand of the guards who had escorted me, the exit door to the reception building was opened onto the starlit night outside.

Just inside the prison gates, an unmarked police car was waiting. I climbed into the back seat, strapped in, and moments later we were off, the Wiltshire nightscape turning to a blur outside my window.

I was already discombobulated. There was something unreal about it being over, something it would take me weeks and months to process and properly accept. For now, all I could think about was the unbelievable madness of travelling at these speeds, hurtling along country lanes, trees and hedgerows and farmland rushing past in a dizzying whirl. Well, it had been years now since I'd travelled in a car, something had washed away in me, and I just wasn't conditioned for it any longer. After a while, I began to feel a sickness rising in my gorge. I'd travelled in all manner of rickety military vehicles across ragged terrain in all four corners of the earth, but these Wiltshire lanes were making me sick. I braced myself and hoped there wasn't far to go.

The truth was, I didn't know. All I knew was that Claire would be waiting for me at the end of this journey, wherever it took me. It had been arranged, some time ago, that I would not be delivered back to the house we shared in Taunton. The media would be camping out there, too, alert to any sign that I was about to return, and we did not want to face it until we were

ready – and nor did we want to visit it upon our neighbours.
Two days ago, Claire had decamped from Taunton to a holiday
cottage somewhere in the wilds of the Cotswolds. I had no idea
where it was. But every mile we drove was a mile closer.

An hour later, the car slowed down, drawing into a service
station where yet another unmarked police car was waiting.
As I transferred vehicles, wishing goodbye to the policeman
who had brought me so far, I drew breath and tried to get the
nausea under control. Whether it was down to travel, or only
anticipation, I was no longer sure. But the clock was still ticking,
so we took off again.

I don't know how far we travelled. To this day, I do not know
which roads we took, which villages we snaked through. But at
last, with the darkness absolute all around, we followed a pitted
farm track and pulled through a gap in the hedgerow. Here a
cottage stood in the grounds of an old farm. It was long after
2am, but the lights still shone in its windows.

The car stopped. The door opened. I stepped out onto the
naked earth. There was a crispness in the air tonight, but all
was perfectly still.

We did not need to knock. As our headlights arced across the
front of the house, the cottage door opened – and two silhouettes
emerged.

With the police driver at my side, I hoisted my pack
over my shoulder and approached the open door. There was
Jonathan, who had run the Justice For Marine A Facebook

group supporting my release. As he reached out his hand, I thought about all the countless strangers who had been moved enough to help me reach this point.

"Welcome home, Al," he said.

Then he stepped aside. Claire was standing in the doorway. I dropped my packs and took her in my arms. There were no words. There still aren't. In the back of my mind was that moment just after my second arrest, when I'd fronted up to her and, unabashedly tearful, told her that I wouldn't hold it against her if she decided to end our marriage, to get on with her life without me as the millstone around her neck. I'd meant every word. There would not have been a shred of resentment or hate had she taken me up on that offer. But for three and a half long years she had stood at my side, marshalling every step of the campaign, organising the groups that had supported me, liaising with my legal team and the champions we somehow acquired from every corner of the country – and, more than any of that, keeping alive the flickering hope that one day all of this would end, and that at the end of that long road there would be a life waiting for me.

Without her love and support, I do not know how I would have endured the years in prison, nor come to accept the diagnosis of "adjustment disorder", nor come to terms with the shell shock of my dishonourable discharge. It is because of Claire that I am who I am, and here she was.

A little while later, we stood again in the doorway as the lights of the police car disappeared around the bend in the track, back into the darkness of the Cotswolds' approaching dawn, Jonathan's car following behind. After that, it was just me and Claire, together at last.

We closed the door and, for two blissful days, not yet ready to face the world, we barely opened it at all.

EPILOGUE

At the time of writing, it is now two years since I was released from prison, having served my sentence and returned to the Taunton home I share with Claire. It is nearly seven years since Claire and I awoke early in that same home to discover military police at our door. And it is eight years since that day in Helmand Province where, in a moment of madness I can still hardly describe, let alone account for, I changed the lives of myself and the four other marines with whom I was charged.

If I have left you with any impression in telling this story in my own words for the first time, I hope it is that I have spent seven long years – and will, I am certain, spend the rest of my life – questioning my actions that day. Uncertain why I did what I did, and unable to recognise, in myself, the man who did them. The journey from my homecoming to England, through the military courts and imprisonment, to the more mundane life I now live with Claire has been fraught with ups and downs. I wish I could say that I kept the faith throughout – faith in the system, yes, but also the faith in myself, which wavered so dramatically from one turn of events to the next.

The acceptance that my experiences in Iraq and Afghanistan, but more particularly my second tour of Helmand Province, led to the development of a mental health condition has been a slow one, and coming to terms with it has been slower still. More than anything else, I have never wanted to be seen as taking the easy option and claiming to have a mental health condition where one did not exist. Warfare is invariably a dangerous, murky business, catapulting you from extremes of boredom and exhaustion to extremes of danger in a matter of seconds – and there are already too many soldiers coming home with undiagnosed mental health problems for me to be content with adding one more to the list.

Accepting my own mental struggles and how they impacted on me in Helmand is a battle I feel that, in some ways, I will be waging for all my years to come. As soldiers we have traditionally been conditioned to believe that, though our bodies are fallible and must be trained correctly to stand the best possible chance of surviving combat, our minds are already well equipped to deal with the traumas of war. More than a century has passed since the battlefields of the first world war threw up terms such as "shell shock" and, later, "combat stress reaction" to describe the effects of warfare on the mind – and yet for me, recognising that I too could be mentally affected by the things I saw, did, and generally experienced in Afghanistan has been an uphill struggle.

But perhaps this is the trajectory of a life. We grow up thinking ourselves impermeable, we launch ourselves into our adult lives, still believing in this myth of our invincibility, at some point we begin to recognise, even at a relatively early age, that our bodies are not immune to the vicissitudes of life, but too many of us refuse to recognise the same things about our minds. We boulder on, pretending that inside we are just the same as ever we were, no matter what we've experienced. We march on, patching up our bodies but pretending we don't even need to think about our minds... until something blows open your world, something you do yourself or something that gets done to you, and suddenly all the king's horses and all the king's men can't put you back together again.

Time and again I come back to the hospital at Camp Bastion. All that state-of-the-art equipment developed and invested in so that doctors and surgeons of the highest calibre could put a broken soldier's body back together, bring them back from the most catastrophic injuries, all the confidence that this was supposed to instil in us – that no matter what dangers we faced in the field, the doctors were better prepared to save us than at any moment in history. And yet, though Camp Bastion did have a dedicated mental health facility, talk of the mental struggles of warfare has always been minimal.

Basic training includes first aid and various medical procedures a soldier might have to perform in the field, but traditionally it contains comparatively little acknowledgement of the mental torment and fatigue that can creep up on a soldier, little by little, increment by increment, changing the way he reacts, the way he performs – and, fundamentally, the way that he *thinks*.

In the First World War, you didn't have to be a coward or a shirker to suffer the effects of shell shock – no matter what the presiding diagnoses of the time may have been. But even in this age, where we acknowledge post-traumatic stress disorder as a real and valid thing, not just for veterans of war but for survivors of any traumatic situation, some of us find it easier to acknowledge the mental health struggles of others than we do our own. This has certainly been my experience.

I have never been faced with a colleague struggling, or a veteran unable to shake off completely their experiences of war, and not believed in the struggle they were going through. Yet, when it came to examining my own mental state, even with a raft of doctors telling me the same thing, I still resisted the diagnosis. Some automatic, inner piece of me reacted against the stigma. Even in this modern age, I thought it diminished me somehow – that it belittled me as an effective Royal Marine in a way that a shrapnel wound, a bullet, the devastation of an IED never would have done.

I cannot rightfully explain what happened in Helmand Province in September 2011. The courts have made their decisions and they are ones that I abide by. But the court and imprisonment process have opened my eyes to the struggles that many veterans face on their discharge from the armed services. Transitioning from one mode of life to another is difficult enough, but when so many veterans are still struggling with the after-effects of their service, bottling up and refusing to reach out for help with the mental health struggles they're going through – and too often, like me, not acknowledging that they have struggles in the first place – the transition back into civilian life can feel an almost insurmountable challenge.

Disproportionate numbers of military veterans end up in trouble with the police after they've returned to civilian life. Disproportionate numbers end up relying on the NHS that treated my father so valiantly because, in order to cope, they turn to the temporary solutions of drink and drugs. In this, I have to count myself fortunate. Throughout everything, I have had Claire – and I truly believe that it is knowing she was there, waiting for me at the end of my tours, at the end of my imprisonment, that kept me resilient. Without Claire to anchor me, would I have been one of those other veterans, directionless in their new lives, unable to settle, not knowing how to properly move on?

Almost a year after I left prison – a year I spent cycling in the fresh air of our Somerset home, putting myself to good use about the house, generally doing my best to show Claire how grateful I was that she had stuck with me in my darkest hours, and how my love for her resounded across the years – all these thoughts came back to me. My 10 months of freedom had hardly been idle, but by the end of 2017 I was close to 45 years of age. There was, and still is, so much of life left to live. All I knew right then was that although my days as a Royal Marine might be behind me, I wasn't yet played out. I still had something to give. Something positive had to come of my experience. There had to be a way I could repay the faith so many thousands had had in me, the support they'd shown, and help contribute to what I was beginning to think of as one of the defining problems of our time.

My second life was about to begin.

In February 2018, not yet a year since I stepped out of prison, I stood outside the Houses of Parliament in London. Gazing up at those hallowed spires, I knew, in my heart, that I was finally looking forward, not back. For so long now I had been gazing into my past, trying to make sense of those days in Helmand. Now, having accepted that I might never properly understand what happened there, I realised I had decades left to do some good in this world – and had started to see what form my contribution would take.

I'd had various offers of work in the months after my release from prison. My military service was certainly in the past, but like many veterans I was offered security positions, both here in the UK and overseas. It wasn't easy to politely decline offers like this. I had already spent too much of my marriage away from Claire, and I did not want to venture far from her again, neither physically nor psychologically. But I did want to contribute to our household expenses – Claire already worked so hard – and the hunger to contribute to the pressing problem of mental health in the military had been growing in me for some time.

I was visiting the Houses of Parliament to attend the launch of ExFor+, the organisation I had recently begun working for. Founded by Simon Adams, himself a former Royal Marine from Dorset, not so far down the road from where Claire and I live, ExFor+'s mission dovetailed exactly with my own – to help troubled servicemen through dark times, to assist in their reintegration into civilian life, with career guidance, transitional employment, education and training – and, perhaps most importantly of all, to provide that sense of community that servicemen of all types and ranks hunger for when they are discharged. My own transition from military to civilian life was atypical, but somehow it still featured the struggles that servicemen often go through. ExFor+ had provided me with the opportunity to do what I needed to do on both a pragmatic and deeper, psychological, level. To give something back.

Simon had joined the Royal Marines in 2006, passing for duty in 2007, after a boyhood and young adulthood spent dreaming of signing up with the armed forces. His life plan had always been to join an elite fighting force and complete a full 22 years of military service – but before he was due to be deployed in 2008, he suffered an accident in training that left him with brain injuries as well as fractures to his spine, scarring and muscle damage. Though he tried to continue with his career after the accident, it was only weeks before he began struggling with his memory and concentration, experiencing recurring nightmares and flashbacks.

From here on, things got incrementally worse for Simon. Retreating within himself, disengaging from family and friends – and, unable to control his emotions, becoming occasionally aggressive at people he had once considered close – he was compelled to acknowledge that his struggles were mental as well as physical. With his dream career coming to an end so soon, he found these circumstances and his transition from service more difficult than he had ever envisaged, but at his lowest point he turned things around.

ExFor+ was his way of remaining part of military society. As he walked for the last time out of his camp gates after being medically discharged, Simon made a promise to himself. That no other service leaver or veteran should ever be in the position of difficulty that he had found himself in, and that he would work towards making this a reality. Simon's promise continues to be his principal motive in life – and, in November 2017, the not-for-profit organisation was awarded a grant from the charitable organisation Help for Heroes, allowing it to start investing more fully in the pursuit of its goals. It was as part of this that I came on board.

At the time of writing, I have been working with ExFor+ for a year. Our mission to help veterans transition properly into new lives will never end – and for me, at this stage of my life, it seems a mission every bit as important as the deployments I was once sent on. If working with Simon and the expanding ExFor+ family is my lasting contribution to society, I will be as proud of it as I have been for serving my country with the Royal Marines. Long may it continue.

There will always be veterans needing assistance with the next steps in their lives. How do I know this? Well, in Afghanistan, the war goes on.

The war that I left behind at the end of 2011 had continued. The feeling that had dogged me – that the six months I had spent patrolling those roads accomplished nothing – was not mine alone. Wars always ebb and flow, but in Afghanistan that ebb and flow seemed endless. Leaving my first tour at Forward Operating Base Inkerman, I could at least take pride in knowing that Sangin was close to thriving once again. But Sangin's upward trajectory was not to last long. In the long hot summer of 2010, the British handed over responsibility for the town to forces from the US, and 40 Commando was repatriated. But over the next few years the Taliban were resurgent in the area, and after a succession of bitter engagements, Sangin was partially retaken by the Taliban in 2015 – in spite of British SAS and American Special Forces being deployed in support of the Afghan National Army. By 2017, the Taliban's hold on Sangin had been completely re-established for the first time since I arrived with 40 Commando in the autumn of 2007. The war was right back where it started.

By 2017, of course, the British presence in Sangin – and indeed Afghanistan more generally – was dramatically reduced. In December 2012, the month after I was arrested for the second time, the UK's prime minister David Cameron announced that half of the force serving in Helmand Province would be withdrawn, leaving only 5,000 British servicemen on the ground. And, by October 2014 – at which point I was approaching my second Christmas in prison – the UK had formally ceased its operations in Afghanistan, withdrawing its combat troops and leaving behind a small force of around 500 in non-combat roles. Camp Bastion, handed over to the new Afghan Ministry of Defence, became Camp Shorabak, a barracks for the Afghan National Army.

As the US began its withdrawal, the Afghan National Army, along with various private military contractors provided by both the US and the United Nations, continued to resist the Taliban. But now reorganised, the insurgents were able to make significant gains, particularly in Helmand. A war that began in 2001 and that has moved through various phases during its long life is still ongoing now, in early 2019 – with more than 15,000 US military still on the ground, and nearly 1,000 troops from the UK.

The methods of attack, the tactics and training, the theatres into which British soldiers are deployed – all these things transform with the passing of the years. But war... war never changes. On a visceral level, war is about one thing – the difference between life and death. It has been that way since time immemorial. And although the British presence in Afghanistan is now a fraction of the size it was when I was out there myself, there remain theatres across the world where our servicemen are called to arms. From Africa to the Baltics, from the Middle East to the islands of the South Atlantic, the British army is actively engaged in operations across the globe.

Every tour, soldiers are seeing their friends killed. Every tour, soldiers are coming home with life-changing injuries.

EPILOGUE

Every tour, others are coming home unable to acknowledge that the things they've seen and done have had a lasting impact on their peace of mind and mental well-being, and every tour, soldiers are being discharged from duties and discovering the civilian world an unfamiliar and even threatening place.

So, wherever there's a war that British servicemen are called upon to fight, wherever there are British soldiers scarred and discharged from their duties, wherever there's a British soldier unsure of his next step on the road to a second life, that's where we'll be.

I can think of no greater service to the armed forces I know and love, and the men who dedicate their young lives to the service of their country. If I found my first vocation as a young man, fresh off the dairy farm and into the Royal Marines, I know now that I have found my second in helping the kind of men I fought alongside find their feet again in an unfamiliar world. This is where I want to be until my time here is through. Far from the scrubland and desert of Helmand Province, this is my new front line.

ACKNOWLEDGEMENTS

There are so many wonderful people who supported Claire and me throughout the campaign for my release: members of the Royal Marines family, veterans and their families from every one of the armed forces and members of the public of every age and from every walk of life. We are immensely grateful to you all.

We would particularly like to say thank you to everyone who gave up their time and travelled to Parliament Square, the CCRC and the Royal Courts of Justice to show their support. We will never forget the 'Sea of Green' that stood beside us and showed us we were not on our own.

To all of those amazing people who donated to the *Daily Mail* campaign fund, the Royal Marines Association and Go Commando charity funds – we simply would not be where we are today without you all – words cannot really express how we feel, but please accept our heartfelt thanks.

The success of the 'Justice for Marine A' campaign relied on the energy and hard work of many fantastic men and women

– too many to mention here, but you know who you are and you know that we will be forever in your debt.

There are of course a few people that we simply have to mention because without them there would have been no campaign and I would probably still be serving time for a murder conviction…

Johnathan Davies, Sue Childs, the campaign team and the RM Mums

Frederick Forsyth

Jonathan Goldberg QC, Jeffrey Israel and Senghin Kong

Richard Drax MP and Lord John Burnett

Major General John Holmes DSO, OBE, MC

Major General Malcolm Hunt OBE

Lieutenant Colonel Ewen Southby-Tailyour OBE

Colonel Oliver Lee OBE

The *Daily Mail* team, especially Sam Greenhill and Richard Pendlebury

Chris Terrill

Pete Hawley and Major Steve Cox

There are so many people to thank – too many to name. We simply do not know how to thank you enough and can only hope that you know how much your support and tireless campaigning continues to mean to both of us. Your never-ending support for Claire during this incredibly difficult time made such a difference – she's not sure she would've survived without you.